THE FIRST GRADE

BIG GET READY

BOOK

AUTHORS

BARBARA GREGORICH
JEAN SYSWERDA
ROBERTA BANNISTER
MARTHA PALMER
JOAN HOFFMAN

ILLUSTRATORS

CHRIS COOK
JOE BODDY

The First Grade **Big Get Ready** Book is a compilation of favorite titles from the **I Know It!** series. The ten titles are listed in the table of contents.

CONTENTS

An answer key is provided at the end of each skill area except Manuscript Writing.

PARENT GUIDE

The skills in the **Big Get Ready Book** for First Grade are those most commonly taught at the first grade level. Here are some suggestions for working with your child at home:

- Don't do too many pages at one sitting. The size of the book could overwhelm the child. Remove a few pages at at time. (Pages are perforated for easy removal.) Praise each completed page. Page by page, day to day, is the best.

- If your child is puzzled by one activity, move on to another. The activities are ordered, but there's nothing magical about that order.

- Do the activities at a particular time of day, perhaps before snack time. Do them when the child is not tired. Discuss the learning experience, be enthusiastic. "Let's work in our school books today! Do you remember what you did yesterday?"

- Enjoy it! Laugh a lot! Discuss the activity. Most activities can be done independently by the child since directions are clear and consistent. Never use an activity as punishment. Don't expect too much. The activities are meant as practice.

- There will be days when your child may not feel like working. This is typical, so accept it. And remember: the communication patterns you establish today will pay off as your child grows older.

© School Zone® Publishing Company. All rights reserved.
Permission is granted teachers to reproduce from this book for their classroom use only.

Look at the arrows. Trace the letters. Now write the letters and words.

B B

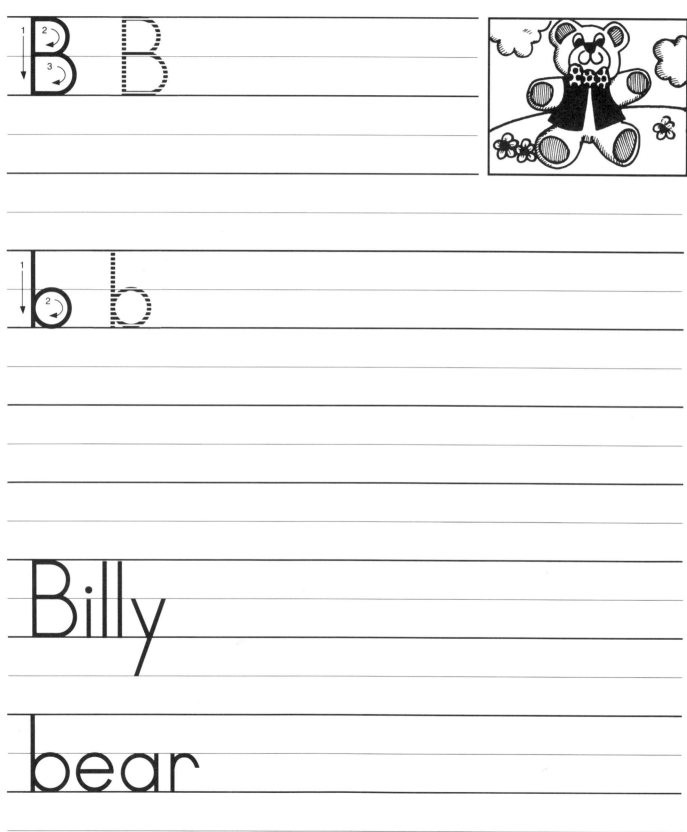

b b

Billy

bear

© School Zone Publishing Company

Look at the arrows. Trace the letters. Now write the letters and words.

A A

a a

Annie

ant

© School Zone Publishing Company

Look at the arrows. Trace the numbers. Now write the numbers.

1 2 3 4 5

6 7 8 9 0

© School Zone Publishing Company

Study the alphabet and number chart.

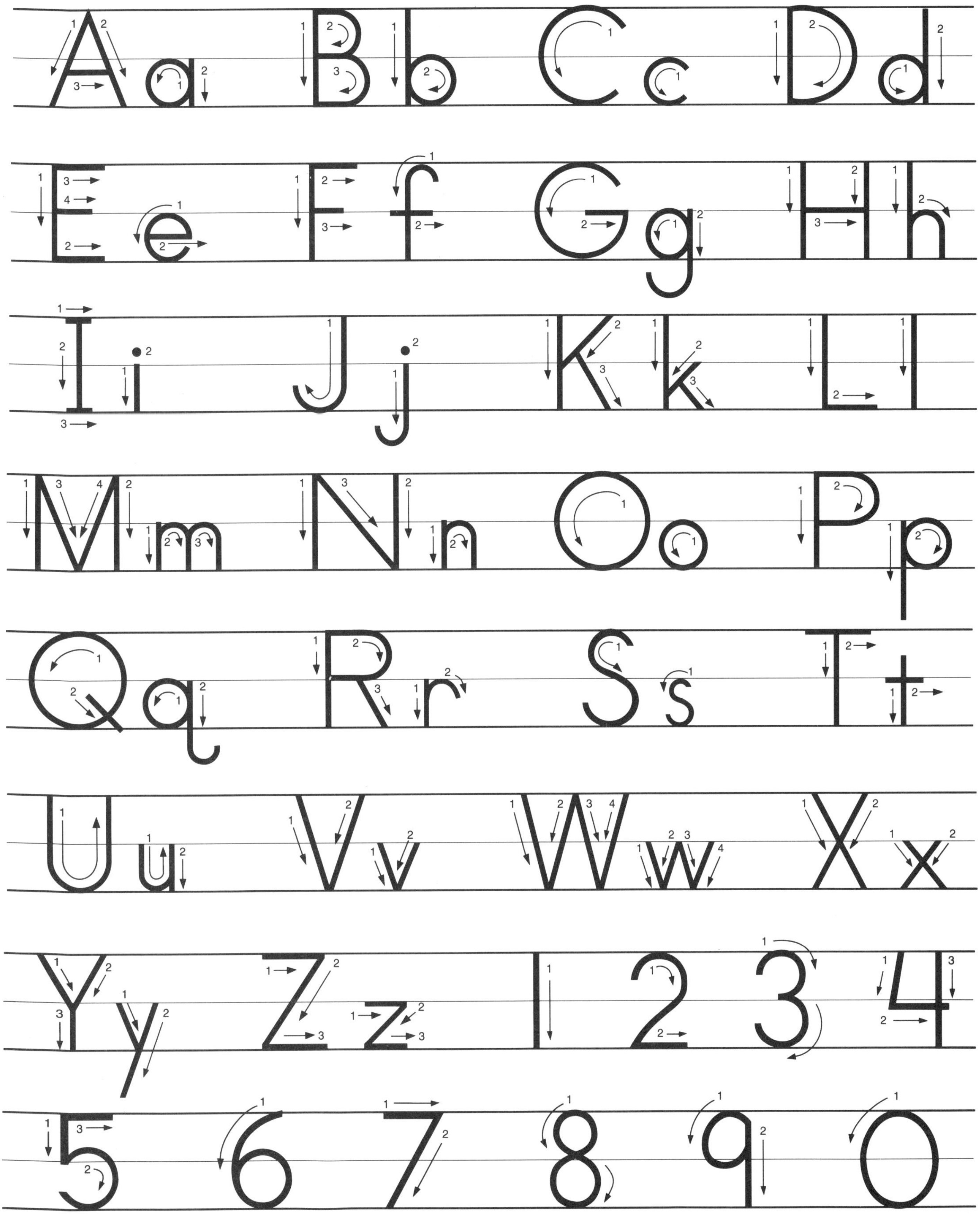

© School Zone Publishing Company

Look at the arrows. Trace the letters. Now write the letters and words.

C C

c c

Cathy

cat

© School Zone Publishing Company

Look at the arrows. Trace the letters. Now write the letters and words.

1 2 D D

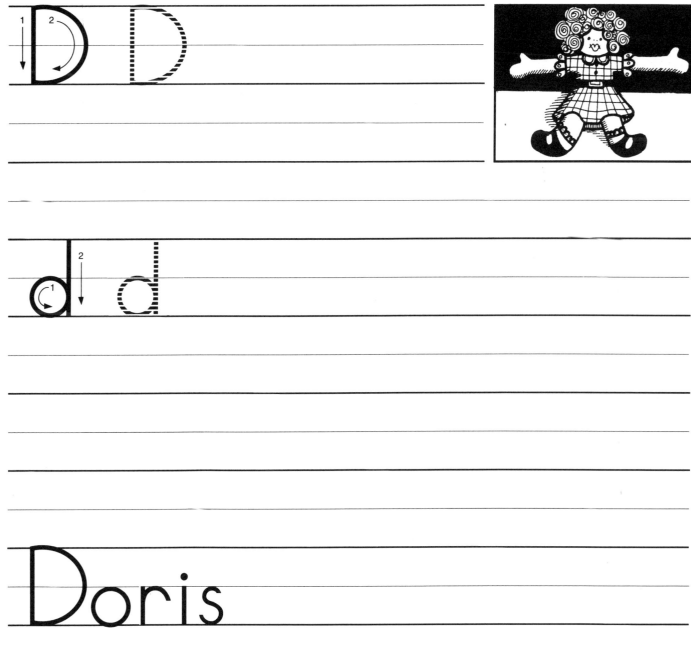

2 1 d d

Doris

doll

© School Zone Publishing Company

Look at the arrows. Trace the letters. Now write the letters and words.

E E

e e

Ellie

elf

© School Zone Publishing Company

Look at the arrows. Trace the letters. Now write the letters and words.

F F

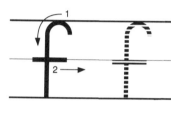

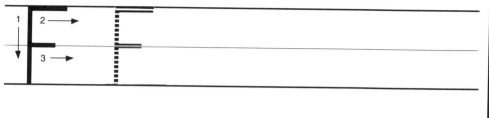

f f

Flora

fairy

© School Zone Publishing Company

Look at the arrows. Trace the letters. Now write the letters and words.

G G

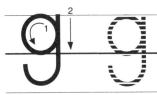

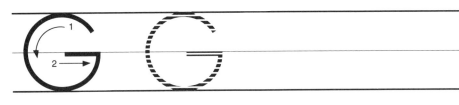

g g

Gary

goat

© School Zone Publishing Company

Look at the arrows. Trace the letters. Now write the letters and words.

1 2 3

H H

1 2

h h

Harry

horse

© School Zone Publishing Company

Look at the arrows. Trace the letters. Now write the letters and words.

I 1 2 3 I

i 1 2 i

Iris

ink

© School Zone Publishing Company

Look at the arrows. Trace the letters. Now write the letters and words.

J J

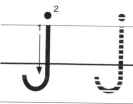

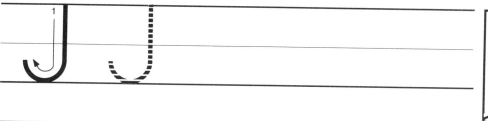

j j

Jenny

jumps

© School Zone Publishing Company

Look at the arrows. Trace the letters. Now write the letters and words.

K K

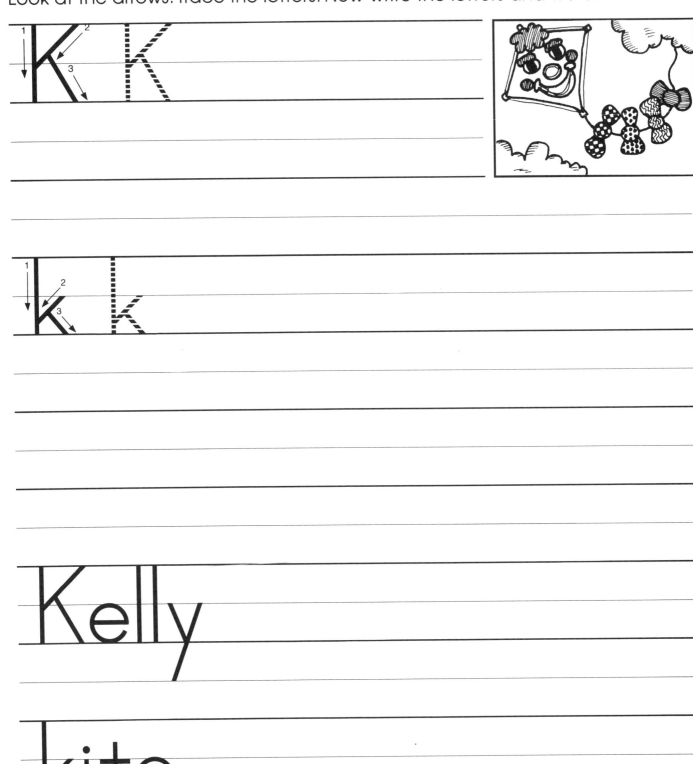

k k

Kelly

kite

© School Zone Publishing Company

Look at the arrows. Trace the letters. Now write the letters and words.

1 2

L L

1

I I

Leroy

lion

© School Zone Publishing Company

Look at the arrows. Trace the letters. Now write the letters and words.

M M

m m

Mary

mouse

© School Zone Publishing Company

Look at the arrows. Trace the letters. Now write the letters and words.

N N

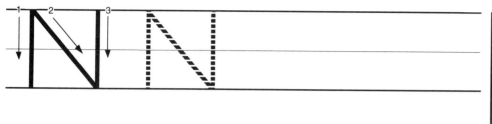

n n

Nancy

nurse

© School Zone Publishing Company

Look at the arrows. Trace the letters. Now write the letters and words.

O O

o o

Owen

owl

© School Zone Publishing Company

Look at the arrows. Trace the letters. Now write the letters and words.

1 2 P P

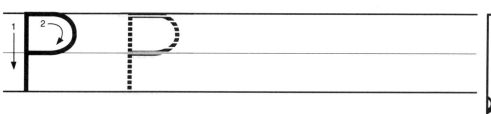

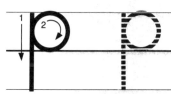

1 2 p p

Peter

pig

© School Zone Publishing Company

Look at the arrows. Trace the letters. Now write the letters and words.

Q Q

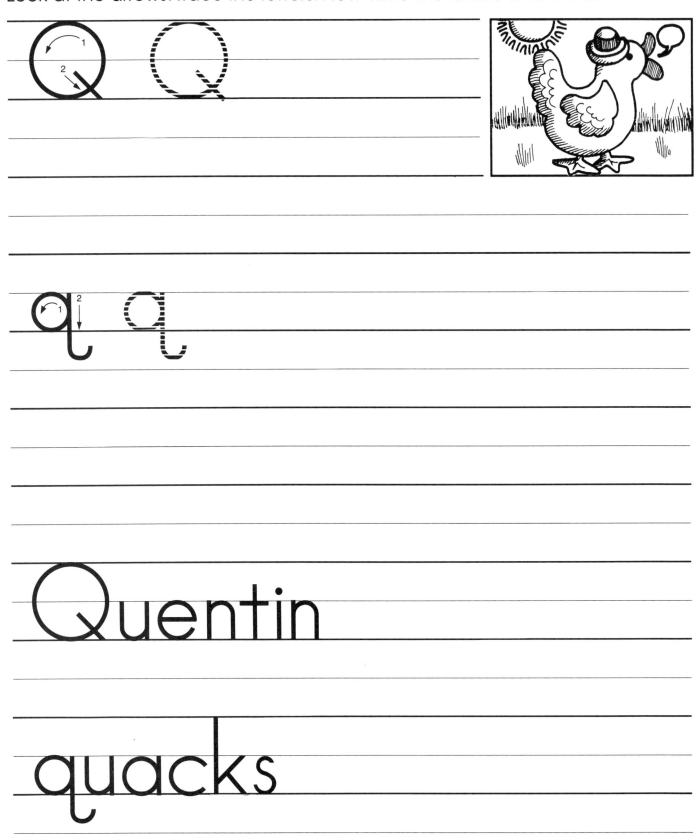

q q

Quentin

quacks

© School Zone Publishing Company

Look at the arrows. Trace the letters. Now write the letters and words.

R R

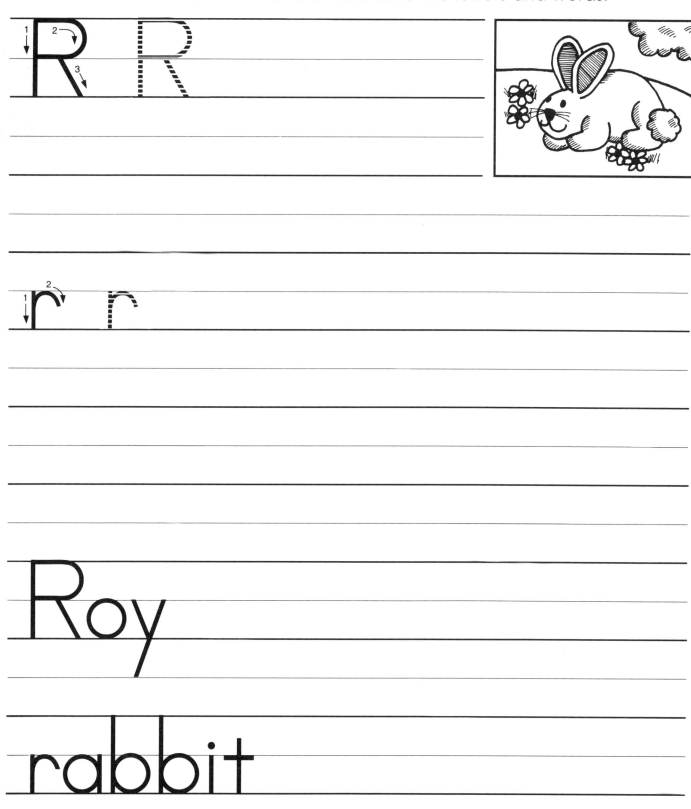

r r

Roy

rabbit

© School Zone Publishing Company

Look at the arrows. Trace the letters. Now write the letters and words.

S S

s s

Sally

seal

© School Zone Publishing Company

Look at the arrows. Trace the letters. Now write the letters and words.

T 1 2→ T

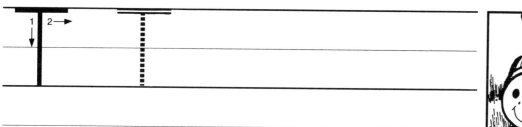

t 1 2→ t

Tommy

turtle

© School Zone Publishing Company

Look at the arrows. Trace the letters. Now write the letters and words.

U U

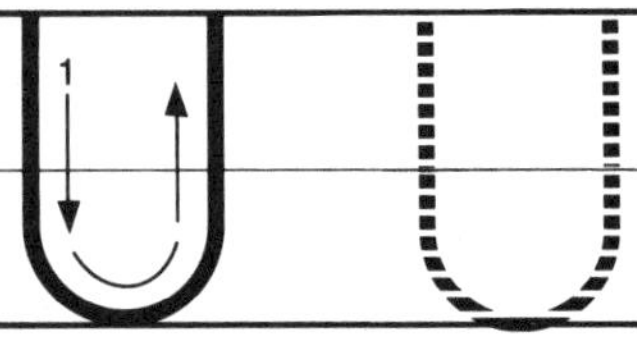

u u

Uncle

unicorn

© School Zone Publishing Company

Look at the arrows. Trace the letters. Now write the letters and words.

V V

v v

Vicky

violin

© School Zone Publishing Company

Look at the arrows. Trace the letters. Now write the letters and words.

W W

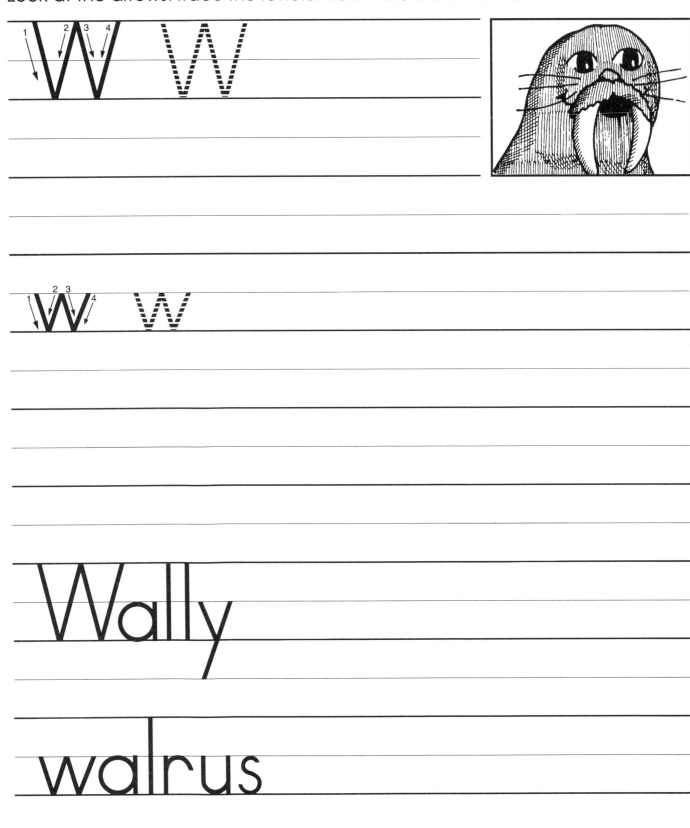

w w

Wally

walrus

© School Zone Publishing Company

Look at the arrows. Trace the letters. Now write the letters and words.

X X

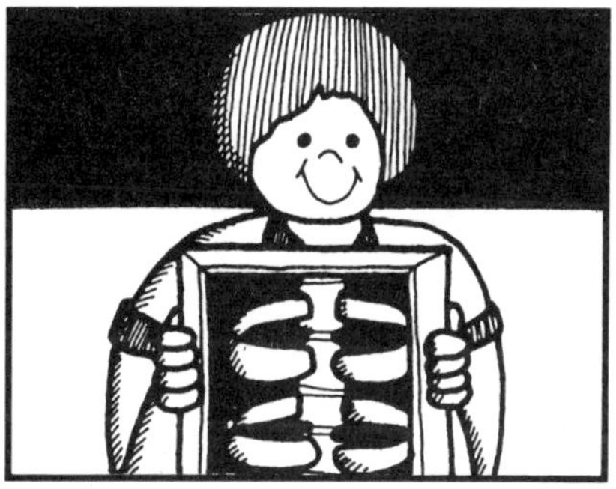

x x

Xavier

x-ray

© School Zone Publishing Company

Look at the arrows. Trace the letters. Now write the letters and words.

Y Y

y y

Yancy

yak

© School Zone Publishing Company

Look at the arrows. Trace the letters. Now write the letters and words.

Z Z

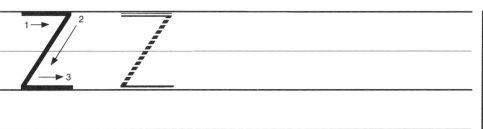

z z

Zippy

zebra

© School Zone Publishing Company

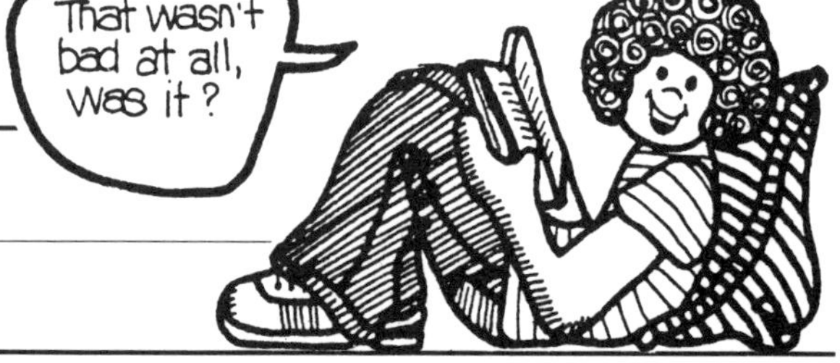
That wasn't bad at all, was it?

© School Zone Publishing Company

Practice writing your name.

© School Zone Publishing Company

Tt

Tammy Turtle likes the letter **t**.
Write the letter **t**.

Tammy Turtle has five words. Each word goes under a picture. Write the correct word under each picture.

© School Zone Publishing Company

Mm

Tammy has a friend. Her name is Myrtle. Myrtle Turtle likes the letter **m**. Write the letter **m**.

Help Myrtle Turtle make it to the moon! Write the correct word by each picture. You can choose from the words in the rocket ship.

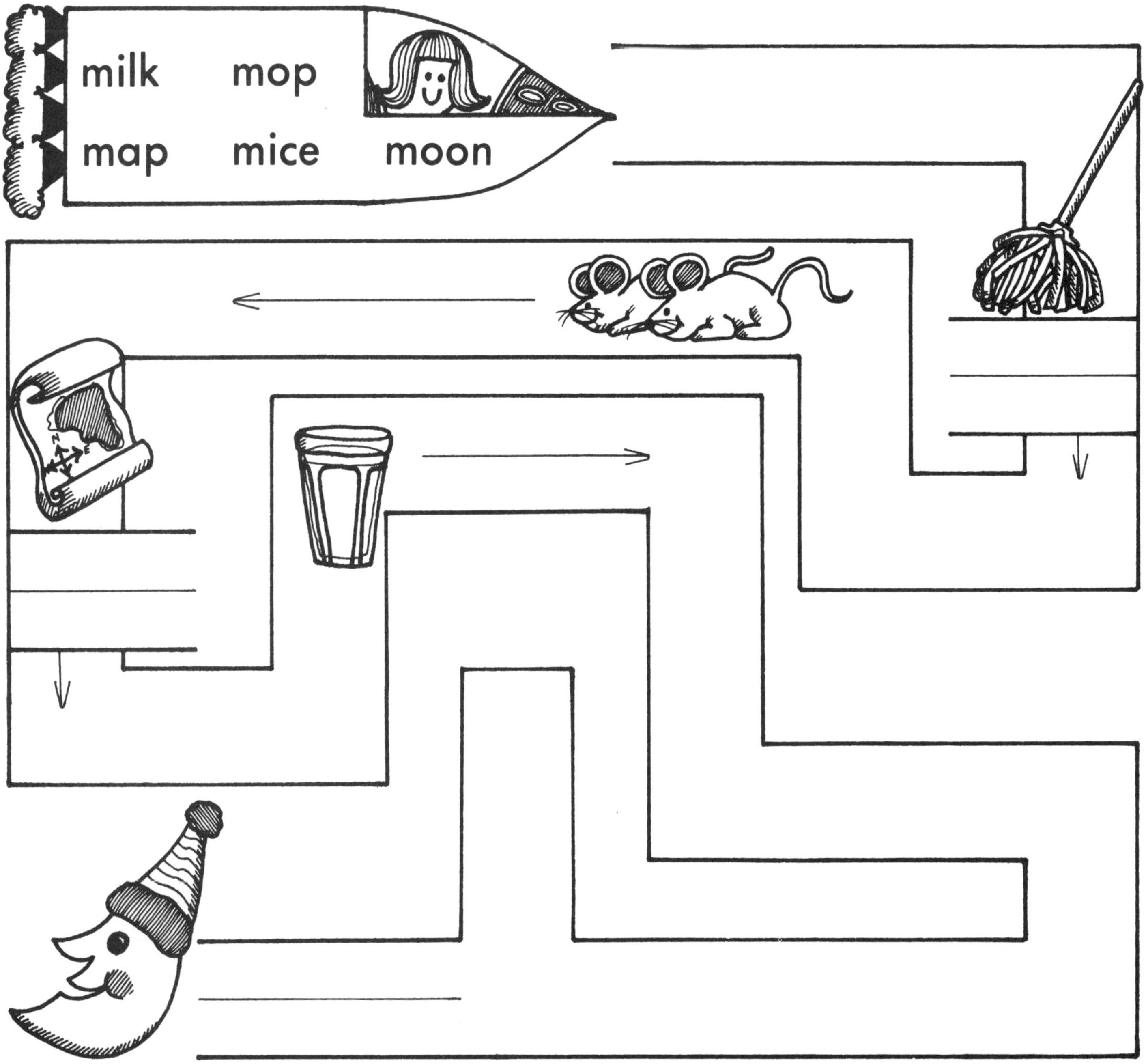

© School Zone Publishing Company

Bb Bb Bb Bb Bb Bb Bb Bb Bb Bb

Write the letter **b**.

Write the correct word next to each picture.

bird	ball	bug	book	bell	bed

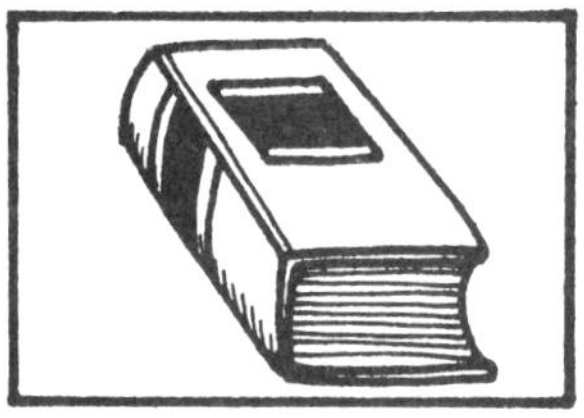

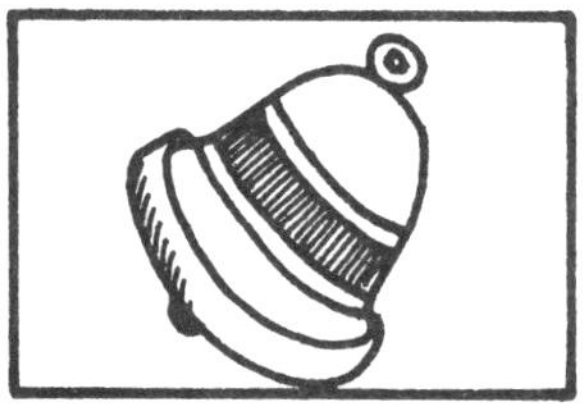

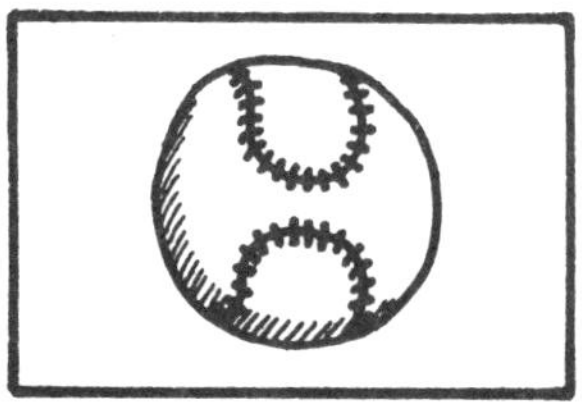

Birds are my buddies, but bugs bug me!

© School Zone Publishing Company

Ss

Silly Sid likes to look like the letter **s**. Silly old Silly Sid! Write the letter **s**.

Silly Sid likes to ask riddles. But first he gives you the answers! Silly old Silly Sid! Write each word next to the riddle it answers.

soap	saw	sand	seal	soup

1. You use this in the tub.

2. This is on the beach.

3. You eat this from a bowl.

4. You cut wood with this.

5. It likes to eat fish.

© School Zone Publishing Company

Pp

P is for parade. All the animals like to be in a parade. Write the letter **p**.

Circle the things that can be in the **P** Parade. Draw a line from the picture to the word. Then write each word.

THE P PARADE

pony pan pig pie pipe

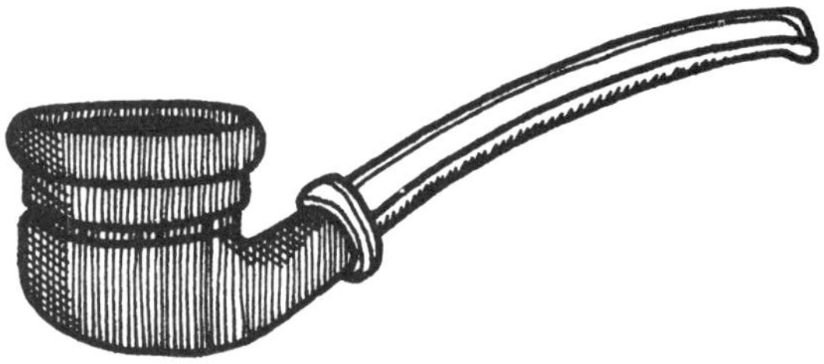

© School Zone Publishing Company

Ll

L is for LOOK! Write the letter **l**.

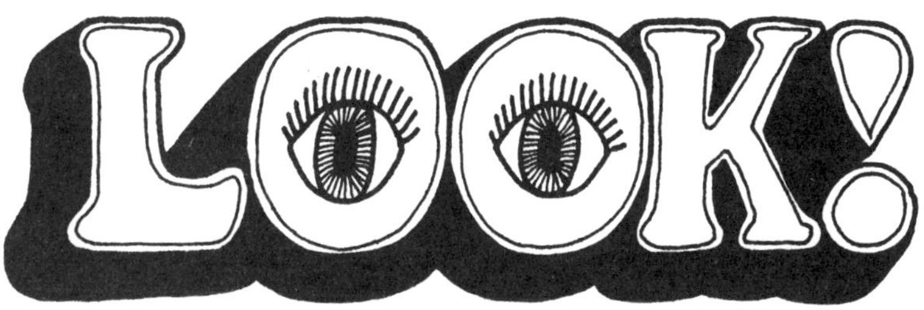

Look! Look and you will see the things hidden in the picture. Six things are hidden. They all begin with the letter **l**. Draw a line around each hidden thing. Draw a line from each hidden thing to the correct word.

letter	lamb	leg	ladder	lamp	lion

© School Zone Publishing Company

Nn

N is for name. **N** is also for Nothing!
Write the letter **n**.

My name is Nothing!

Nothing wants to eat these words! Then there will be nothing left on the page! Quick! Write the letter **n** in front of each word. Then say the word.

____othing

____ext

____ight

____ame

____ever

Nothing is nice, but you never know what he'll eat next!
n

© School Zone Publishing Company

Dd

D is for Doctor Duck. Write the letter **d**.

Look at the picture. Say the word. Draw a line around the letter that starts the word.

Color each space that has the letter **d**. What is the picture?

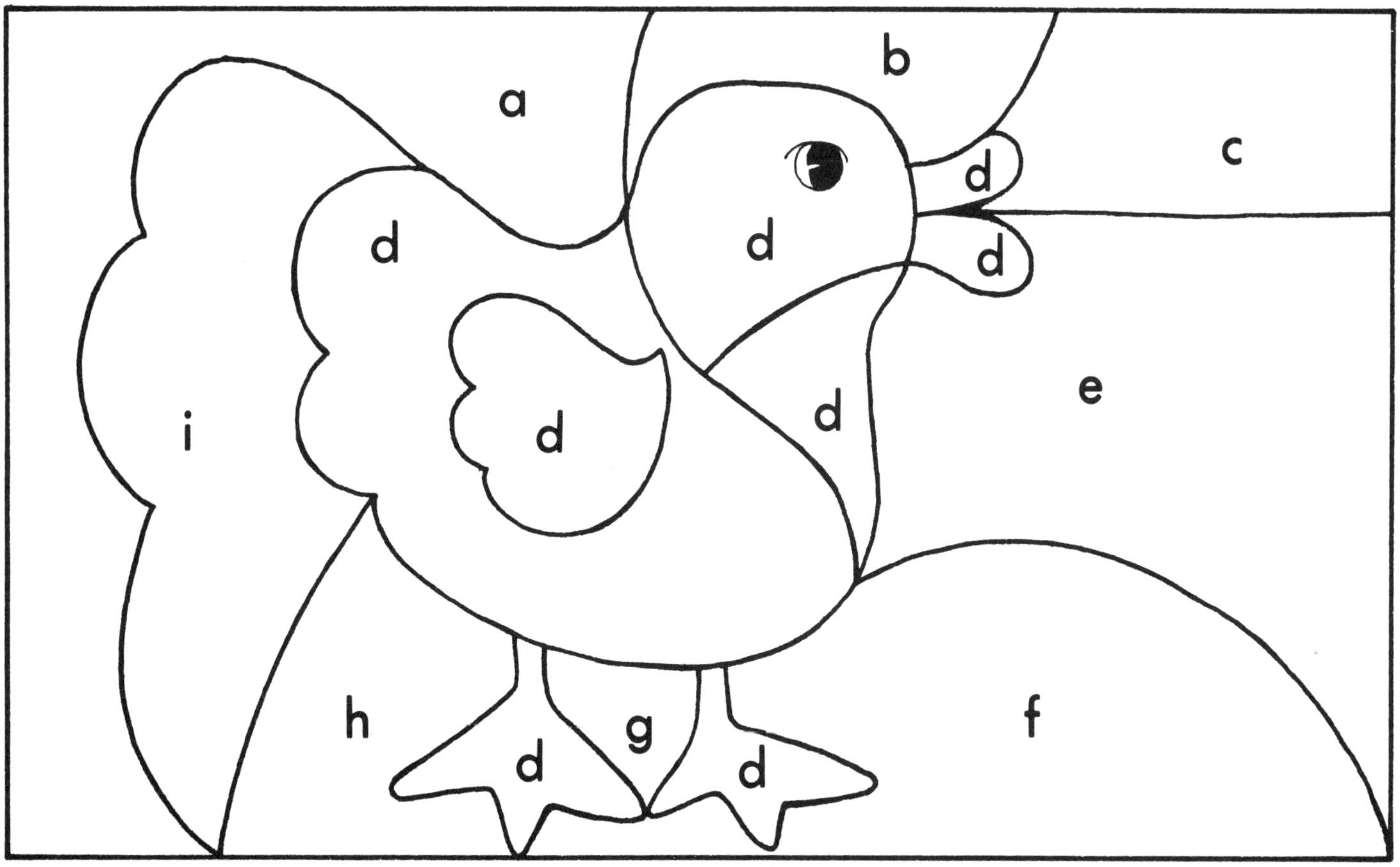

This is a picture of a (doctor dog duck).

© School Zone Publishing Company

Ff

Four fast fish want you to write the letter **f**.

Look at the picture. Write the correct word on the line.

fox	fish	fire	food	farm	feet

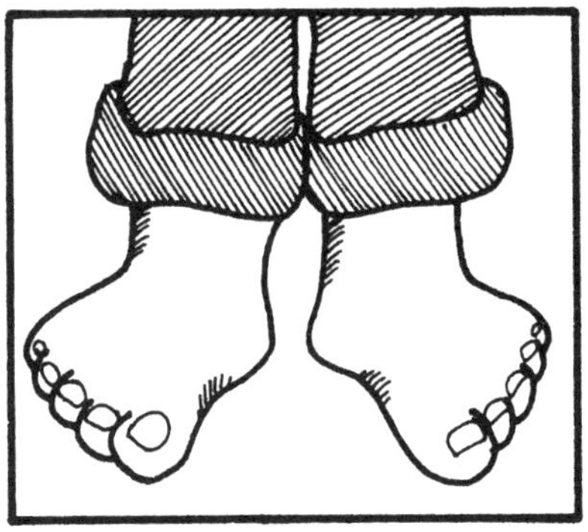

© School Zone Publishing Company

Hh

H is for Happy Horse, of course.
Write the letter **h**.

Help Happy Horse get home to his hay! Write the correct word by each picture.

© School Zone Publishing Company

Rr

R is for rain. Write the letter **r**.

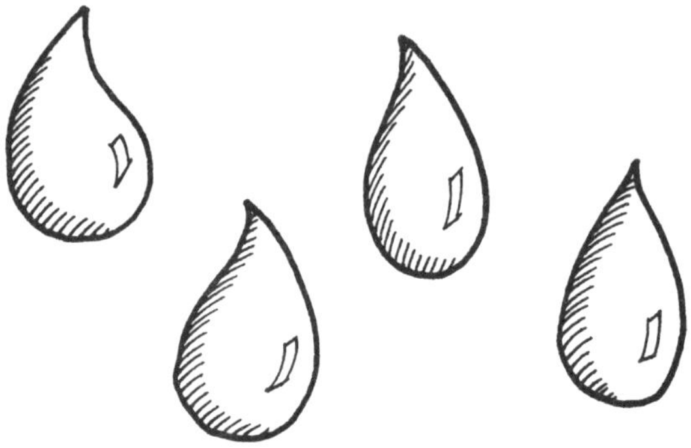

R is also for riddle. Read the riddle. Write the correct word on the line.

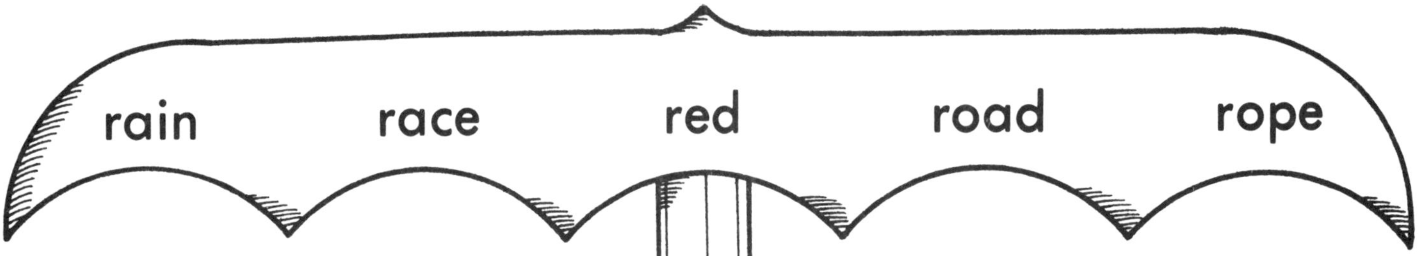

1. It is a color.
2. It is wet.
3. You can jump with it.
4. You can drive a car on it.
5. You can run in it.

© School Zone Publishing Company

Jj

J is for jump. Write the letter **j**.

Jack can jump. He can jump over words that start with **j**! Circle each word that Jack can jump over.

jump bear just

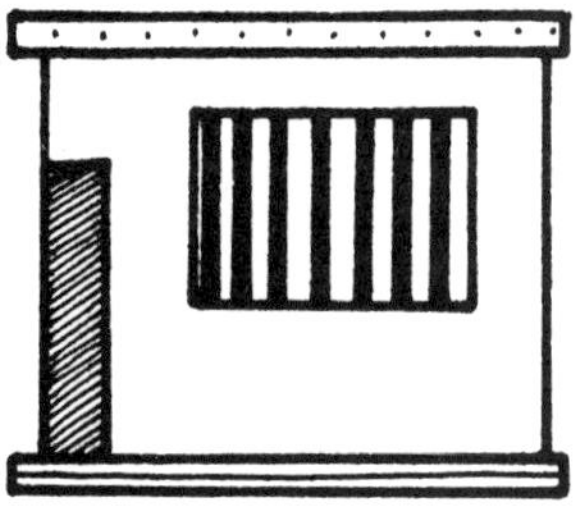

jail

horse

jar

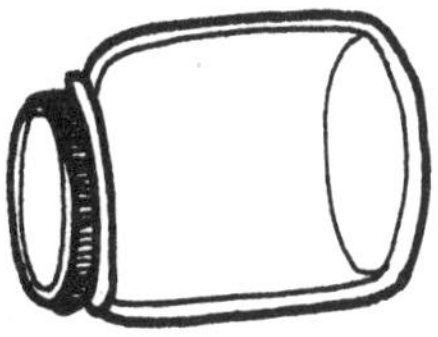

turtle job

car

joke

© School Zone Publishing Company

Kk

K is for Kelly Kitten. Write the letter **k**.

Kelly Kitten knows all about the letter **k**. You can, too. Draw a line from each picture to the correct word. Then write the word.

keep

kite

king

kiss

key

© School Zone Publishing Company

Ww

W is for the Word Wagon. Write the letter **w**.

The Word Wagon wants **w** words. Draw a line around the words that begin with **w**. Then write them in the Word Wagon.

west happy snake word web wall

cow

jump

walk

wet

Wow! The Word Wagon is full of wonderful words!

© School Zone Publishing Company

Yy

Y is for You! Yes, it is! Write the letter **y**.

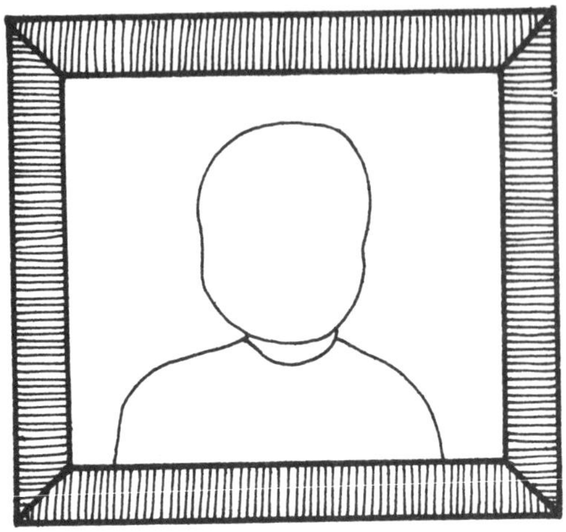

Now draw a picture of yourself!

Write the letter **y** in front of each word. Then say the word. Read the sentence to someone.

1. Sam likes to ____ell.

2. Pat plays in her ____ard.

3. Jay is seven ____ears old.

4. Dan is too ____oung to go to school.

5. Mary's favorite color is ____ellow.

6. ____es! I want ice cream!

© School Zone Publishing Company

Vv

V is for Valentine. Write the letter **v**.

Look at each picture. Say the word. Circle the pictures that begin with **v**.

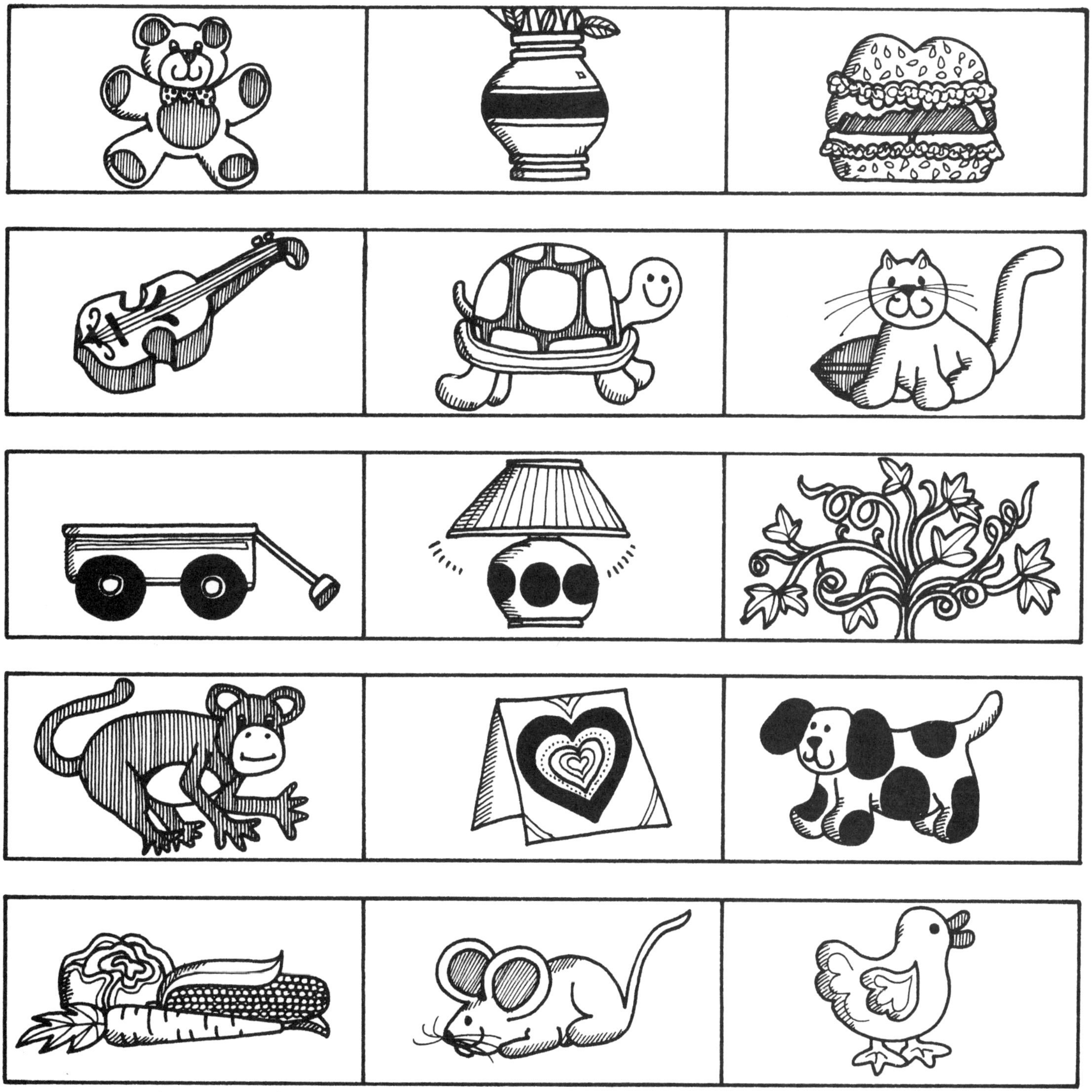

© School Zone Publishing Company

Zz

Z is for Zippy Zebra. Write the letter **z**.

Zippy Zebra likes the letter **z**. But not many words start with **z**. Look at the pictures. Say each word. Write the word on the line.

zipper

zebra

zoo

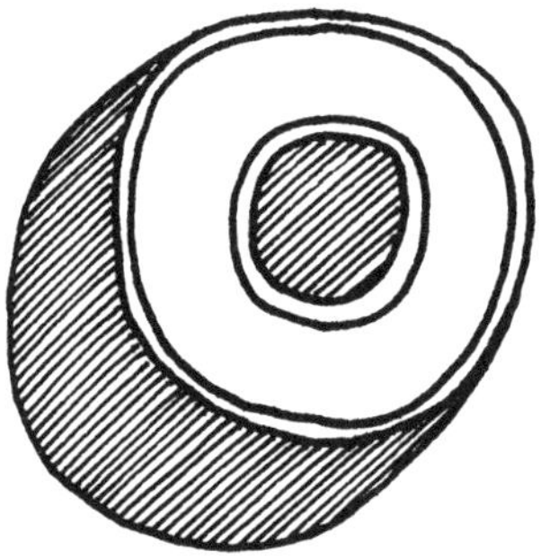

zero

© School Zone Publishing Company

Qq

Q is for Quiet Quentin. Shhh! Write the letter **q**. Write it quietly.

Color all the words that start with **q**. What is the picture?

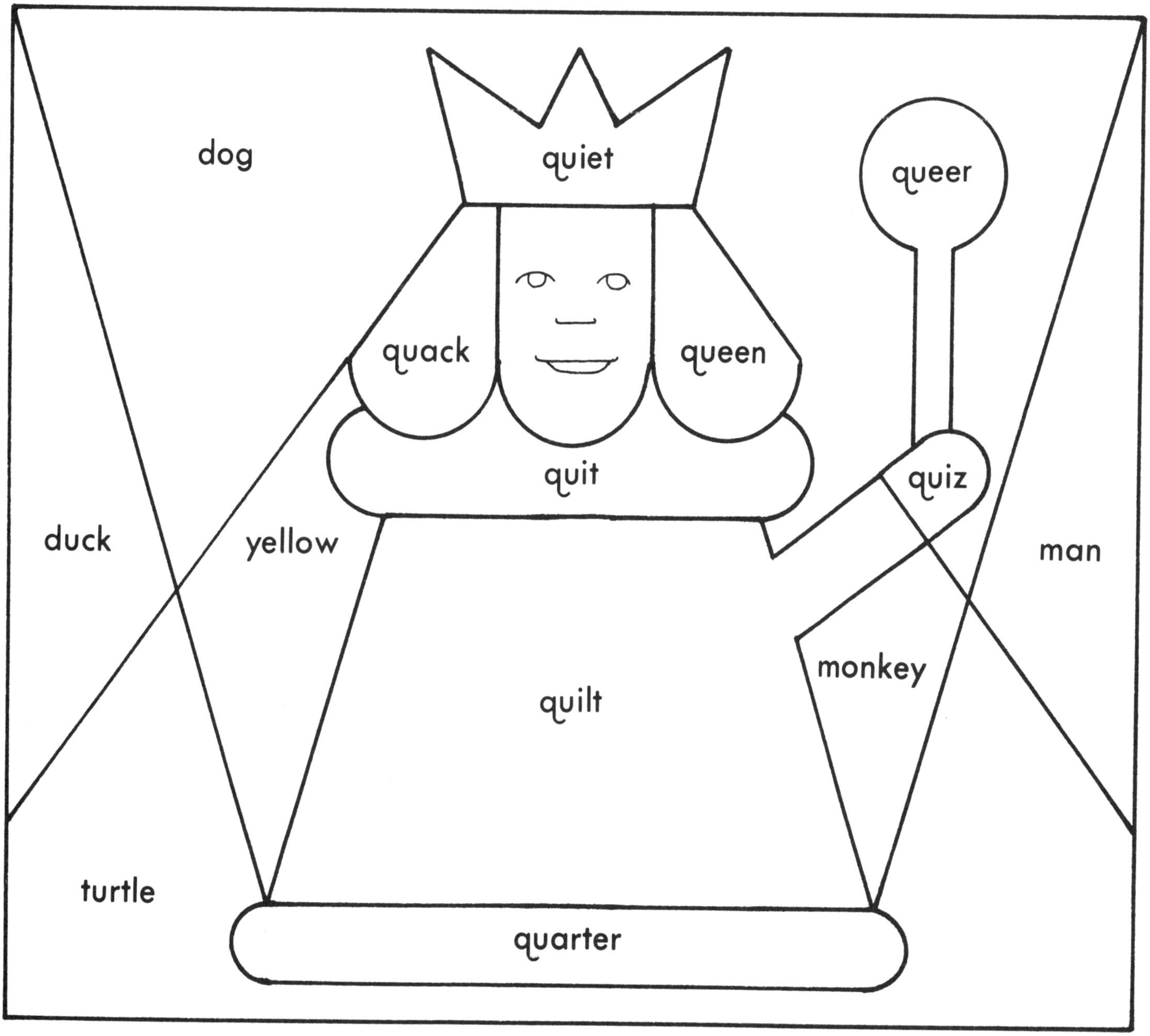

This is a picture of a (queen   quarter   duck).

© School Zone Publishing Company

Cc

C is for Cold Cat. Write the letter **c**.

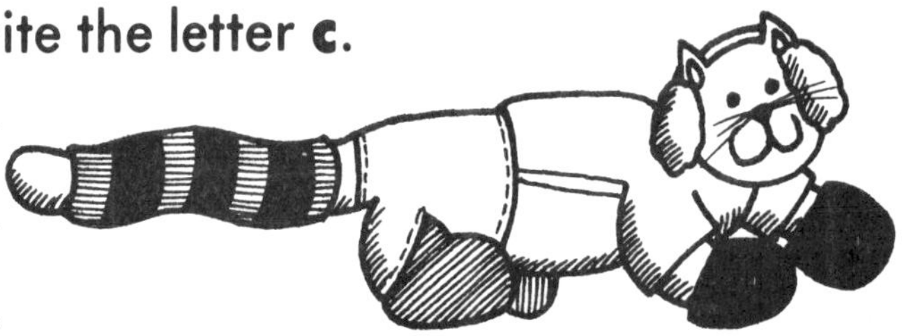

Cold Cat wants his coat. Help him find it. Write the correct word by each picture.

cake	cow	cat	coat	car	can

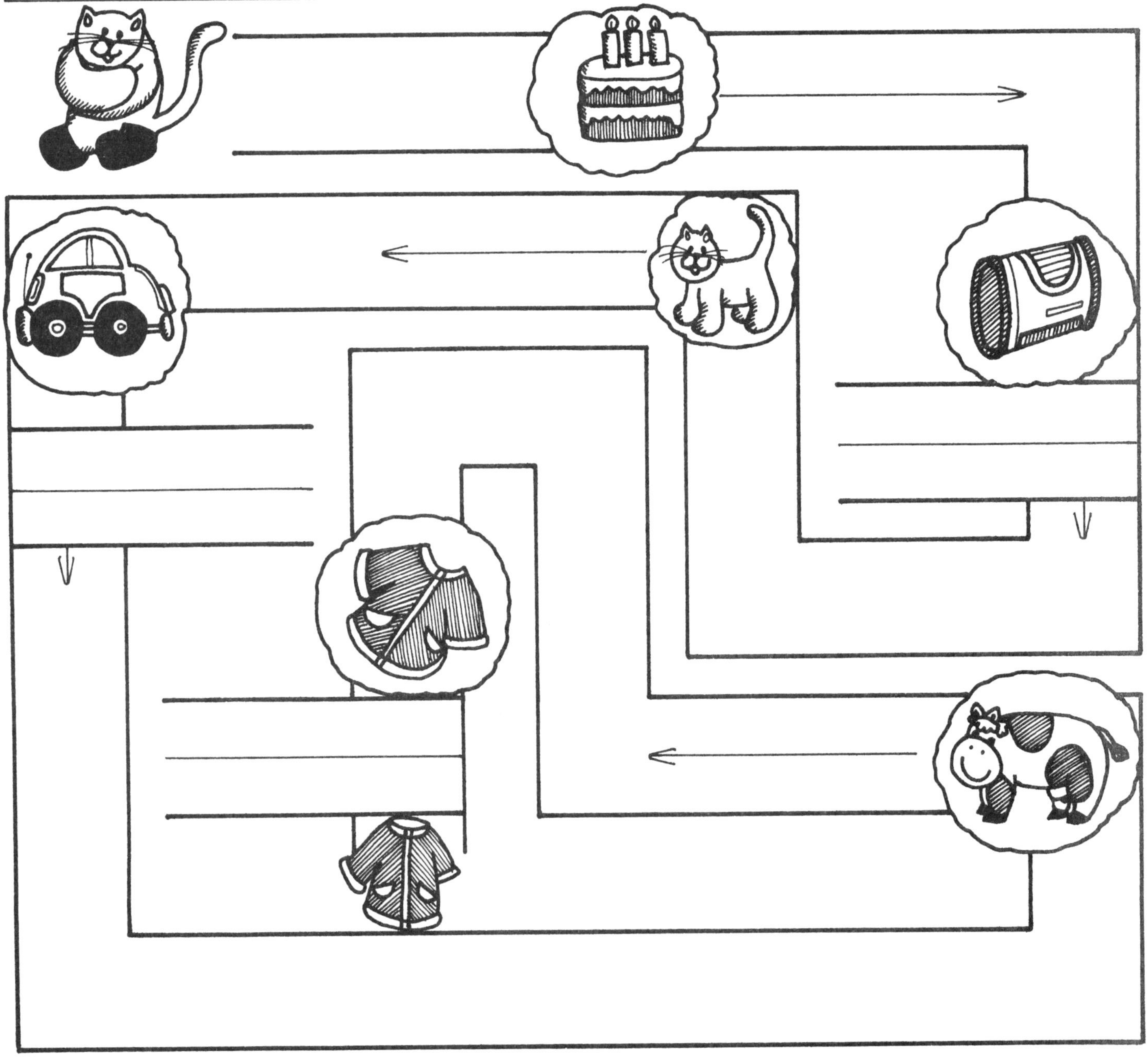

© School Zone Publishing Company

Cc

C also stands for circus. Write the letter **c**.

When the letter **c** is followed by **e**, **i**, or **y**, it usually has the soft sound. It sounds like the **c** in city.

Write the letter **c** in front of each word. Say the word. Read the sentence to a friend.

1. The ____ity has tall buildings.

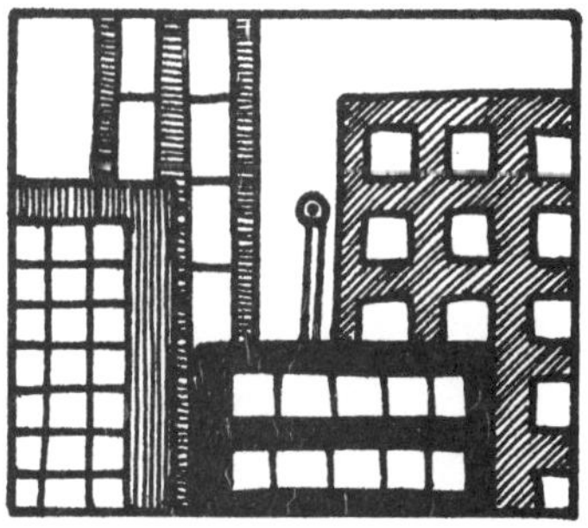

2. Mary drew a ____ircle on the paper

3. Mark stood in the ____enter of the circle.

4. We will go to the ____ircus.

© School Zone Publishing Company

Gg

G stands for Gary Goat. Write the letter **g**.

Gary Goat eats anything! Quick! Finish each word before Gary Goat eats it! Write the letter **g** in front of each word. Say the word.

____irl

____ate

____ood

____oat

____oose

____old

© School Zone Publishing Company

Gg

G also stands for Giant Giraffe. Write the letter **g**.

When **g** is used with **e**, **i**, or **y**, it has a soft sound. It sounds like the **g** in giraffe.

Giant Giraffe wants to be a General! Help him be a General. Connect the dots and he will be General Giant Giraffe! Then trace the words. Say each word.

general

giant

giraffe

© School Zone Publishing Company

Xx

X is used at the end of some words. Write the letter **x**.

Look at each picture. Say the word. Then finish each word by adding the letter **x**. Say the word again.

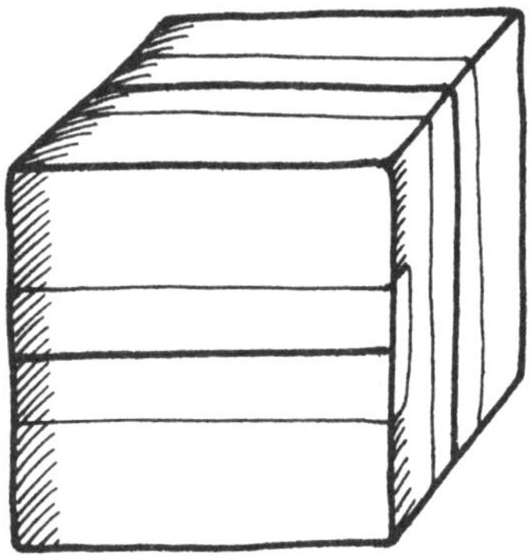

bo____

fo____

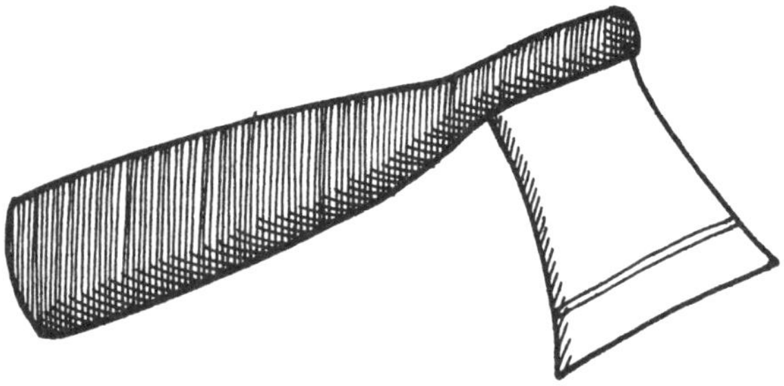

a____

si____

© School Zone Publishing Company

Pp

Nn

Sometimes **p** and **n** end words.

Draw a line around the pictures that end with the letter **p**.

Draw a line around the pictures that end with **n**.

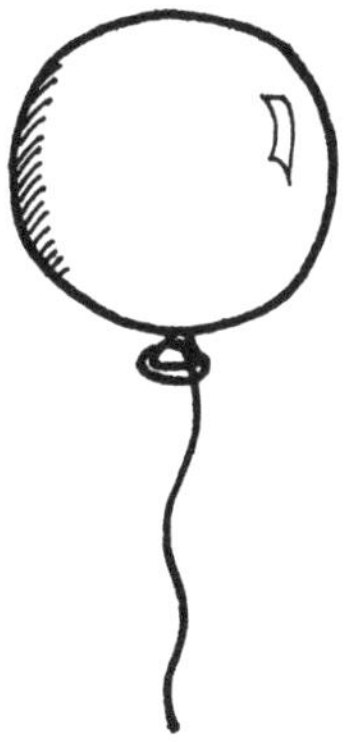

© School Zone Publishing Company

Dd

Rr

The letters **d** and **r** are sometimes used to end words.

Put an X next to the words that end in **d**.

________cow

________dad

________rocket

________pet

________told

________bird

________read

Put an X next to the words that end in **r**.

________bear

________money

________car

________turtle

________under

________fast

________sister

© School Zone Publishing Company

Ss 

Tt 

Sometimes the letter **s** ends a word. Sometimes the letter **t** ends a word. Draw a line from the letter to the picture word that ends in that letter.

jet	boat	cat	boots	dress	glass

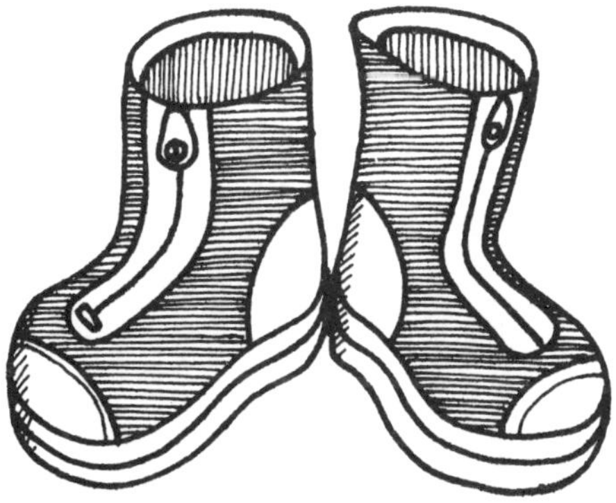

s

t

s

t

s

t

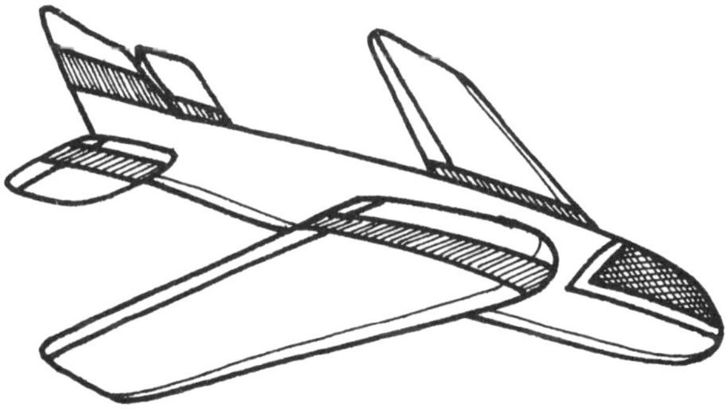

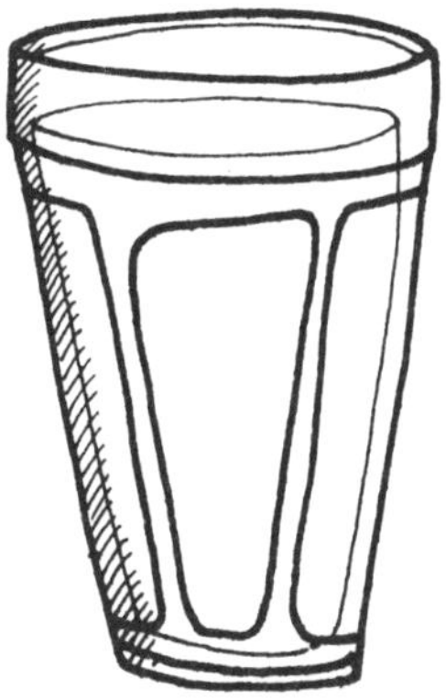

© School Zone Publishing Company

Yy

A lot of words end in **y**.

Circle the word or the picture that ends in **y**.

girl	big	funny	**y**
			**y**
tiger	why	never	**y**
			**y**
fun	game	play	**y**
			**y**
sad	happy	like	**y**
			**y**

© School Zone Publishing Company

Ll 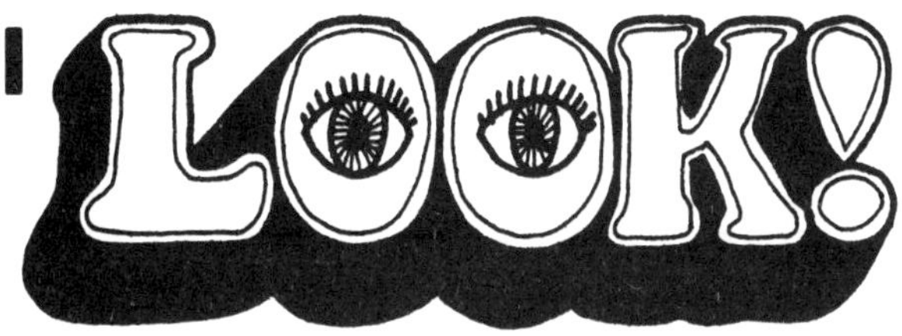

Ww 

The letter **l** can end words. The letter **w** can end words.

Draw a line around the picture or pictures whose name ends in the box letter.

© School Zone Publishing Company

WORD ENDING REVIEW

Draw a line around the picture or pictures whose name ends in the box letter.

n

s

p

t

d

r

© School Zone Publishing Company

REVIEW

Play word tick-tack-toe! Draw a line through the three pictures that have the same beginning sounds.

1.

2.

3.

4.

© School Zone Publishing Company

REVIEW

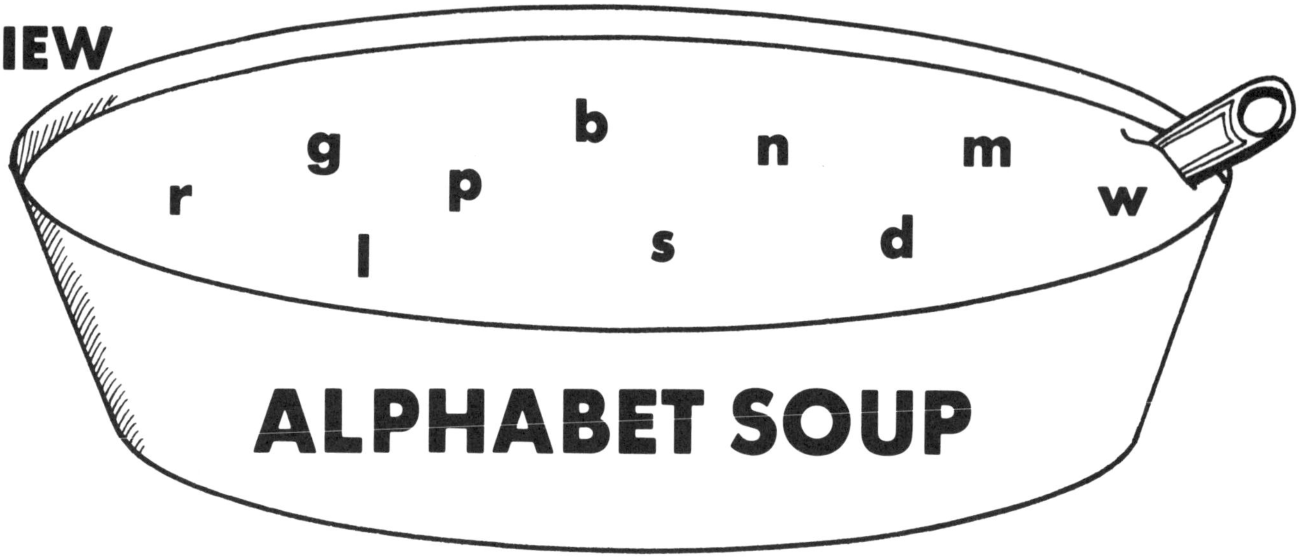

Find the right letter to make a word. Write the letter on the line.

____ird

____abbit

____any

____even

____iraffe

____ion

____othing

____octor

____icture

____agon

© School Zone Publishing Company

Page 33
Automatic
fill-in.

Page 34
mop
mice
map
milk
moon

Page 35
book
bug
bed
bird
bell
ball

Page 36
1. soap
2. sand
3. soup
4. saw
5. seal

Page 37
Automatic
fill-in.

Page 38
Automatic
fill-in.

Page 39
Automatic
fill-in.

Page 40
All words begin
with d.
Picture of a
duck.

Page 41
food
fox
feet
fire
farm
fish

Page 42
hat
hill
hand
hen
head

Page 43
1. red
2. rain
3. rope
4. road
5. race

Page 44
jump
just
jar
job
joke
jail

Page 45
king
kite
key
keep
kiss

Page 46
west
word
web
wall
walk
wet

Page 47
1. yell
2. yard
3. years
4. young
5. yellow
6. yes

Page 48
vase
violin
vine
Valentine
vegetables

Page 49
Automatic
fill-in.

Page 50
quack
quilt
quiet
queer
queen
quiz
quarter
quit
Picture of
a queen.

Page 51
cake
can
cat
car
cow
coat

Page 52
1. city
2. circle
3. center
4. circus

Page 53
girl
gate
good
goat
goose
gold

Page 54
Automatic
fill-in.

Page 55
box
fox
ax
six

Page 56
soap   balloon
sleep   train
mop   pan
cup   fan
man

Page 57
dad   bear
told   car
bird   under
read   sister

Page 58
t – boat, jet, cat
s – dress, glass, boots

Page 59
funny
baby
why
boy
play
money
happy
pony

Page 60
l – ball, hill
w – cow
l – owl, bell
w – saw

Page 61
n – man, train
s – dress
p – cup
t – cat, goat
d – bird
r – bear, car

Page 62
1. cat   2. dog   3. bird   4. fork
   car   duck   book   fish
   coat   doctor   bee   feet

Page 63
bird   lion
rabbit   nothing
many   doctor
seven   picture
giraffe   wagon

© School Zone Publishing Company

Answer the riddle. The answer to each riddle rhymes with cat.

pat
hat
bat
sat
rat

1. Fat Cat plays ball with this.
   It is a ___ ___ ___.
2. Fat Cat runs after this.
   It is a ___ ___ ___.
3. People do this to Fat Cat. Then he purrs.
   They ___ ___ ___.
4. Fat Cat wears one on his head.
   It is a ___ ___ ___.
5. Fat Cat did this when he was tired.
   He ___ ___ ___.

© School Zone Publishing Company

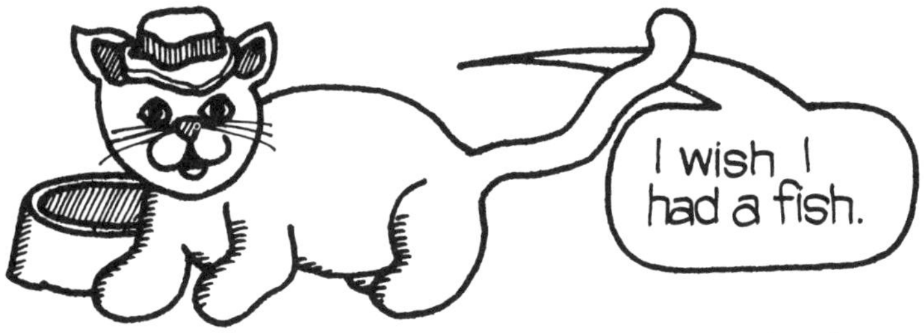

Read the sentence. Circle the words that rhyme. Then draw a picture.

The fish was in the dish.

The goat in the boat wore a coat.

© School Zone Publishing Company

Read the word in the box. Circle the picture that rhymes with the word. Write the name of the picture on the line.

thing

____

sing

____

sing

____

thing

____

© School Zone Publishing Company

Here is a story about Jake. Circle every word that rhymes with Jake.

Jake liked to bake. What should he make?

He would make a cake! A cake is what Jake would bake! Jake made the cake. He put it in to bake.

Then he went out. Jake went to the lake. He picked up a rake. Poor Jake! You cannot rake a lake!

But Jake said the lake was fake! He said he would take the rake. Take the rake and make a lake!

Jake! Stop, for goodness' sake! Go and check your cake! Forget about the fake lake!

I don't think Jake is awake!

© School Zone Publishing Company

Read the words. Write each word next to the correct picture. Say the word out loud.

book	cook	hook	look	took

 ________________

 ________________

 ________________

 ________________

 ________________

© School Zone Publishing Company

Look at the picture. Circle the word that names the picture.

let

pet

met

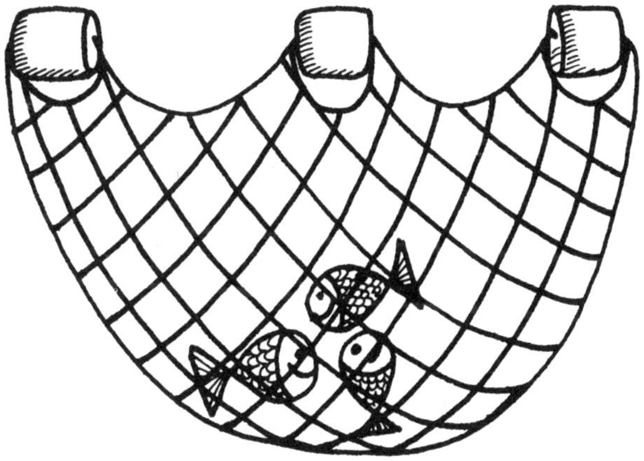

let

bet

net

vet

met

bet

net

pet

met

I'll bet the vet has a net to catch a pet.

© School Zone Publishing Company

Play tick-tack-toe. Draw a line through the three words that rhyme. Then write the three rhyming words on the line.

well	bend	send
boat	coat	goat
toy	look	dime

____
____
____

wish	cake	log
right	fish	cold
rake	bill	dish

____
____
____

thing	dog	hook
ring	time	coat
sing	cat	make

____
____
____

fish	like	sat
take	mat	ball
bat	bike	log

____
____
____

© School Zone Publishing Company

Read each sentence. Write the correct word on the line.

1. A __________ is green.
   dog hog frog

2. The __________ ran after the ball.
   dog log hog

3. A __________ is a big pig.
   frog dog hog

4. The woman cut the __________ with a saw.
   log hog frog

The frog sat on a log in the bog.

© School Zone Publishing Company

Say the word. Circle the picture that rhymes with the word.

big	
den	
fig	
pen	
big	
den	

© School Zone Publishing Company

Say the words. Draw a line from the words to the correct picture.

1. bed

2. sled

3. Ned and Ted

4. Ned fled.

5. Ned, Ted, and Jed

6. Ted led Jed.

Ned fled on a sled. Ted led Jed to another sled.

© School Zone Publishing Company

Make your own poem! Fill in the blanks with the words given.

town Brown crown gown down

Brenda ____________
Went to ____________.
She bought a ____________
And a ____________.

Brenda ____________
Fell right ____________.
She tore her ____________
And broke her ____________.

© School Zone Publishing Company

Read each sentence. Two words in each sentence rhyme. Circle the two words that rhyme.

1. The ball went over the wall.

2. The wall was tall.

3. Did you fall in the hall?

4. Did the ball fall on the cat?

5. She will call over the wall.

6. We play ball in the fall.

© School Zone Publishing Company

Read each word. Draw a line from the word to the correct picture.

1. jam

2. ham

3. Sam

4. Sam and ram

5. Sam and ham

6. Sam at the dam

Sam spread the jam on the ham, and fed it to the ram!

© School Zone Publishing Company

Look at the picture. Say the picture word. Circle the word that names the picture.

fat mat cat	bake cake lake	dish wish fish	king thing swing

goat boat coat	fall hall ball	wall tall call	sled bed red

brown gown crown	pig wig dig	bake take lake	hen pen men

ten men hen	dog frog hog	net pet let	look book cook

© School Zone Publishing Company

Answer the riddle. Write the correct word on the line.

block	clock	lock	dock	sock

1. It tells you the time.
   It is a ______________________.

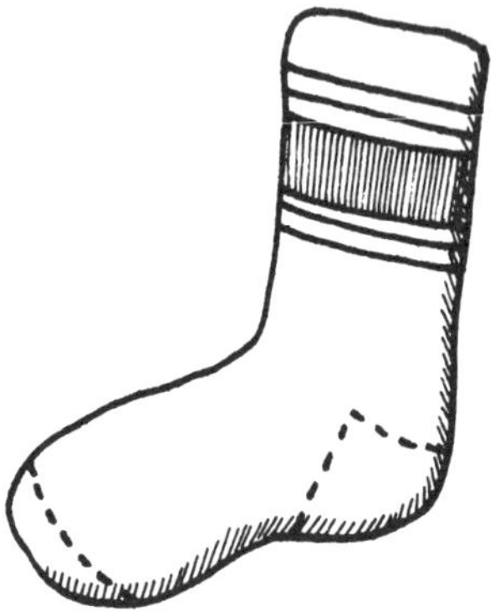

2. A key opens it.
   It is a ________________.

3. You wear it on your foot.
   It is a ____________________.

4. You play with it.
   It is a ______________________.

5. A boat can be here.
   It is a ____________________.

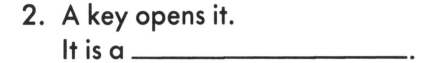

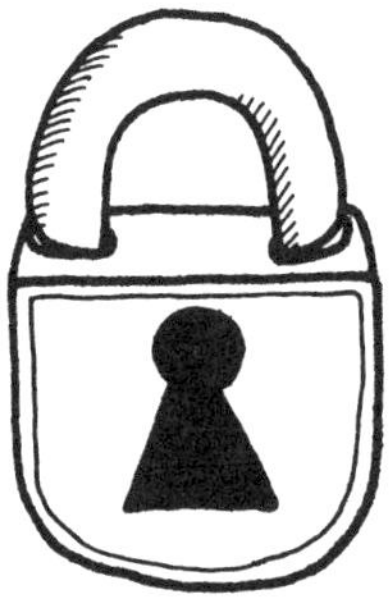

© School Zone Publishing Company

Read the sound in the box. Circle the word or picture that rhymes with the sound in the box.

un

cat

fun

dog

and

un

win

did

run

and

bell

said

land

un

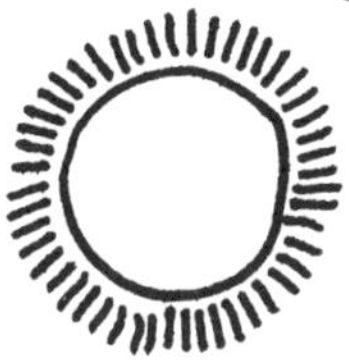

and

un

and

sand

mister

right

un

© School Zone Publishing Company

Read each sentence. Write the correct word on the line.

1. Jenny drank the ________________.

mop pop hop

2. Dad cleaned the floor with a ________________.

top hop mop

3. Mike said hello to the ________________.

cop top hop

4. That rabbit sure can ________________.

mop hop cop

5. The lid of the jar is the ________________.

hop cop top

© School Zone Publishing Company

Color blue all the words that rhyme with **an**.

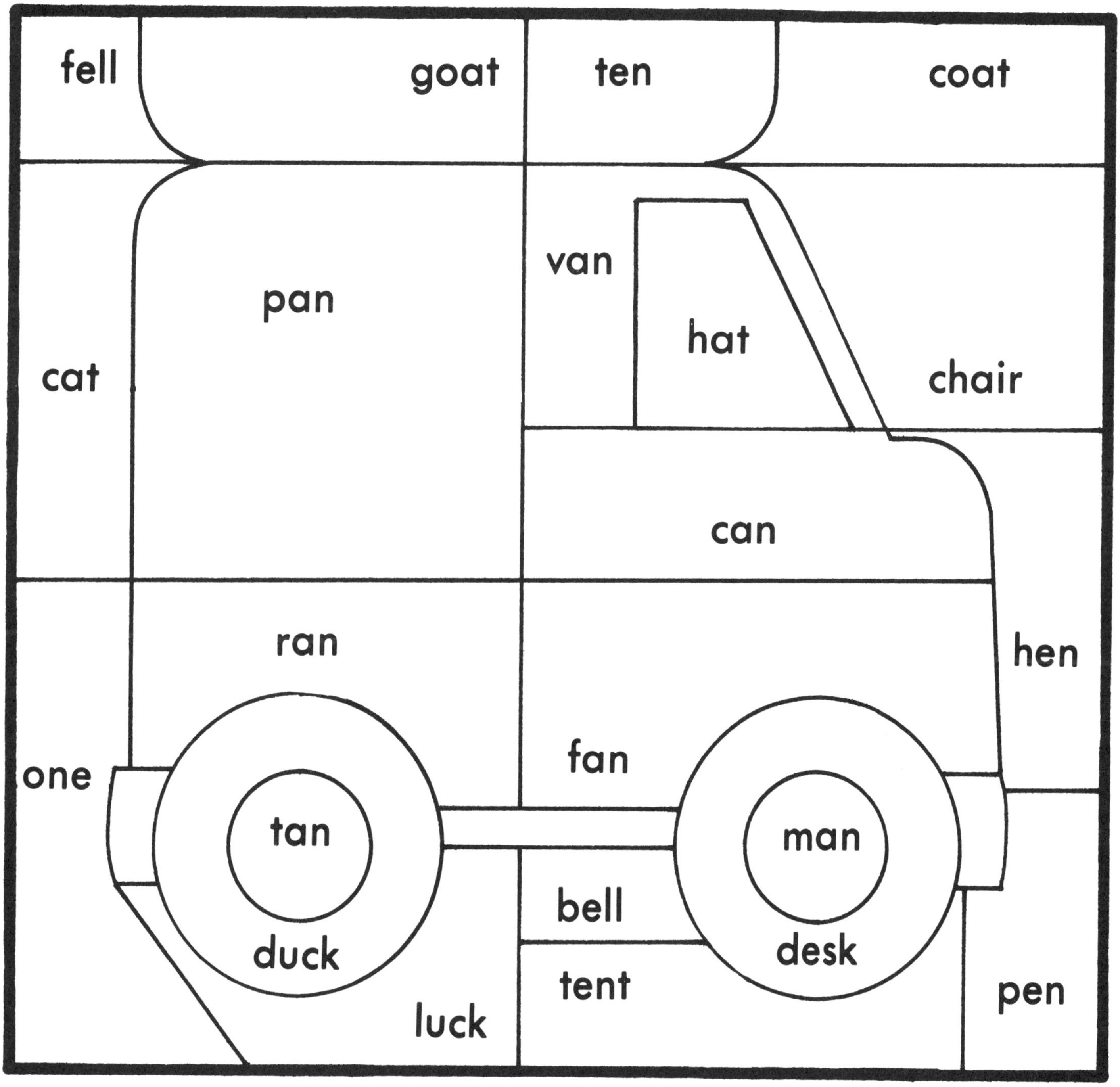
fell
goat
ten
coat
van
pan
hat
cat
chair
can
ran
hen
fan
one
tan
man
bell
duck
desk
tent
pen
luck

This is a picture of a (man fan van).

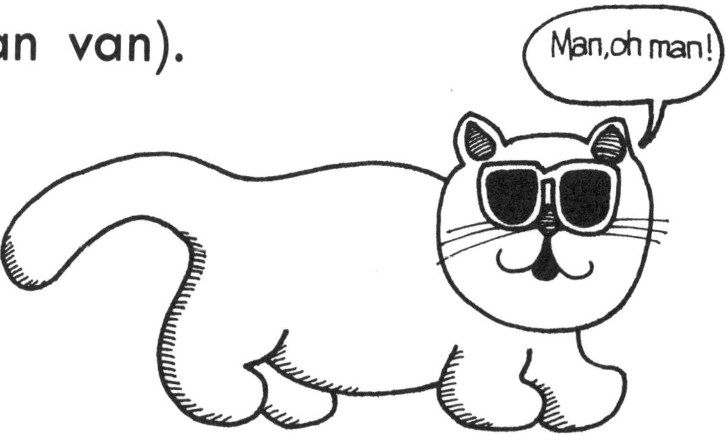
Man, oh man!

© School Zone Publishing Company

Mack the Hack is a Lumberjack! He wants you to have fun with the **ack** sound. Follow the directions.

p	cr	J	bl	b	t

1. Add one letter to ack. The word means "not in front."
   It is in ______________________.
2. Add two letters to ack. The word is a color.
   It is ______________________.
3. Add a capital letter to ack. It is a boy's name.
   It is ______________________.
4. Add two letters to ack. It is in a sidewalk.
   It is a ______________________.
5. Add one letter to ack. It is very sharp.
   It is a ______________________.
6. Add one letter to ack. You do this to a suitcase.
   You ______________________ it.

Mack and Jack lack a tack!

© School Zone Publishing Company

A lot of words rhyme with **old.** Find the way to the gold.
Write all the **old** words.

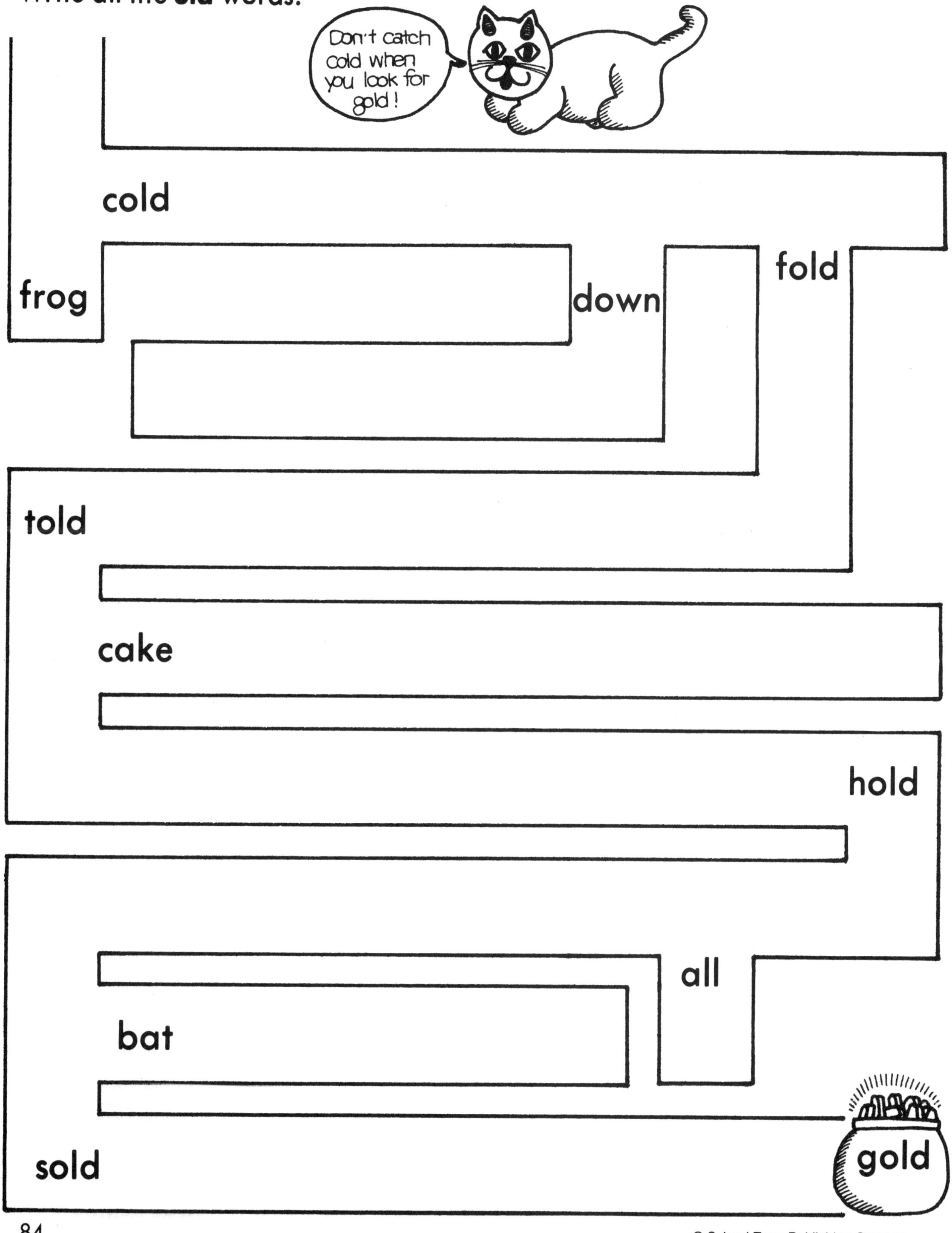

© School Zone Publishing Company

Look at the picture. Add one letter to the first line to make a word. The word tells what the picture is. Then add letters to the other lines to make words that rhyme.

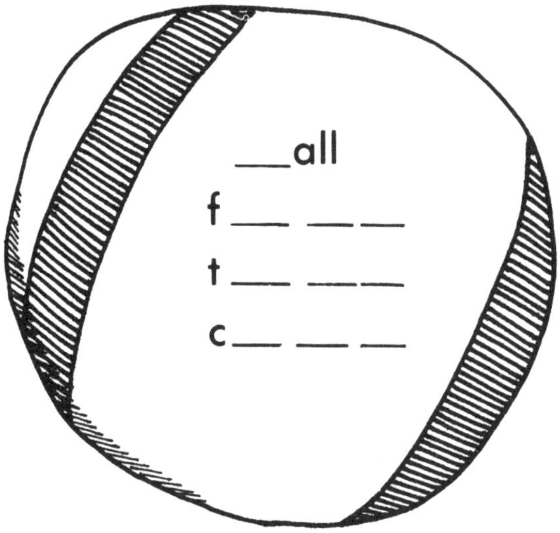

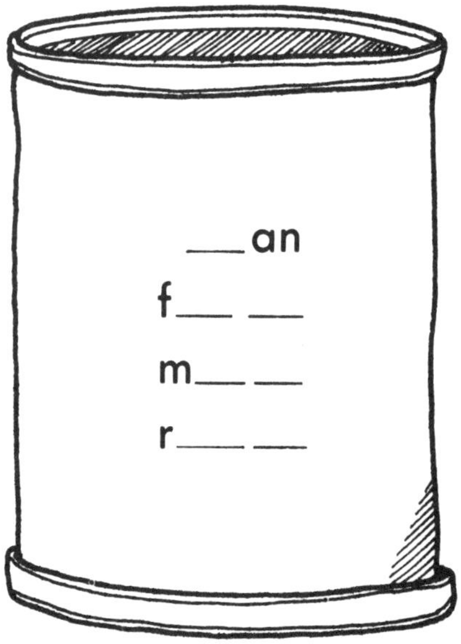

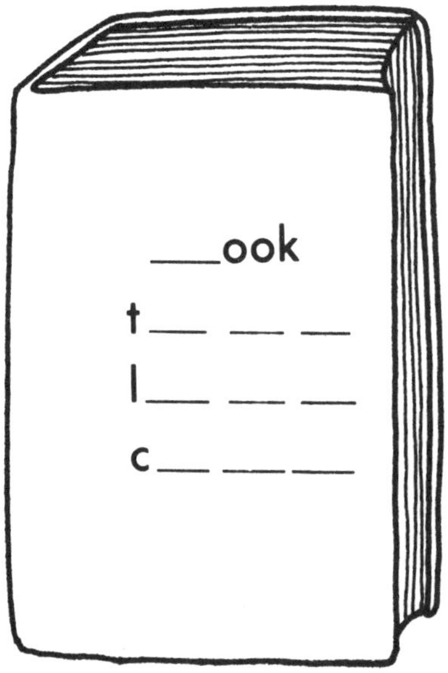

© School Zone Publishing Company

Draw a line from the word to the correct picture. Say each word.

dot

Spot

pot

knot

hot

Scott

© School Zone Publishing Company

Read the sentence. Circle the words that rhyme. Then draw a picture.

Nell fell in the well.	Yell when I ring the bell.

© School Zone Publishing Company

Look at the words. Write a word next to the correct picture. Say the word.

lap	cap	trap	map	nap

____

____

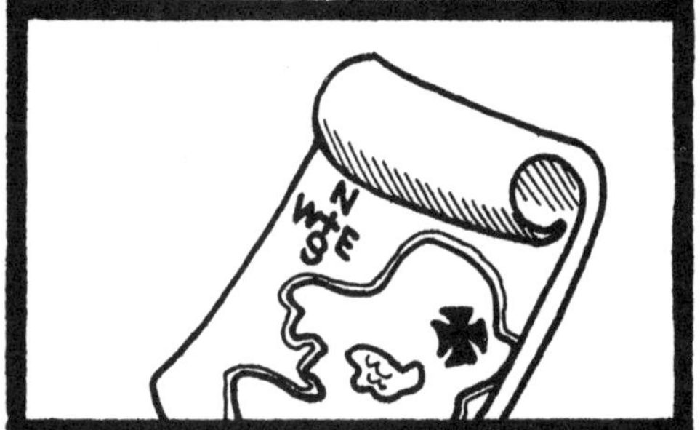
N
W
E
S

____

____

____

I like to wear a cap when I take a nap.

© School Zone Publishing Company

Help the jay hide in the hay! Write all the words that rhyme with jay and hay on the lines.

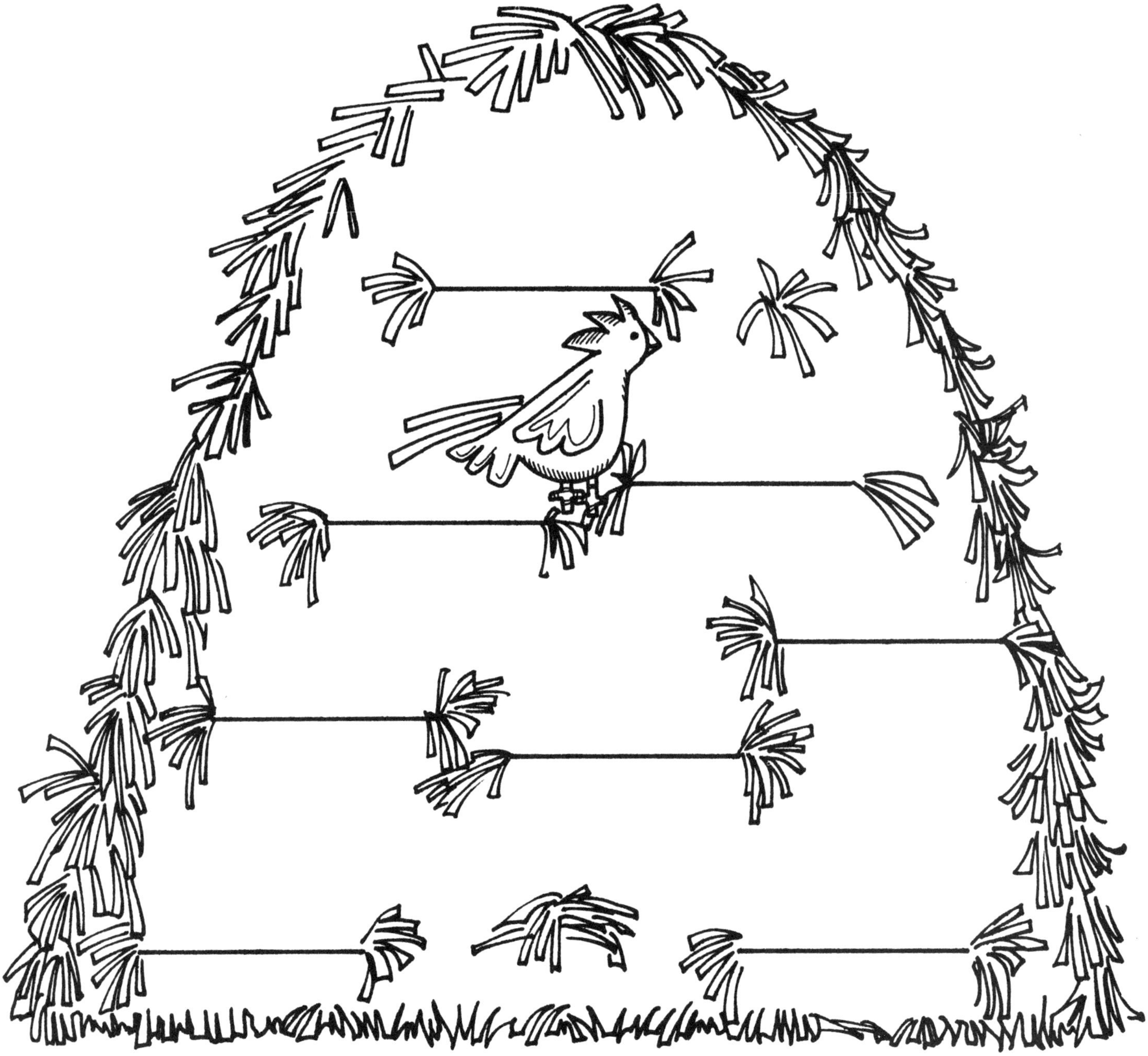

dig	bay	pay	lay	hop	log	way
day	bird	into	ray	fat	say	may

© School Zone Publishing Company

This is a story about Bug. Fill in the lines with the correct words. All the words rhyme with Bug.

1. Bug liked to sleep on a ____________.

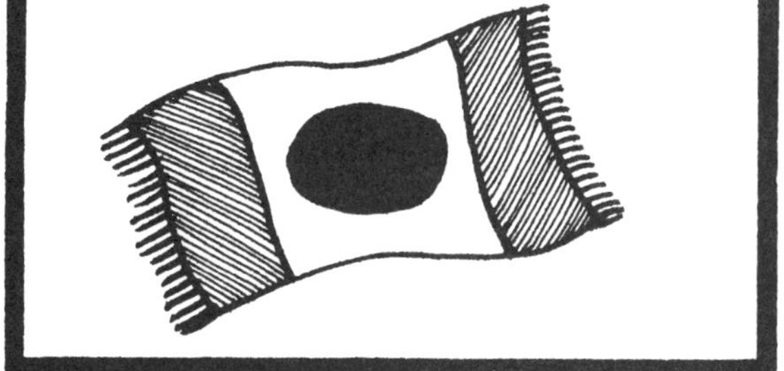

2. Bug drank her milk from a ____________.

3. When Bug liked somebody, she gave them a ____________.

4. One day Bug saw a long rope. She gave it a __________.

Oops! Dirt dropped on Bug!

5. Bug had to get out! So Bug ____________ her way out.

6. Then she went home. Bug went back to sleep on her _______.

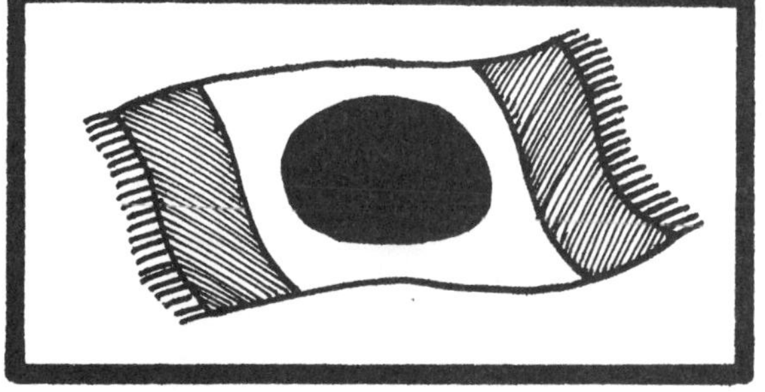

© School Zone Publishing Company

This is a tent game. Write all the words that rhyme with tent on the lines.

rent go bent cent away dent chair bird sent

REVIEW

Look at the pictures. Say the picture words. Circle Yes if the picture words rhyme. Circle No if they do not rhyme.

Yes No

Yes No

Yes No

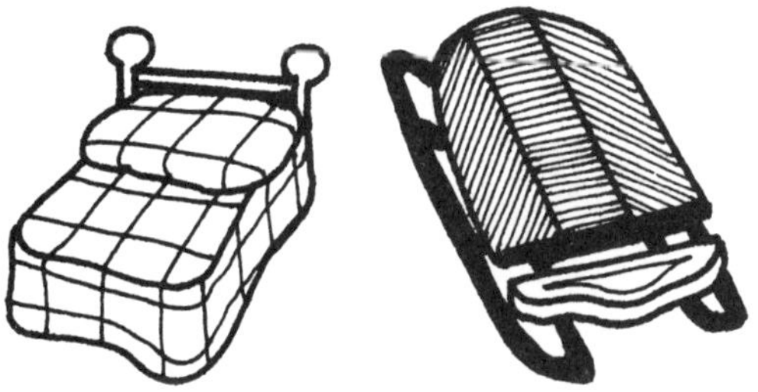

Yes No

Yes No

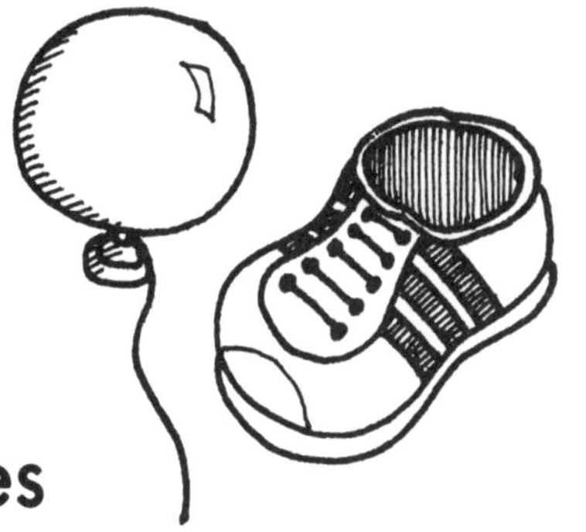

Yes No

Yes No

Yes No

© School Zone Publishing Company

REVIEW

Draw a line from the rhyming words to the correct picture.

fat cat

ten men

hot pot

goat coat

wet pet

bug mug

frown clown

fish dish

bell fell

bent tent

© School Zone Publishing Company

REVIEW

Read the sentence. Say the word in the box. Then put a box around the word that rhymes with it.

1. I fell into the well.

2. Look at my new book.

3. The boy had a new toy.

4. I like your red bike.

5. I told you I had a cold.

6. The vet helped my pet.

7. Did Nell tell you a joke?

8. Ten men went to work.

© School Zone Publishing Company

REVIEW

Read each riddle. Write the answer on the line. Then draw a picture of your answer.

1. It rhymes with red.
   You sleep in it. ____________

2. It rhymes with dish.
   It can swim. ____________

3. It rhymes with lake.
   You eat it. ____________

4. It rhymes with hall.
   It is a toy. ____________

5. It rhymes with boat.
   It is something to wear. ____________

6. It rhymes with tell.
   It rings. ____________

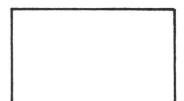

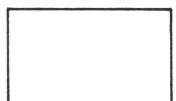

It rhymes with send. This is the ________.

© School Zone Publishing Company

Page 65
1. bat
2. rat
3. pat
4. hat
5. sat

Page 66
fish – dish
goat – boat – coat

Page 67
thing – ring
sing – king
sing – wing
thing – swing

Page 68
bake, make
make, cake, cake, bake,
cake, bake
lake, rake, rake, lake,
lake, fake, take, rake, take,
rake, make, lake
sake, cake, fake, lake

Page 69
cook
took
book
hook
look

Page 70
pet, net
vet, met

Page 71
boat, goat, coat
wish, fish, dish
thing, ring, sing
bat, mat, sat

Page 72
1. frog
2. dog
3. hog
4. log

Page 73
big – pig
den – hen
fig – wig
pen – men
big – dig
den – ten

Page 75
Brown
town
gown/crown
crown/gown
Brown
down
gown
crown

Page 76
1. ball, wall
2. wall, tall
3. fall, hall
4. ball, fall
5. call, wall
6. ball, fall

Page 78
cat, cake, fish, king
coat, ball, wall, sled
crown, wig, lake, men
ten, frog, net, book

Page 79
1. clock
2. lock
3. sock
4. block
5. dock

Page 80
un – fun, and – hand, un – run
and – land, un – sun, and – band
un – gun, and – sand, un – bun

Page 81
1. pop
2. mop
3. cop
4. hop
5. top

Page 82

pan	fan
van	man
can	tan
ran	(van)

Page 83
1. back
2. black
3. Jack
4. crack
5. tack
6. pack

Page 84
cold
fold
told
hold
sold
gold

Page 85

cake	cat
rake	bat
bake	rat
take	sat
hen	ball
pen	fall
ten	tall
men	call
can	book
fan	took
man	look
ran	cook

Page 87
Nell, fell, well
yell, bell

Page 88
cap
nap
map
trap
lap

Page 89
day, bay, lay
may, pay, ray
say, way

Page 90
1. rug
2. mug
3. hug
4. tug
5. dug
6. rug

Page 91
rent, bent
cent, dent
sent

Page 92
cat – hat, yes
cake – foot, no
pig – wig, yes
hook – book, yes
log – dog, yes
bed – sled, yes
balloon – shoe, no
bug – mouse, no

Page 94
1. fell
2. book
3. boy
4. like
5. cold
6. vet
7. Nell
8. Ten

Page 95
1. bed
2. fish
3. cake
4. ball
5. coat
6. bell

© School Zone Publishing Company

SHORT A WORDS

Short a sounds like the a in apple.
It also sounds like the a in ant.

Say the picture word. Write the word. Add the correct letters.

___ a ___

___ a ___

___ ___ ck

st ___ mp

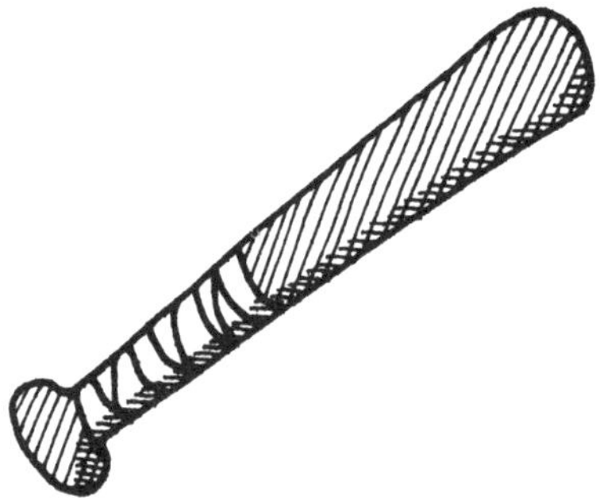

b ___ t

l ___ mp

___ a ___

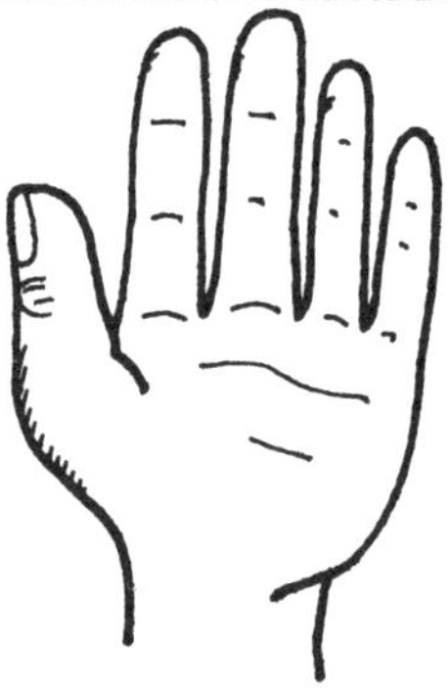

___ a ___ ___

___ a ___ ___

My Aunt Ann is an ant who eats apples.

SHORT A WORDS

Say the picture word. Does the word have a short a sound? Circle Yes if it does. Circle No if it does not.

No 	Yes No 	Yes No 
Yes No 	Yes No 	Yes No 
Yes No 	Yes No 	Yes No 
Yes No 	Yes No 	Yes No 

© School Zone Publishing Company

Color all the words that have a short a sound red.

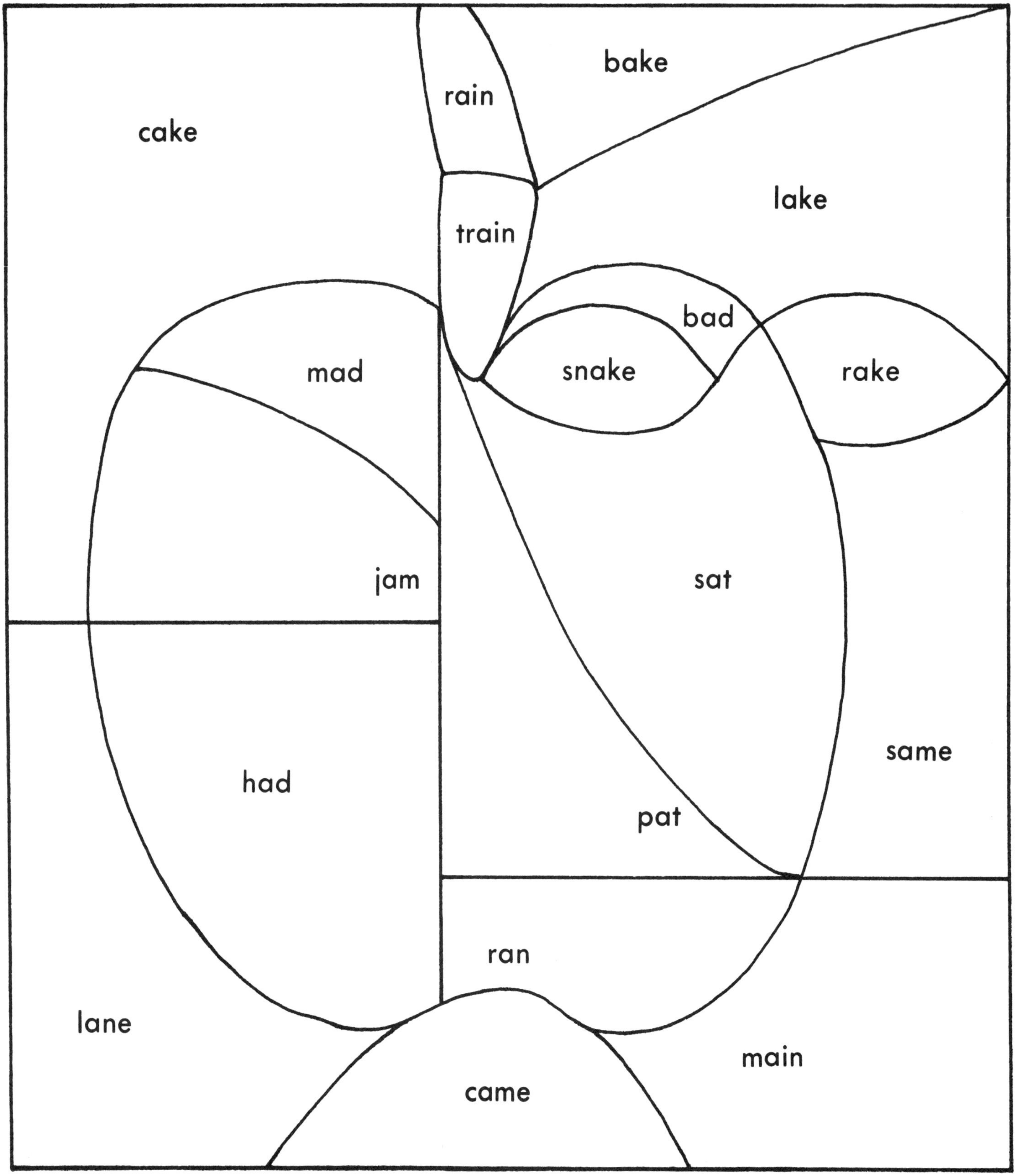

This is a picture of an ___ ___ ___ ___ ___.

Ants eat an apple a day to keep doctors mad!

© School Zone Publishing Company

SHORT A WORDS

____

Answer the riddle. Write the correct word on the line. Then draw a picture of your answer.

mask	bat	hand	fan	cat

1. You need a ball and ______ to play baseball.

2. A ______ blows air on you.

3. On Halloween, you could wear a ________ .

4. The mother of a kitten is a ______ .

5. Hold my ________ when we cross the street.

© School Zone Publishing Company

SHORT E WORDS

Short e sounds like the first sound in Edward Elephant.

Help Edward Elephant find his way home. Write the correct short e word by each picture.

tent	nest	sled	bell	ten	bed

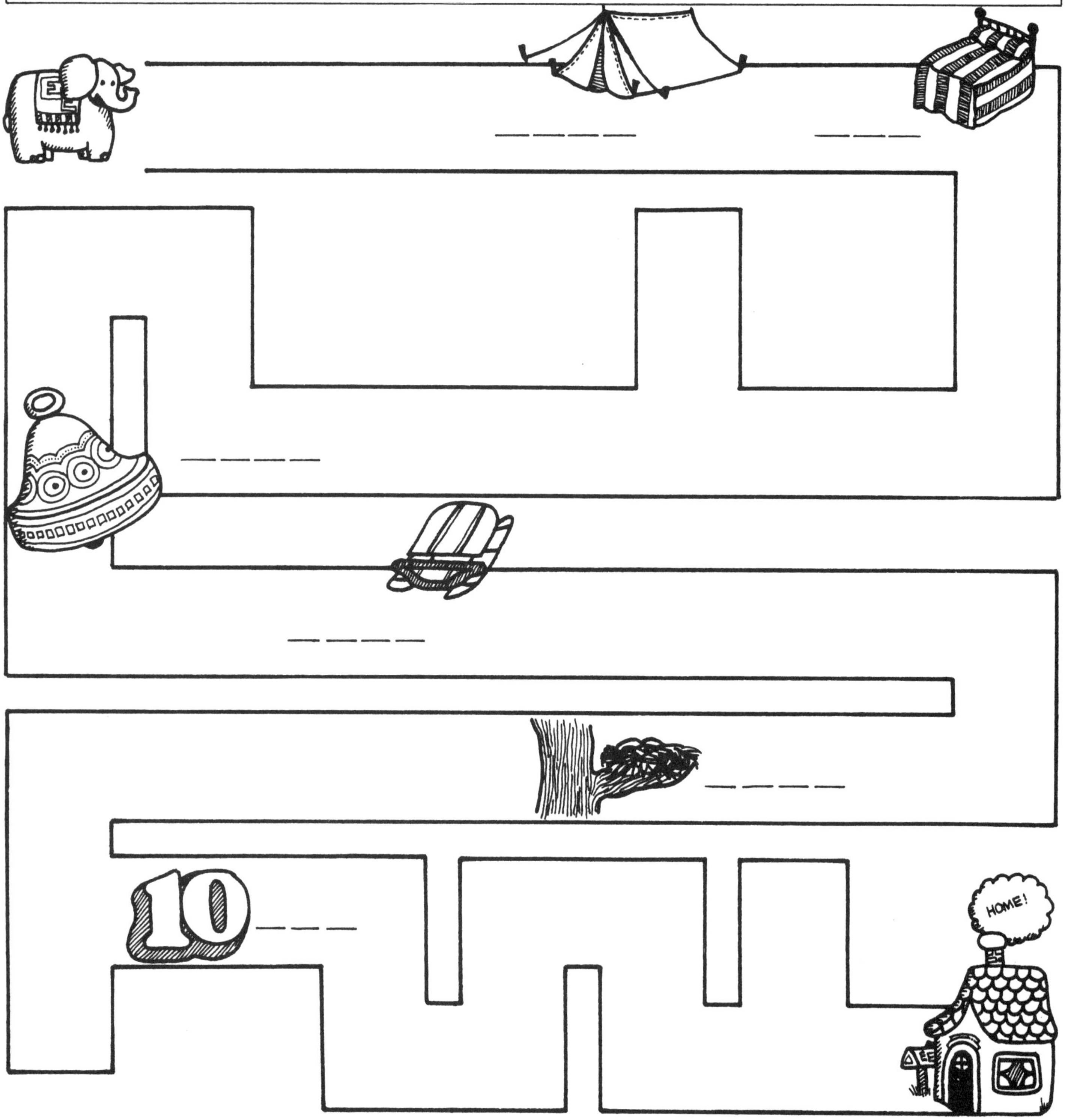

© School Zone Publishing Company

SHORT E WORDS

Draw a line from the short e word to the correct picture. Write each word under the picture.

leg

belt

pen

dress

desk

hen

wet

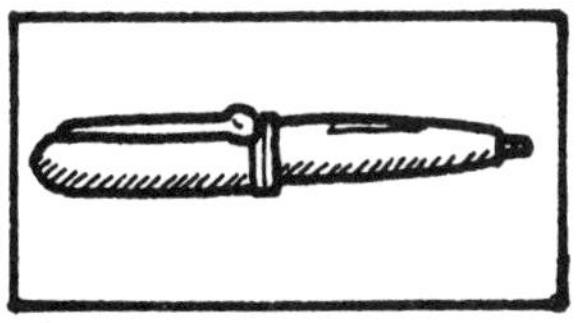

© School Zone Publishing Company

Edward Elephant has a lot of words! Some of them have the short e sound. Put an x next to the words that have the short e sound.

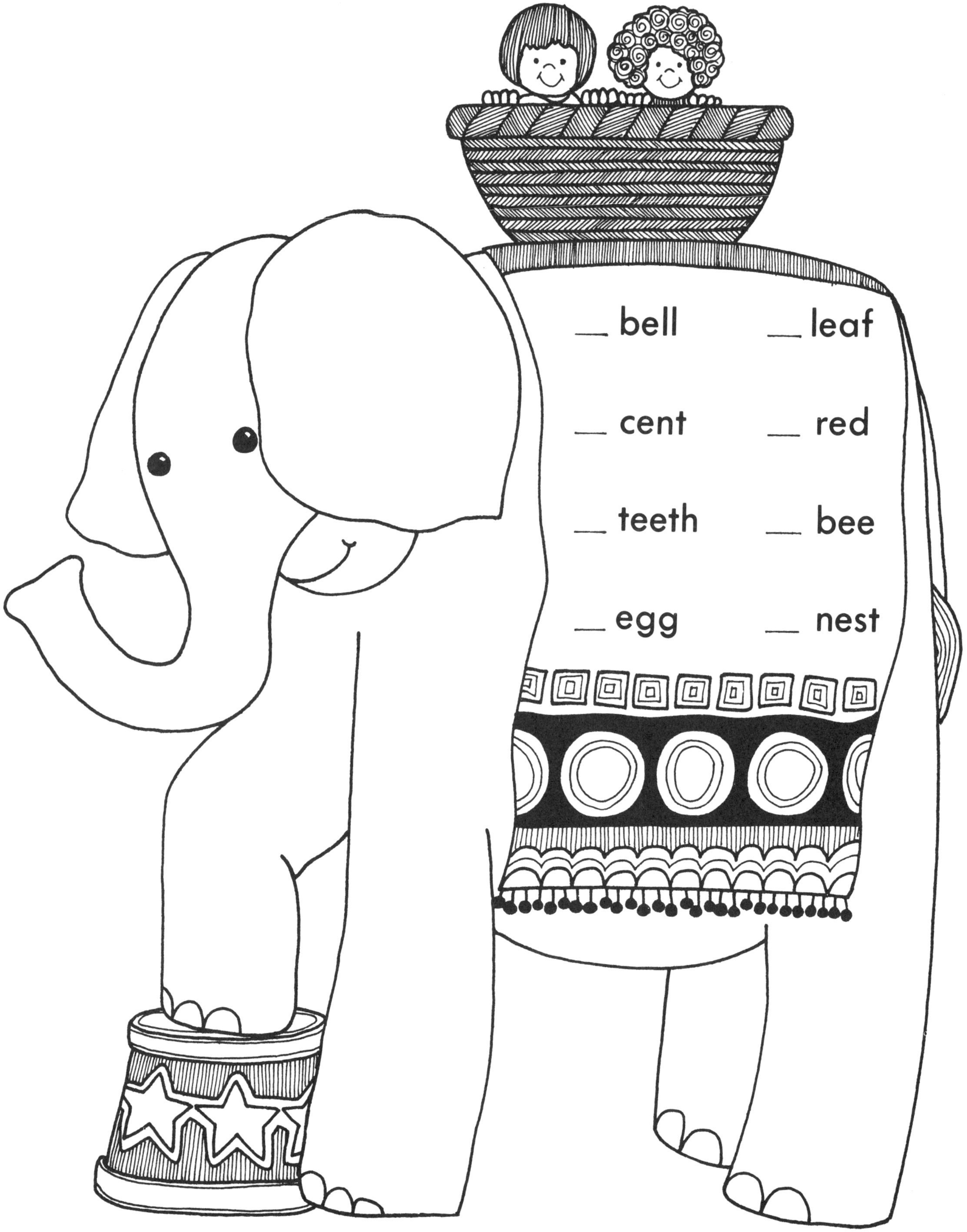

© School Zone Publishing Company

REVIEW: <u>a</u>, <u>e</u>

Answer the riddle. Add an <u>a</u> or an <u>e</u> to get the correct answer. Say the word.

1. You cook food in this. p___n

2. You write with this. p___n

3. It makes a ringing sound. b___ll

4. It is a good fruit. ___pple

5. It is a bright color. r___d

6. It lays eggs. h___n

7. You hit a ball with this. b___t

8. This has five fingers on it. h___nd

© School Zone Publishing Company

REVIEW: a, e

Write a in the space if it is a short a word. Write e if it is a short e word. Say the word. Then draw a line from the word to the picture.

1. t____ n

2. f ____ n

3. ____ pple

4. ____ nt

5. m ____ n

6. t ____ nt

7. d ____ sk

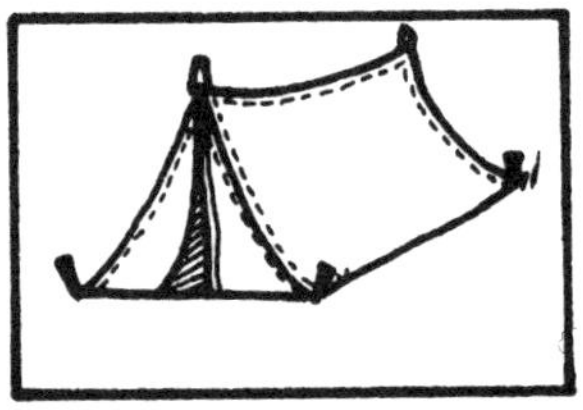

© School Zone Publishing Company

SHORT I WORDS

Short i sounds like the i in it.

Look at the picture. Say the word. Write in the missing letters. Say the word again.

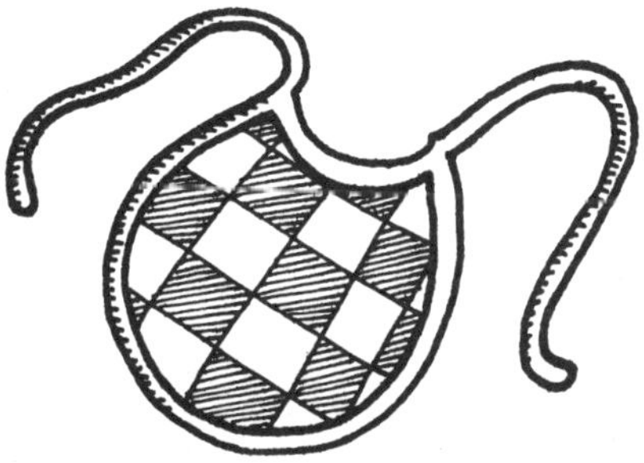 b ___ b	 f ___ sh	 p ___ g
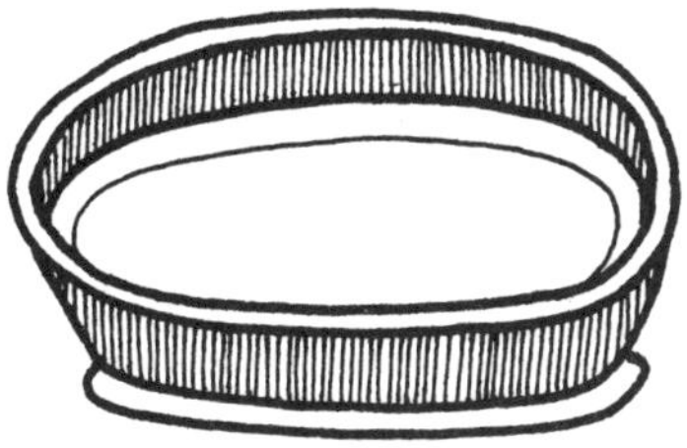 ___ i ___ ___	 ___ i ___ ___	 ___ t
 l ___ d	 w ___ g	 g ___ ft

© School Zone Publishing Company

SHORT I WORDS

Look at the picture. Say the picture word. If it has a short i sound, circle Yes. If it does not have a short i sound, circle No.

 Yes No	 Yes No	 Yes No
 Yes No	 Yes No	 Yes No
 Yes No	 Yes No	 Yes No
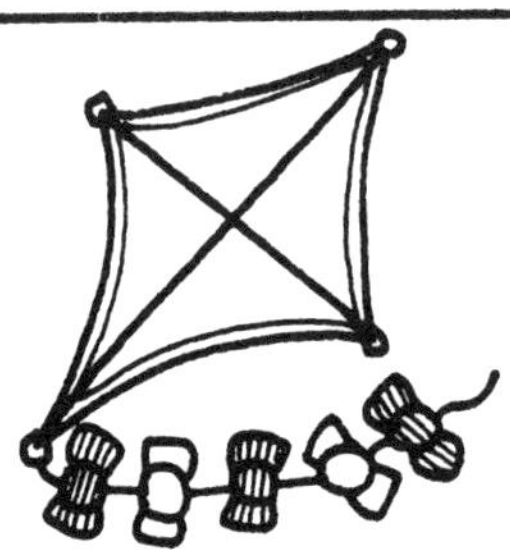 Yes No	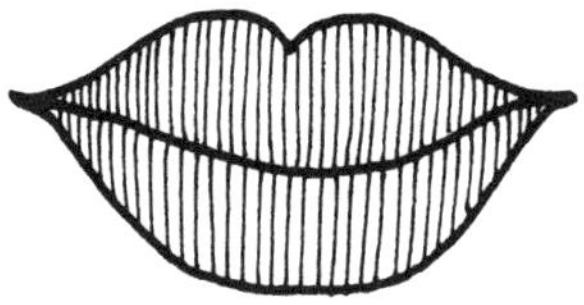 Yes No	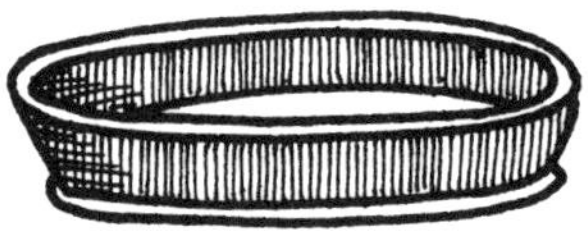 Yes No

© School Zone Publishing Company

SHORT I WORDS

Color all the short i words. Color them pink.

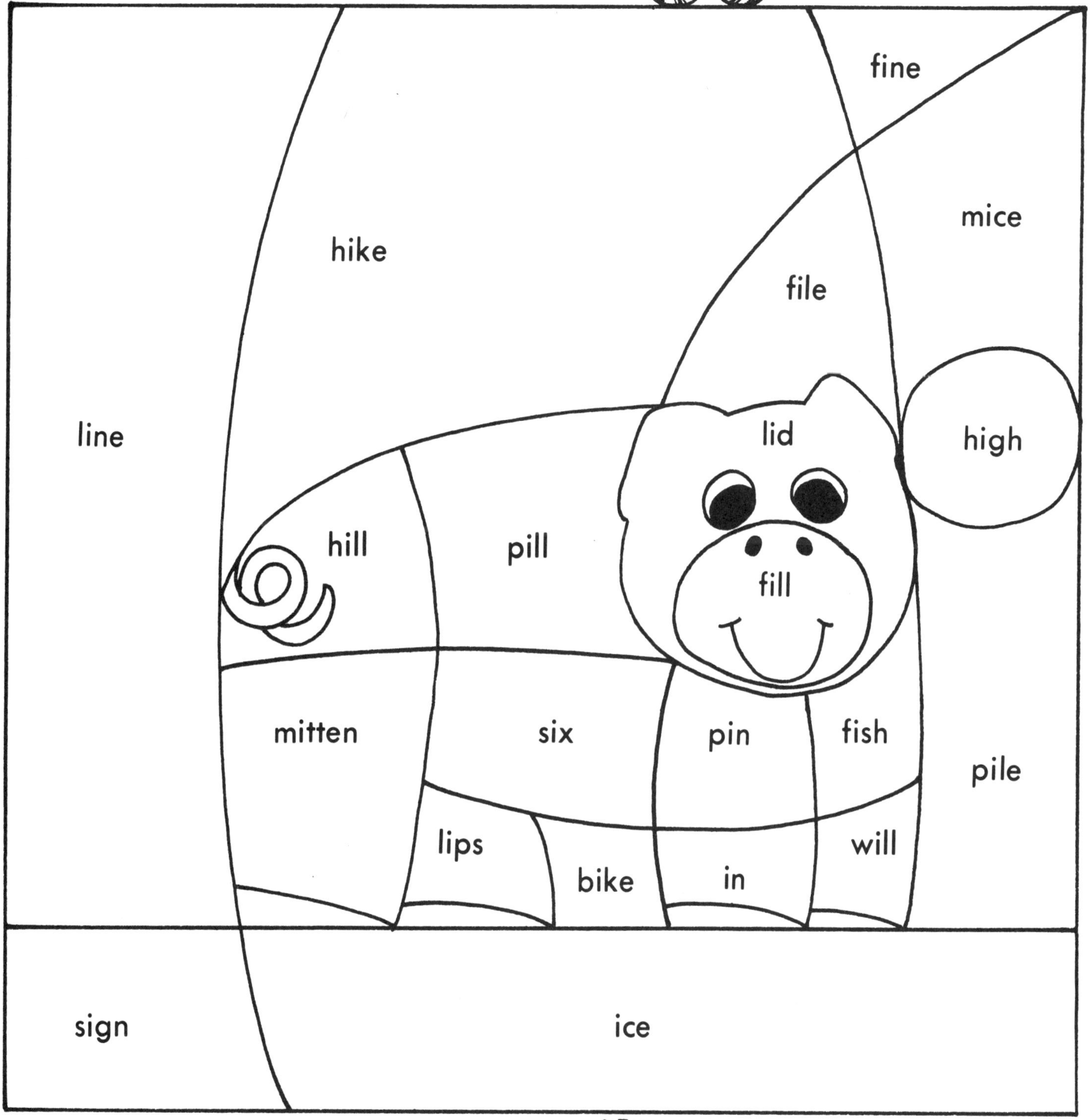

This is a picture of a ___ ___ ___ .

© School Zone Publishing Company

REVIEW: a, i

Ant and It have their words all mixed up! Write the words that have a short a sound in Ant's house. Write the words that have a short i sound in It's house.

pig	hat	lamp	six
hill	hand	fish	bad

© School Zone Publishing Company

REVIEW: e, i

Help Edward Elephant and It stop fighting! Draw a line from Edward Elephant to the things that have a short e sound. Draw a line from It to the things that have a short i sound.

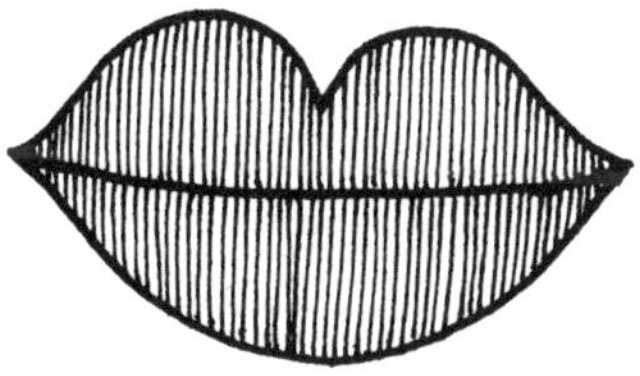

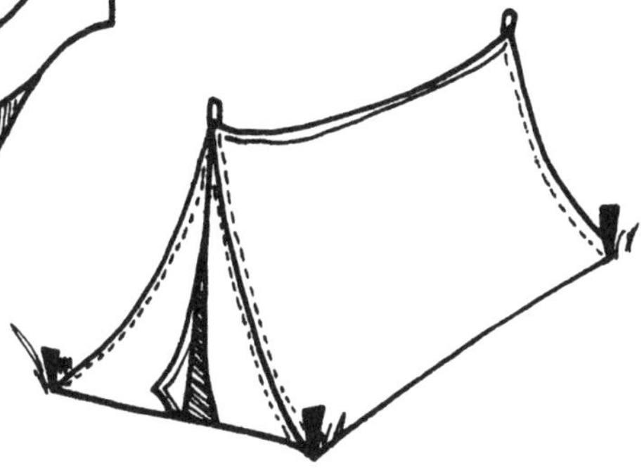

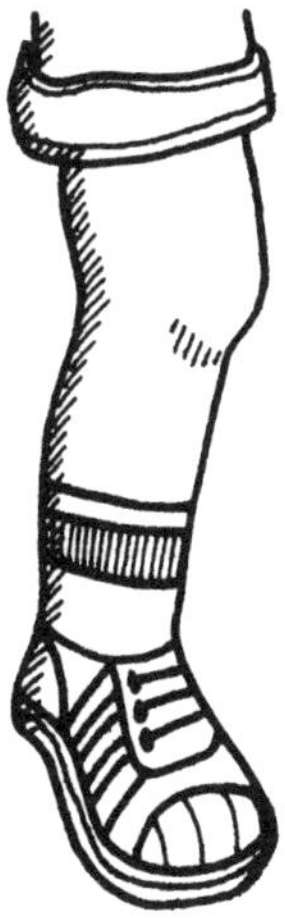

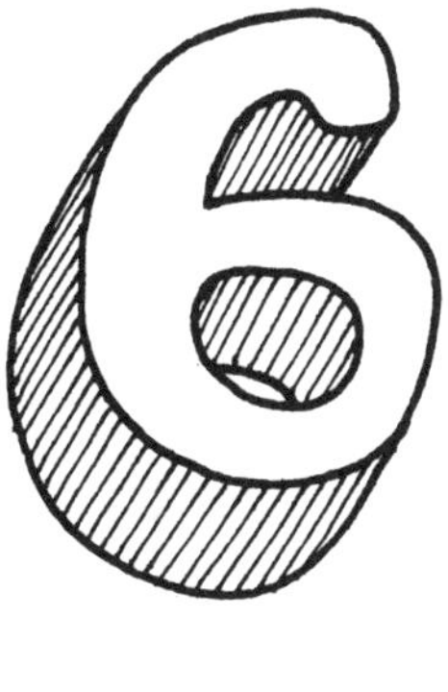

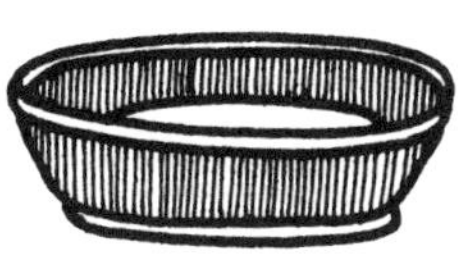

The sled belongs to (It, Edward Elephant).

© School Zone Publishing Company

REVIEW: a, e, i

There are six things hidden in the picture. Circle each hidden thing.
Write the word on the correct line.

bat	gift	pen	tent	fan	fish

Short a sound	Short e sound	Short i sound
____________	____________	____________
____________	____________	____________

© School Zone Publishing Company

SHORT O WORDS

Short o sounds like the beginning sound in Olive Octopus.

Olive Octopus has something in each arm! But she forgot what she has! Put an o in each blank. Then Olive Octopus will know what she is holding!

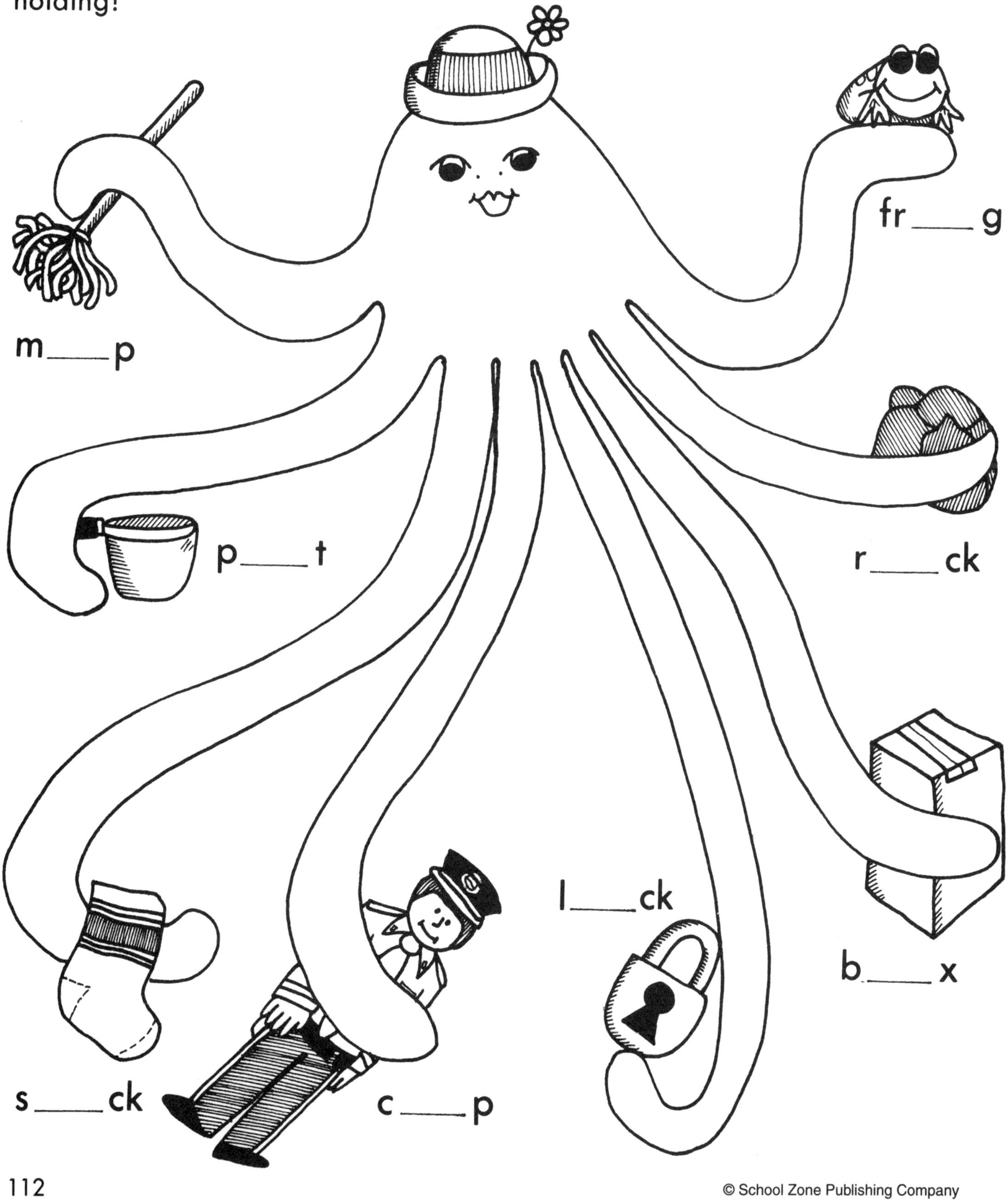

© School Zone Publishing Company

SHORT O WORDS

Circle the picture in each row whose word has a short o sound.

1.
2.
3.
4.
5.
6.
7.

© School Zone Publishing Company

Color all the words that have a short o sound red.

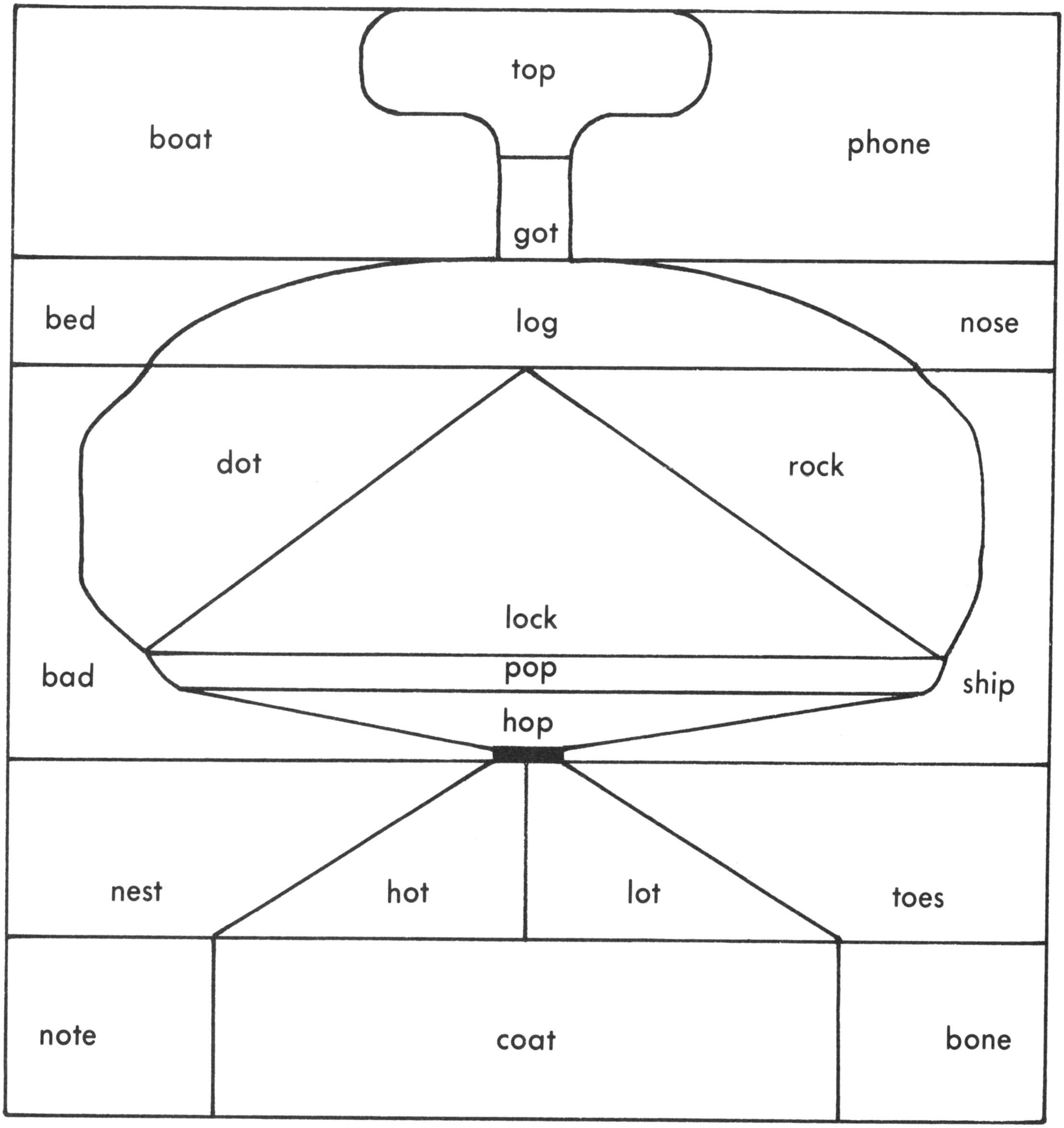

This is a picture of a ___ ___ ___ .

© School Zone Publishing Company

REVIEW: a, o

Answer the riddle. Write an a or an o in the blank. Say the word.

1. You wear this on your head. h____ t

2. A fire feels like this. h____ t

3. You play with it. bl____ck

4. This is a color. bl____ck

5. A drawing of the world. m____p

6. You clean the floor with this. m____p

7. You put it on your foot. s____ck

8. You carry things in it. s____ck

My, my! I hope they don't mix us up!

© School Zone Publishing Company

REVIEW: e, o

There are six hidden things in the picture. Draw a line around each thing. Then write the words below.

clock	bell	hen	pot	bed	mop

Short e words

____

____

____

Short o words

____

____

____

© School Zone Publishing Company

REVIEW: i, o

Look at each picture. Say the picture word. Circle i if the word has a short i sound. Circle o if the word has a short o sound.

i o 	i o 	i o 
i o 	i o 	i o 
i o 	i o 	i o 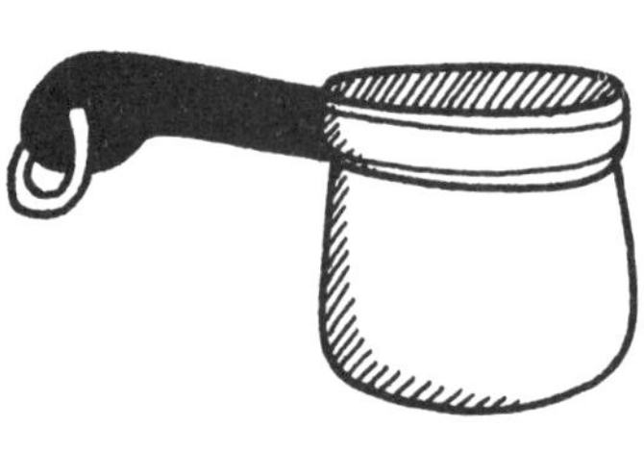

© School Zone Publishing Company

REVIEW: a, e, i, o

Circle the picture in each row that has the short vowel sound.

short a		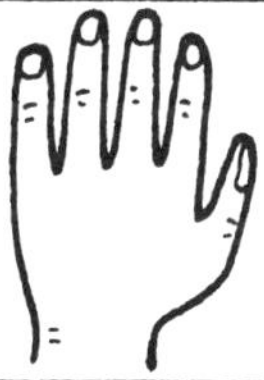	
short e			
short e			
short i			
short a			
short o			
short i			
short o			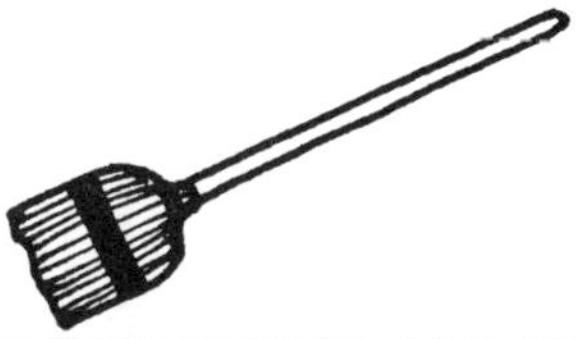

© School Zone Publishing Company

SHORT U WORDS

Short u sounds like the first sound of Uppity Up.

Look at the picture. Say the picture word. Write the missing letters on the line. Say the word.

 c ___ p	 b ___ s	 b ___ g
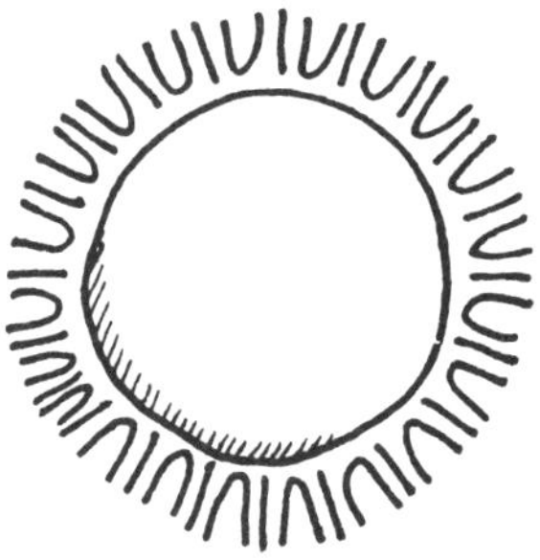 ___ u ___	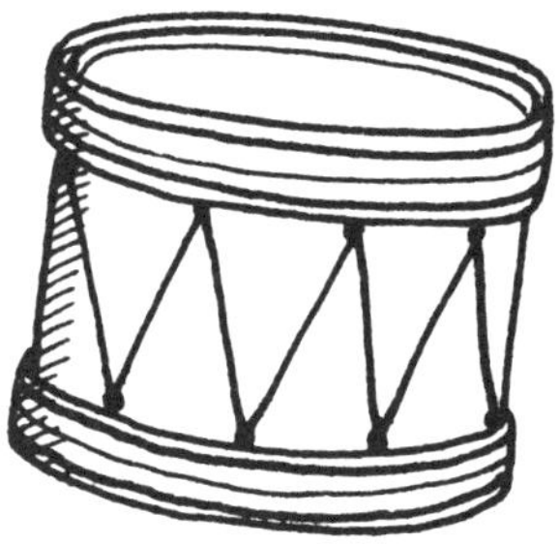 ___ ___ u ___	 ___ u ___ ___
 g ___ m	 s ___ b	 br ___ sh

© School Zone Publishing Company

Uppity Up has lost his words! Circle the pictures that have a short u sound. They belong to Uppity Up.

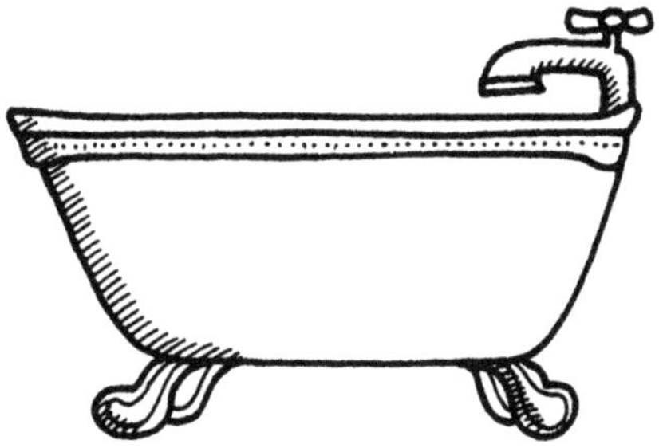

© School Zone Publishing Company

Color all the short u words orange.

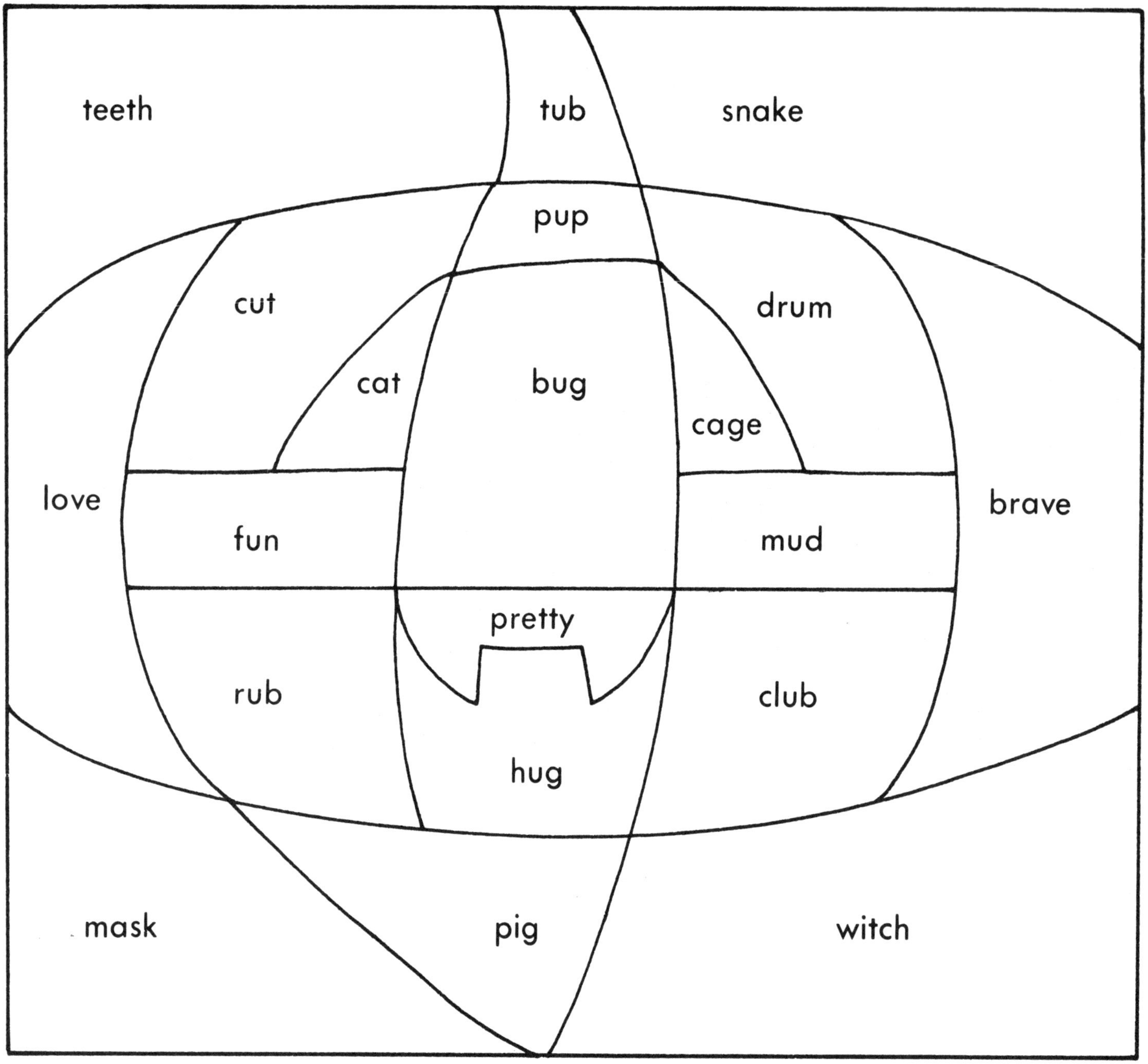

This is a (sun, bus, pumpkin).

© School Zone Publishing Company

REVIEW: a, u

Answer the riddle. Write a or u on the line. Say the word.

1. It goes on your head. c___p

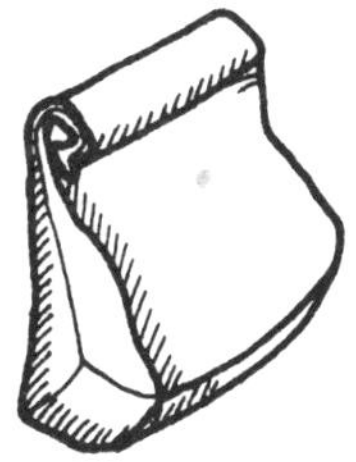

2. You drink from it. c___p

3. It is wet dirt. m___d

4. It means the same as angry. m___d

5. It is small. b___g

6. You can keep a lunch in it. b___g

7. It blows cool air. f___n

8. You have this when you play. f___n

© School Zone Publishing Company

REVIEW: e, u

Circle the words or pictures that have the sound in the box.

Short e	Short u
  	hug lot tub

Short e	Short u
bet feet lips tent	  

© School Zone Publishing Company

REVIEW: i, u

Draw a line from the letter to a picture that has the short vowel sound.

i

u

i

u

i

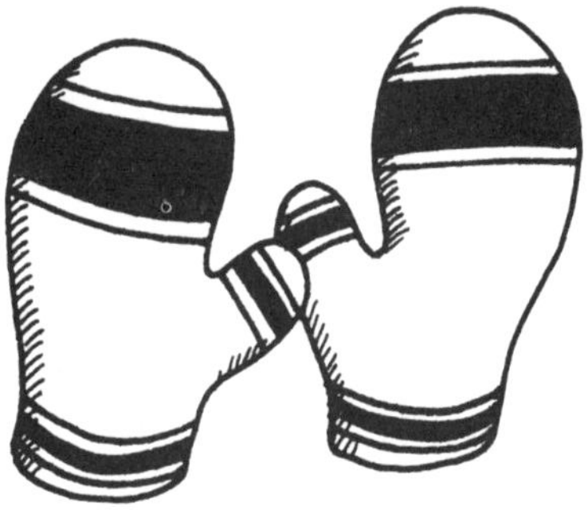

u

i

u

© School Zone Publishing Company

REVIEW: o, u

Help Olive Octopus and Uppity Up find their way home. Write the correct word by the picture.

REVIEW: a, e, i, o, u

Add a short vowel to make a word. Then write the words on the correct line. Say each word.

a	e	i	o	u

c___p b___lt p___g d___ll d___ck

p___nts sl___d f___sh s___cks dr___m

b___t f___x

Things to wear Things to play with Animals

______________ ______________ ______________

______________ ______________ ______________

______________ ______________ ______________

______________ ______________ ______________

© School Zone Publishing Company

REVIEW: a, e, i, o, u

Look at the picture. Say the picture word. Circle the short vowel that has the same sound as the picture word.

e a 	e i 	i o 	o u 
e a 	e o 	e i 	e u 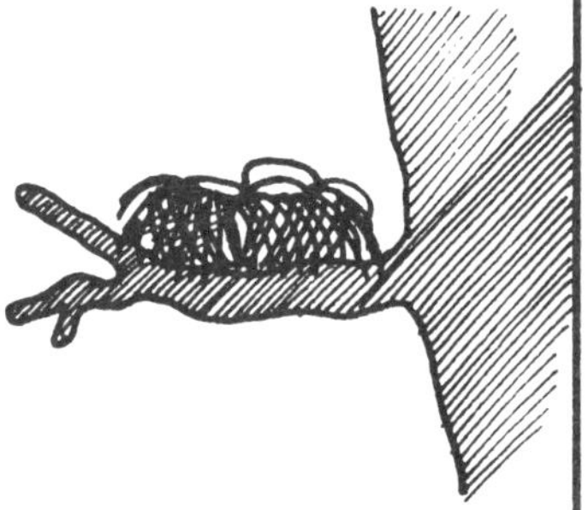
i o 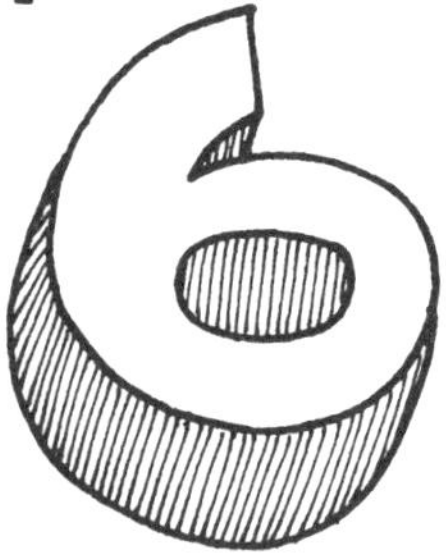	i u 	i a 	i e 
o u 	o a 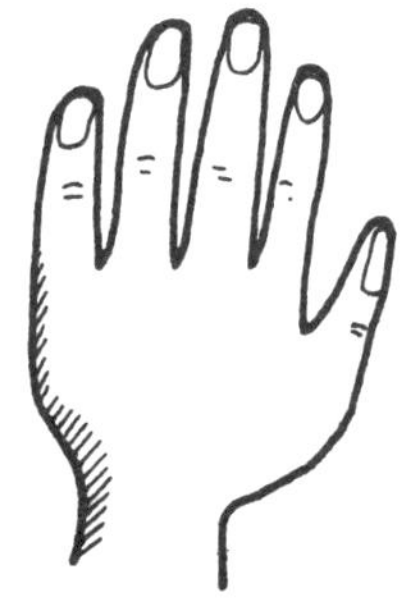	o e 	o i 

© School Zone Publishing Company

Page 97
hat, fan, tack, stamp, bat, lamp, cat, hand, mask

Page 98
train – no, ant – yes, bag – yes, man – yes, fan – yes, cake – no, rake – no, lamb – yes, rain – no, snake – no, lamp – yes, cat – yes

Page 99
ran, bad, had, mad, sat, pat, jam, (apple)

Page 100
1. bat
2. fan
3. mask
4. cat
5. hand

Page 101
tent, bed, bell, sled, nest, ten

Page 102
dress, leg, hen, belt, desk, wet, pen

Page 103
bell, cent, egg, red, nest

Page 104
1. pan
2. pen
3. bell
4. apple
5. red
6. hen
7. bat
8. hand

Page 105
1. ten
2. fan
3. apple
4. ant
5. man
6. tent
7. desk

Page 106
bib, dish, lid, fish, hill, wig, pig, It, gift

Page 107
fish – yes, slide – no, six – yes, kite – no, fire – no, witch – yes, lid – yes, lips – yes, pie – no, ship – yes, pig – yes, dish – yes

Page 108
fish, pin, six, mitten, lips, in, will, pill, hill, lid, fill, (pig)

Page 109
Short a words: hat, hand, lamp, bad
Short i words: pig, six, hill, fish

Page 110
Short e words: dress, tent, leg, ten
Short i words: lips, ship, dish, six
Sled belongs to Edward Elephant.

Page 111
1. Short a – bat, fan
2. Short e – pen, tent
3. Short i – gift, fish

Page 112
Automatic fill-in.

Page 113
1. sock
2. clock
3. fox
4. top
5. mop
6. block
7. cop

Page 114
top, hot, log, lot, dot, hop, rock, pop, got, (top), lock

Page 115
1. hat
2. hot
3. block
4. black
5. map
6. mop
7. sock
8. sack

Page 116
Short e words: bell, hen, bed
Short o words: clock, pot, mop

Page 117
ship – i, witch – i, cop – o, fox – o, socks – o, mittens – i, clock – o, six – i, pot – o

Page 118
Short a – hand
Short e – belt
Short e – desk
Short i – pig
Short a – bat
Short o – lock
Short i – bib
Short o – dog

Page 119
cup, sun, gum, bus, drum, sub, bug, duck, brush

Page 120
sun, drum, duck, tub, hut, cup

Page 121
pup, club, mud, rub, fun, drum, hug, cut, bug, (pumpkin), tub

Page 122
1. cap
2. cup
3. mud
4. mad
5. bug
6. bag
7. fan
8. fun

Page 123
Short e: desk, nest
Short u: hug, tub
Short e: bet, tent
Short u: truck, duck

Page 124
Short i words: pig, witch, fish, mittens
Short u words: bus, cup, duck, drum

Page 125
mop, cop, bus, lock, duck, fox

Page 126
Things to wear: cap, pants, belt, socks
Things to play with: bat, sled, doll, drum
Animals: pig, fox, fish, duck

Page 127
desk – e, six – i, lips – i, cup – u, octopus – o, ant – a, duck – u, ship – i, cat – a, drum – u, elephant – e, hand – a, pig – i, fox – o, nest – e, It – i

© School Zone Publishing Company

LONG A SOUND: ai

The Great Longo is a magician! He makes long vowel words! Sometimes he makes words with a long a sound. He makes them by putting ai together! What magic!

Help the Great Longo. He wants you to add long a words to his magic chain. Look at each picture. Say the picture word. Write the letters ai on the blank lines. Say the word. Then write the words on Great Longo's magic chain.

tr ___ ___ n

sn ___ ___ l

r ___ ___ n

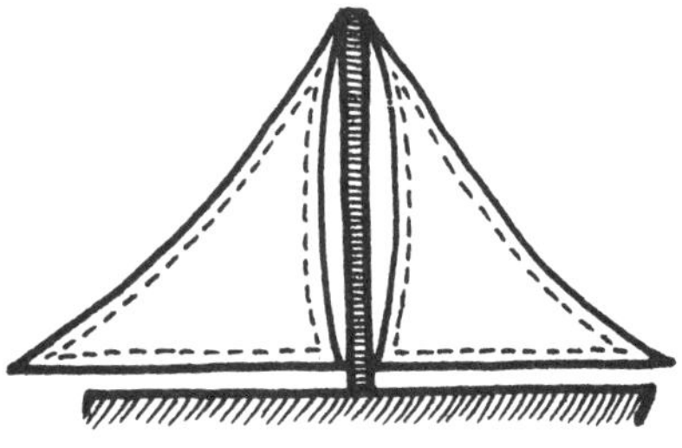

s ___ ___ l

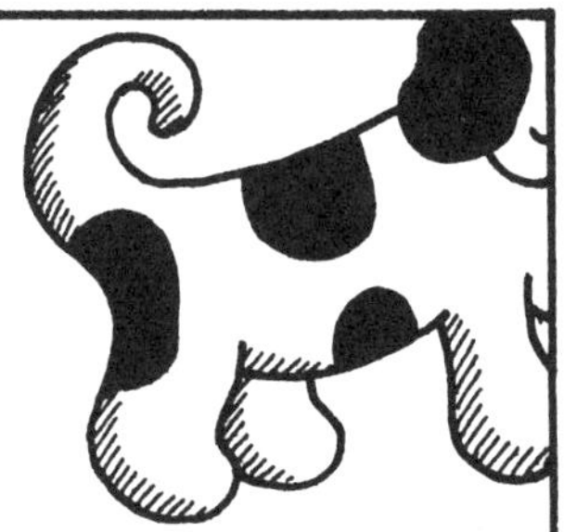

t ___ ___ l

p ___ ___ l

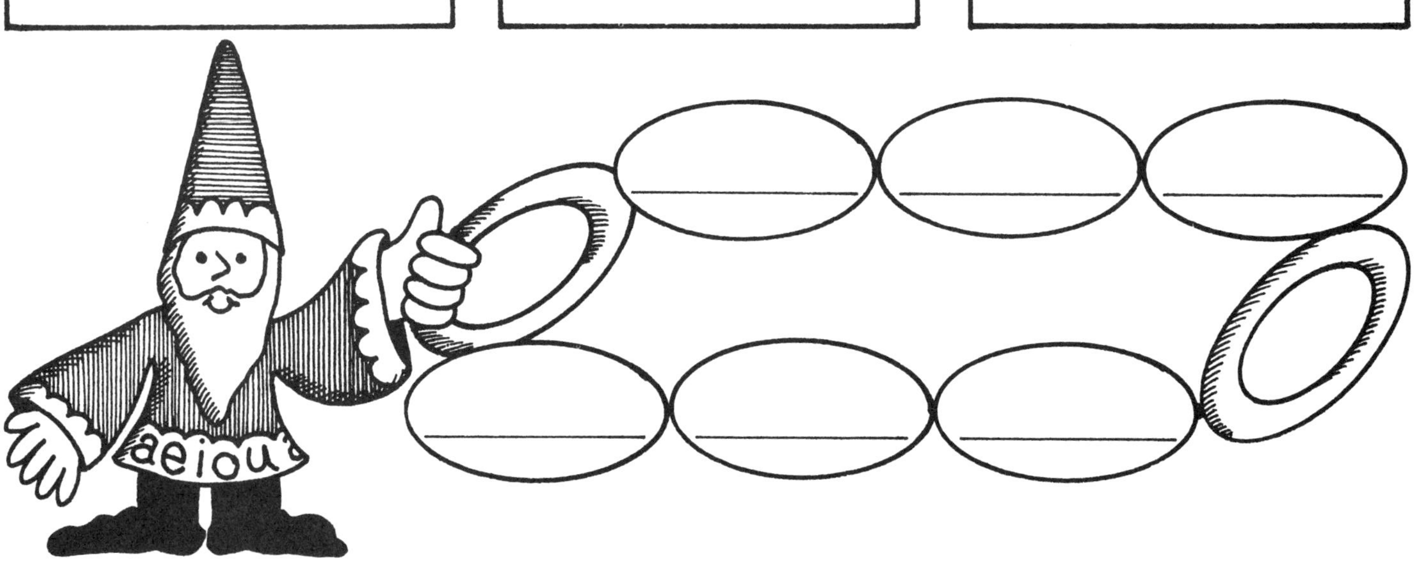

© School Zone Publishing Company

LONG A SOUND: ay

Make a long a playhouse! Make it with ay bricks! Look at the pictures at the bottom of the page. Say the picture word. Then write ay on the line to finish the word. The letters ay help make a long a sound! Write a long a word on each brick of the playhouse.

h__ __

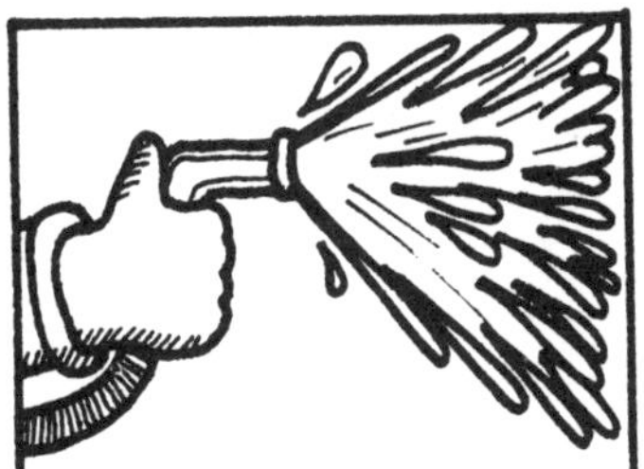

spr__ __

pr__ __

cr__ __on

tr__ __

j__ __

M__ __

© School Zone Publishing Company

LONG A SOUND: eigh

Once the Great Longo had a long a party. He called it the eigh party. Fill in the blanks to find out what happened. Use the eigh words at the bottom of the page to help you.

1. First, Longo had _ _ _ _ _ big cakes.

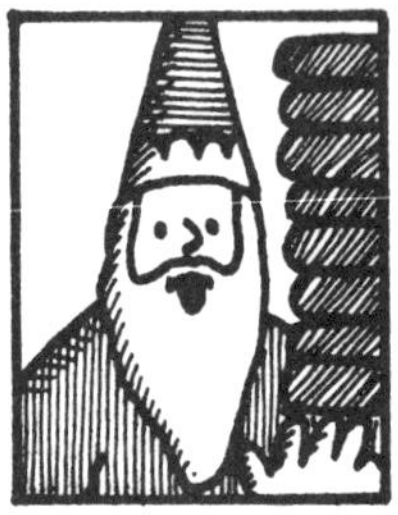

2. Then he started to _ _ _ _ _ himself.

3. "Oh, no!" he said. "My _ _ _ _ _ _ is over 200 pounds!"

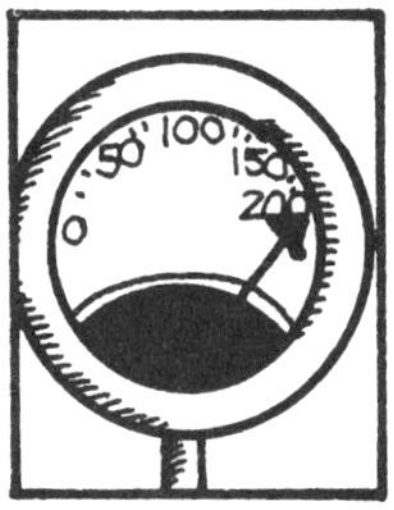

4. "I'll be as big as a _ _ _ _ _ _ _ train," he added.

5. "I've got to stop. I won't eat for _ _ _ _ _ days!"

eight	weight	weigh
freight	eight	

© School Zone Publishing Company

LONG A SOUND: silent e

The Great Longo has a magic wand! It is called the silent e wand! The silent e wand changes words. You can help the Great Longo change words. Look at the pictures. Say the first picture word. See how it is spelled. Say the second picture word. Write the letters of the first word on the lines. Then add an e. Say the new word. Do you hear what the magic e wand can do?

man

__ __ __ __

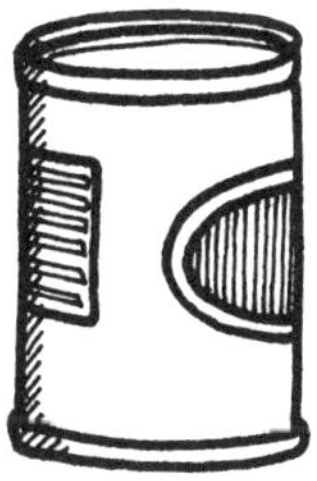

can

__ __ __ __

pan

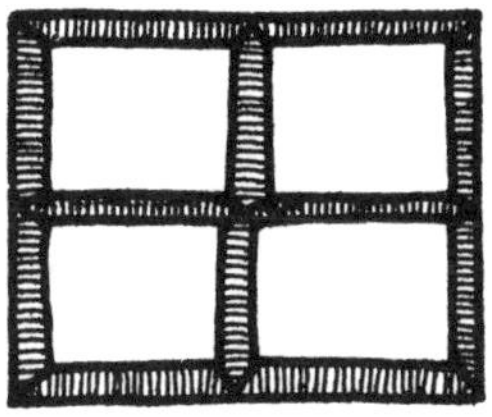

__ __ __ __

cap

__ __ __ __

© School Zone Publishing Company

LONG A SOUND: silent e

The Great Longo is still using his silent e wand! He is making long a words out of other words by adding a silent e! Read each sentence. Write in the blank the silent e word that begins like the underlined word. Say the silent e word. Hear the long a sound!

pale	hate	pane	plane	cane

1. I ____________ to wear this hat.

2. He threw the pan through the window ______.

3. You can walk with a ____________________.

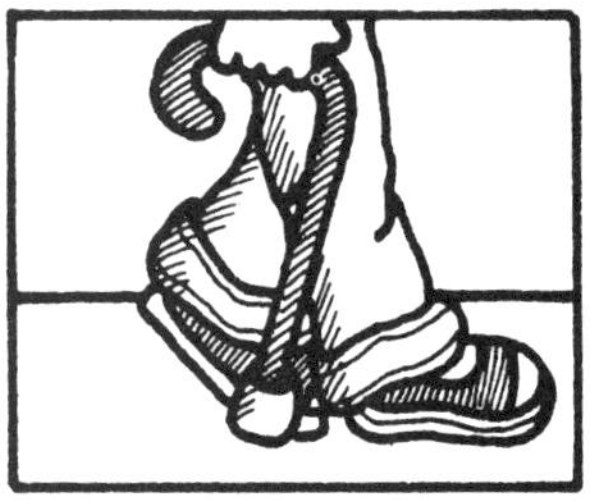

4. My pal looked sick and _______________.

5. I plan to fly on a ____________.

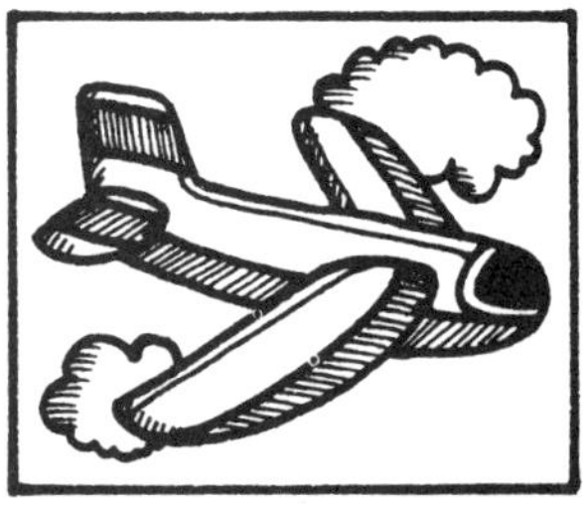

© School Zone Publishing Company

LONG A SOUND REVIEW

Color each long a word blue. Then see what you find!

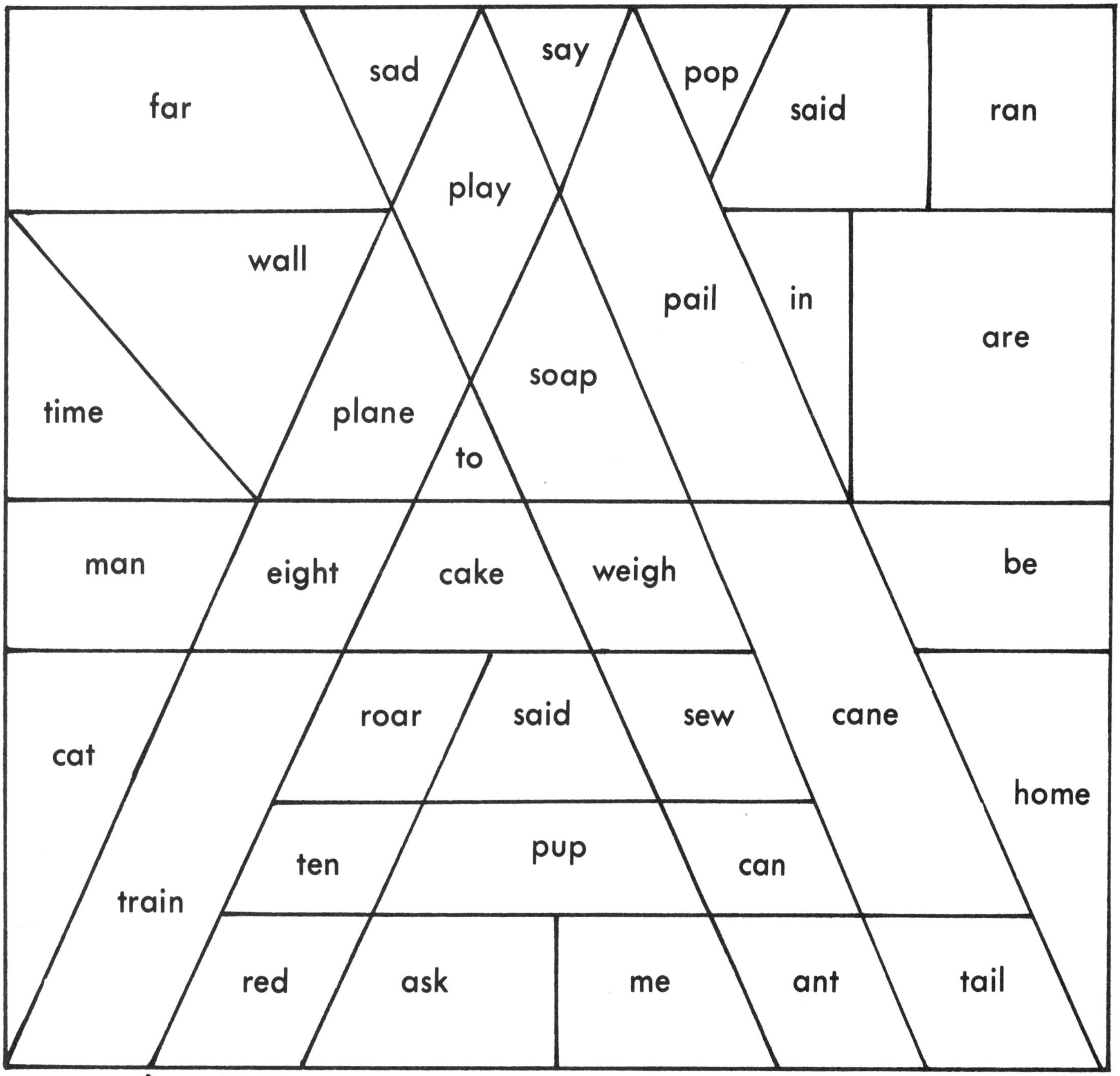

© School Zone Publishing Company

LONG A SOUND: REVIEW

The Great Longo is driving a long a train. He wants to fill the train cars with long a words. Look at the list at the bottom of the page. Then write only the long a words on the cars of the train.

stay	ran	rain	made	take	mad
hat	car	day	bake	pail	gray

© School Zone Publishing Company

LONG E SOUND: ee

Help the Great Longo trap the buzzing bee! Help the Great Longo block all the doors with long e words. The long e words are made by the letters ee together. Look at each picture. Then write the correct word by the picture.

sheep three wheel teeth teepee tree

© School Zone Publishing Company

LONG E SOUND: ea

Sometimes the letters ea make the long e sound. Look at each picture. Say the name of the picture. Write ea in the blanks. Then write the word below the picture. Say the word.

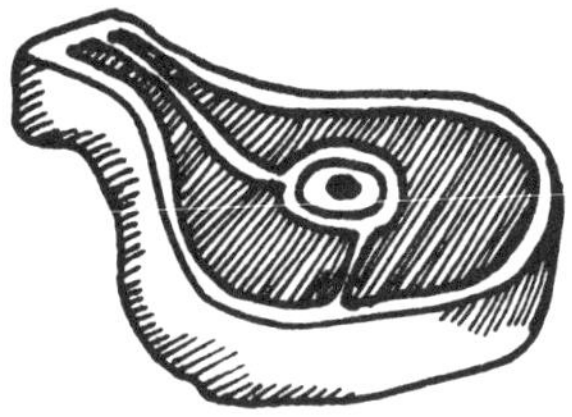

m ___ ___ t

____

l ___ ___ f

____

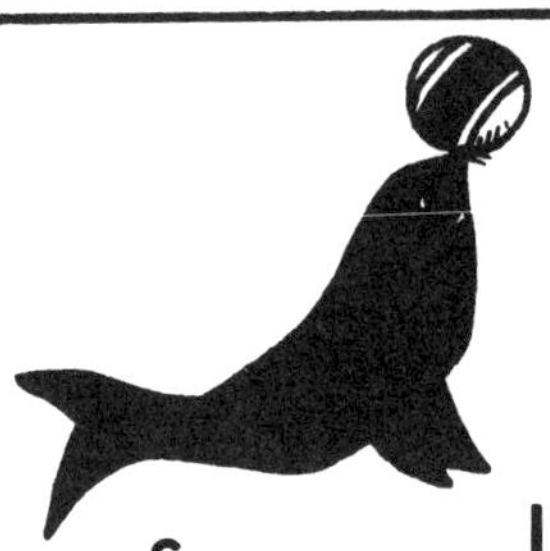

s ___ ___ l

____

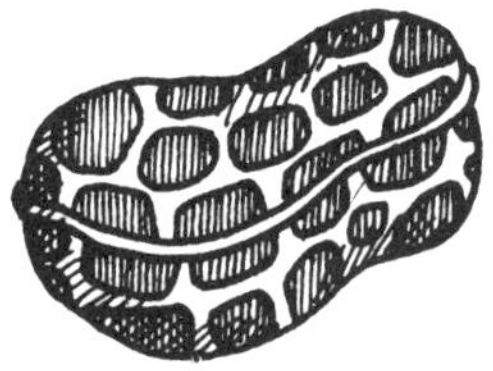

p ___ ___ nut

____

___ ___ gle

____

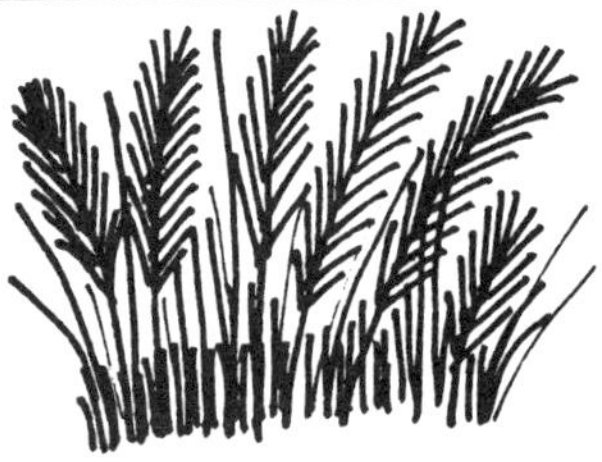

wh ___ ___ t

____

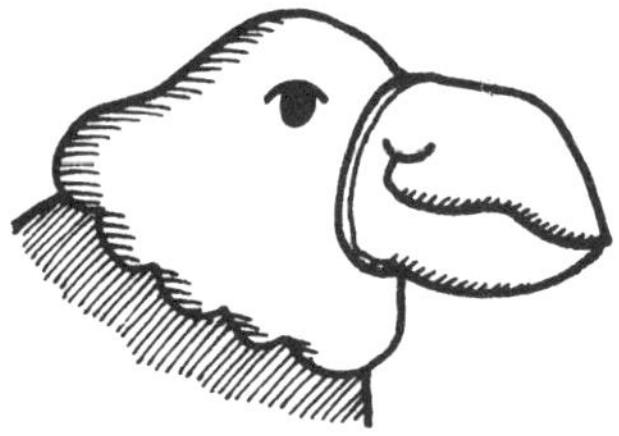

b ___ ___ k

____

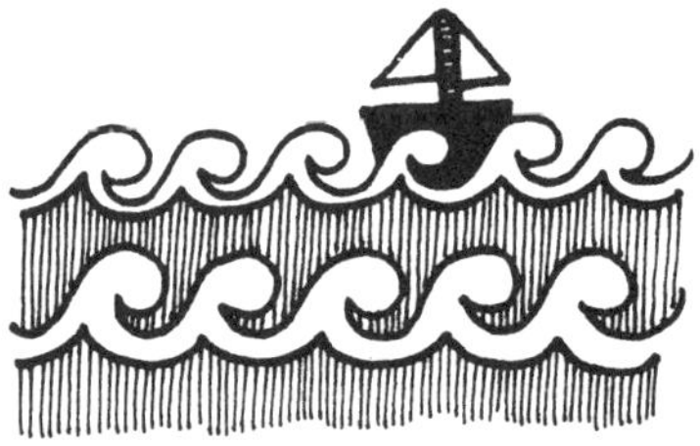

s ___ ___

____

s ___ ___ t

____

© School Zone Publishing Company

LONG E SOUND: ey

The Great Longo makes magic with the letters ey. They make the long e sound at the end of some words. Look at each picture. Draw a line from the picture to the word. Write the word.

key

____

monkey

____

donkey

____

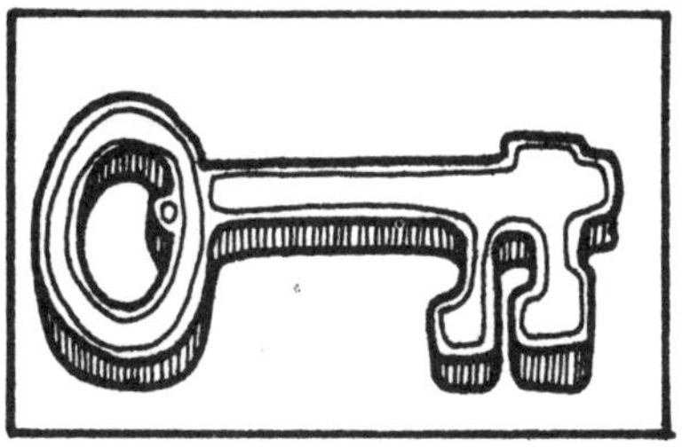

hockey

____

money

____

turkey

____

ey
Don't ask me why, but it works!
a e i o u a

© School Zone Publishing Company

LONG E SOUND: ie, e

Help the Great Longo catch a thief! Look at each picture. Then write the correct word by the picture. Say the word. Hear the long e sound.

field	chief	cookie	thief	priest	he	she

© School Zone Publishing Company

LONG E SOUND REVIEW

The Great Longo is hiding things! He is hiding things that are spelled with a long e sound! Look at the words at the bottom of the page. Then look at the picture. Find the things that have a long e sound. Circle them.

bee	tree	cookie	turkey	penny
key	leaf	peanut	wheel	teepee

© School Zone Publishing Company

LONG E SOUND REVIEW

Look at each picture. Say the word. Circle Yes if the word has a long e sound. Circle No if it does not.

thief
Yes No

sheep
Yes No

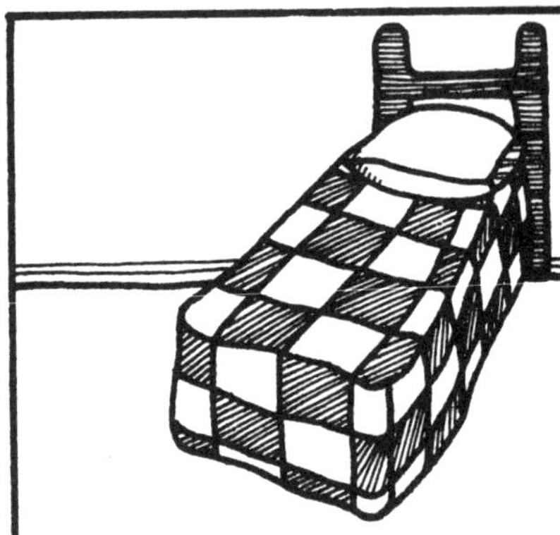
bed
Yes No

peach
Yes No

net
Yes No

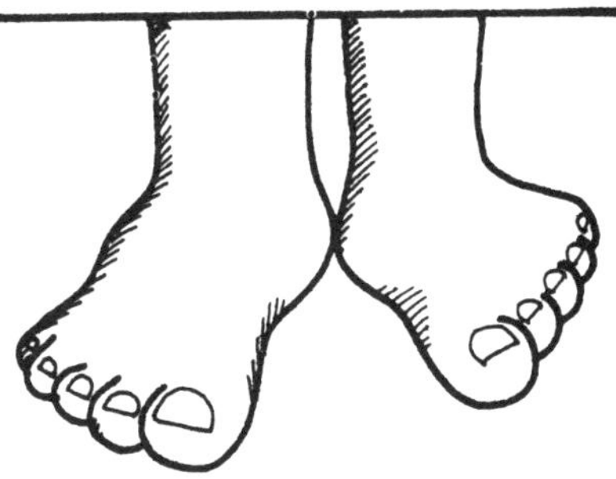
feet
Yes No

men
Yes No

bee
Yes No

monkey
Yes No

© School Zone Publishing Company

LONG I SOUND: ie, y

The Great Longo makes the long i sound in words. He does it by using the letter y or the letters ie! The Great Longo is tricky!

Look at each picture. Then fill in the blanks next to each picture with two words that rhyme. Use the words at the bottom of the page.

	Birds ________ in the ________.
	A ____________ must be very ________.
	________ sister is very ________.
	Some animals ________ down and seem to ________.
	Some ________ fell on my ________.
	________ not to ________.

fly	pie	spy	my	try	lie
die	sky	cry	shy	tie	sly

© School Zone Publishing Company

LONG I SOUND: igh

The Great Longo is being chased by Mighty Moose! Help the Great Longo get away. Write the correct word by the picture.

knight	night	light	thigh	high	fight	fright

© School Zone Publishing Company

LONG I SOUND: ild, ind

The Great Longo is making riddles. The answers are long i words that end in ild or ind. Read each riddle. Then write in the blank the correct long i word from the list at the bottom of the page.

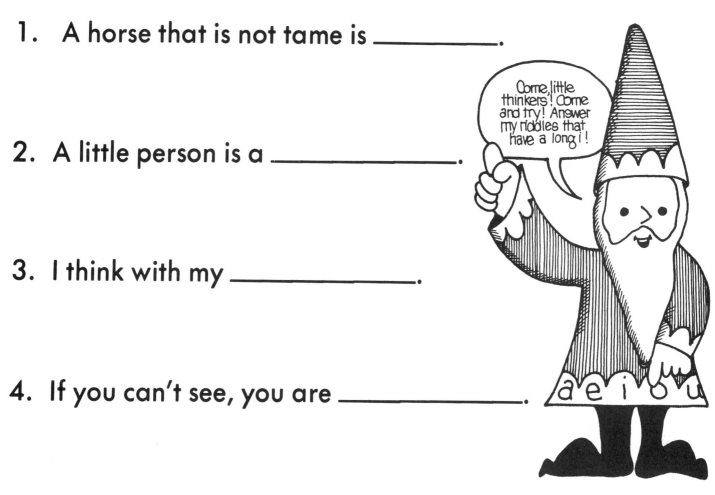

Come, little thinkers! Come and try! Answer my riddles that have a long i!
a e i o u

1. A horse that is not tame is ________.

2. A little person is a ________.

3. I think with my ________.

4. If you can't see, you are ________.

5. If you lose something, someone may ________ it.

6. If you help people, you are ________.

blind	wild	child	mind	find	kind

© School Zone Publishing Company

LONG I SOUND: silent e

The Great Longo is making silent e words again! This time his words all have the long i sound. Look at the pictures. Write the i in the blank space inside each word. Then draw a line from each word to the right picture.

d ___ m e

t ___ m e

b ___ k e

k ___ t e

w r ___ t e

t ___ r e

f ___ r e

p ___ p e

These words will be mine, if you draw the right line!
a e i o u a

© School Zone Publishing Company

LONG I SOUND: REVIEW

The Great Longo is on a long i butterfly chase! Help him by coloring each butterfly that has a long i word written on it. Try to catch all the long i butterflies!

© School Zone Publishing Company

LONG I SOUND: REVIEW

Read each word and say each picture word. Put a circle around the word or picture in each row that has a long i sound.

i			
i	give	pie	whip
i	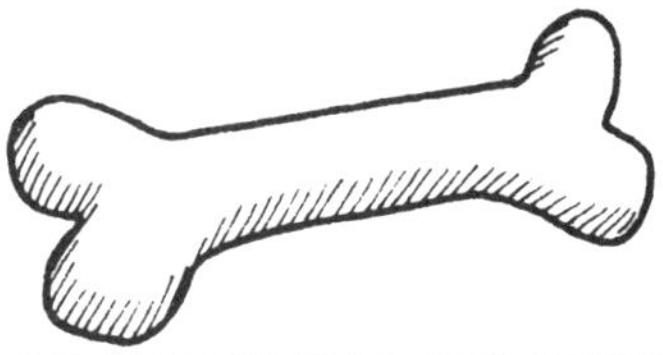		
i	gift	tire	dig
i			
i	baby	bee	dime
i			
i	five	eight	six

© School Zone Publishing Company

LONG O SOUND: oe, oa

The Great Longo makes long o words in many tricky ways. Sometimes he uses oe to make the long o sound. Sometimes he uses oa to make the long o sound!

Look at each picture. Write in the missing letters. Say the word. Then write all the long o words on the Great Longo's boat.

t ___ ___

h ___ ___

d ___ ___

r ___ ___ d

c ___ ___ t

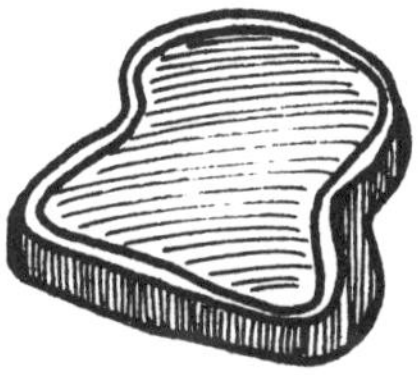

t ___ ___ st

b ___ ___ t

g ___ ___ t

t ___ ___ d

© School Zone Publishing Company

LONG O SOUND: o, ow, old, ost

The Great Longo is making long o riddles! He makes the long o sound with o, ow, old, or ost! How tricky! Read the riddle. Then write in the correct answer.

1. Get ready, get set, ________________!

2. I eat my soup from a ________________.

3. White ________________ fell from the sky.

4. ________________ is bright and shiny.

5. Did you see a ________________ on Halloween?

6. The black bird in the tree was a ________________.

7. If it's not yes, it is ________________.

8. If you are not young, you are ________________.

bowl	old	no	gold
go	ghost	crow	snow

© School Zone Publishing Company

LONG O SOUND: silent e

The Great Longo is lost! He wants to go home! Help him find the way home. Draw a line from the Great Longo to the first word that has the long o sound. Then draw a line to the next word with the long o sound. Pretty soon, you will get the Great Longo home!

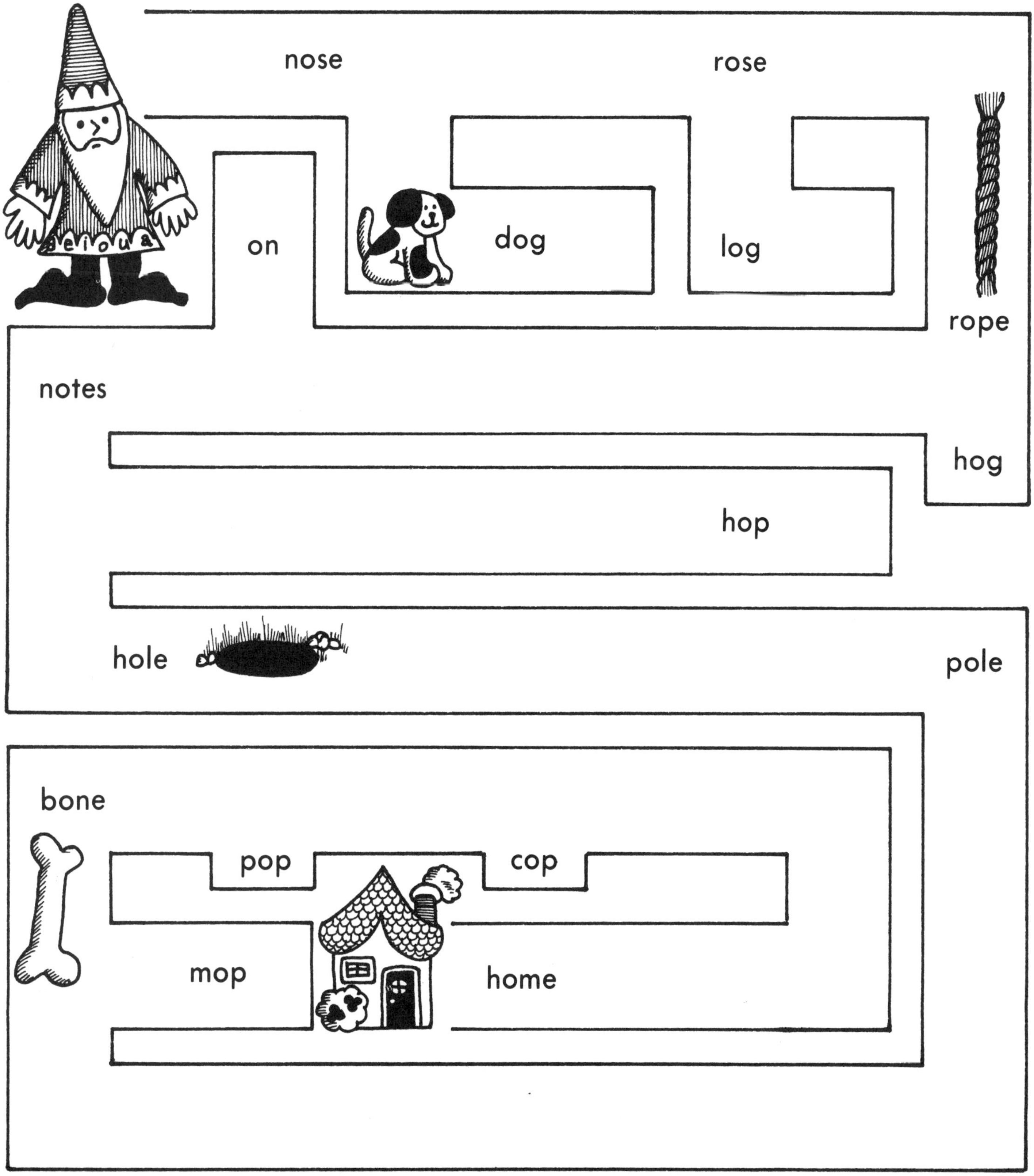

© School Zone Publishing Company

LONG O SOUND: REVIEW

Help the Great Longo put long o words inside his giant o! Look at the words at the bottom of the page. Write only the words that contain the long o sound inside Longo's o. Let's go!

globe	know	now	told	rode	row	rope
note	not	goat	get	top	home	toe

© School Zone Publishing Company

LONG O SOUND: REVIEW

Color in each space that contains a long o word. The Great Longo has a secret message waiting for you!

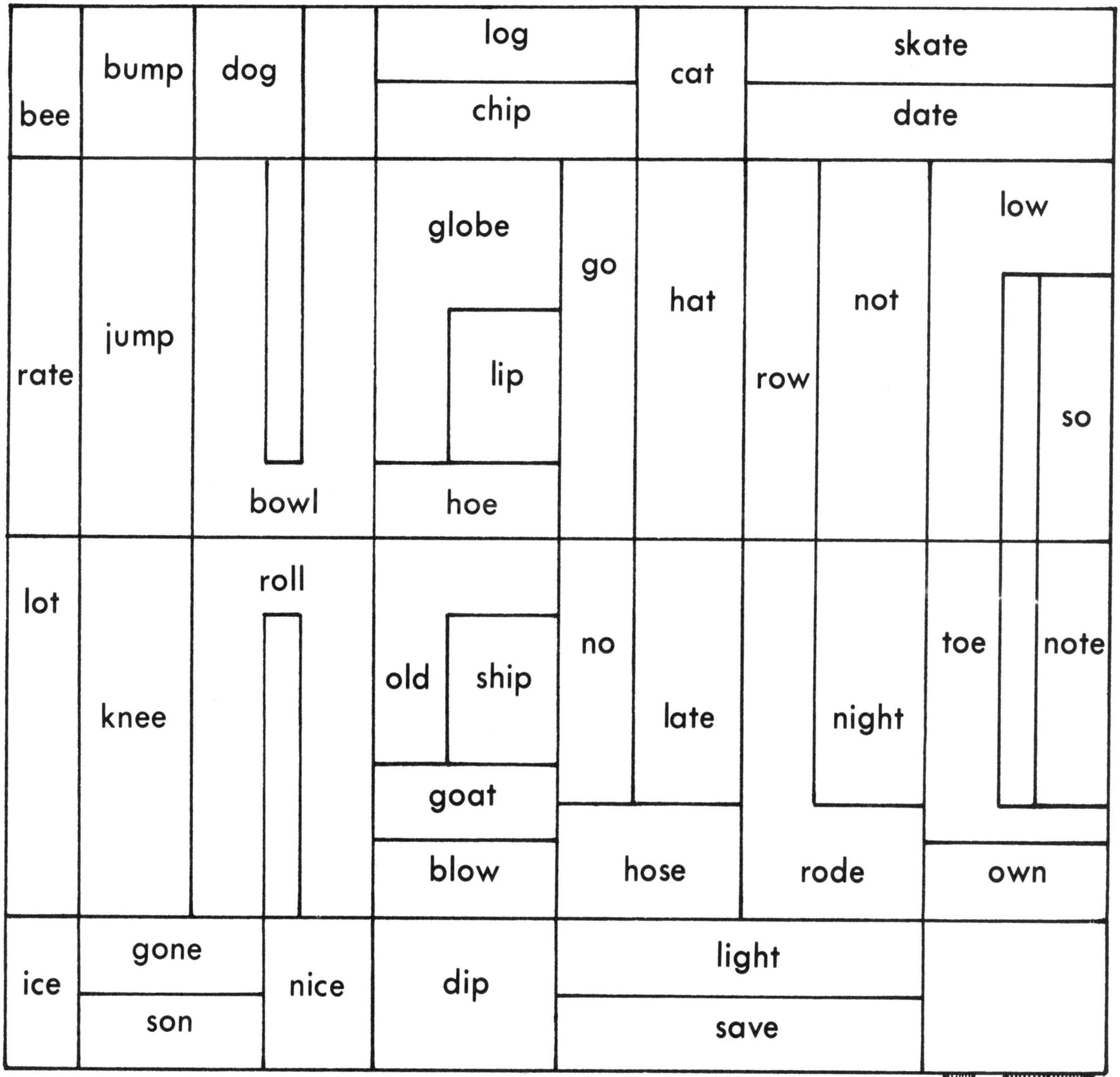
bee
bump
dog
log
chip
cat
skate
date
rate
jump
bowl
globe
lip
hoe
go
hat
row
not
low
so
lot
knee
roll
old
ship
goat
blow
no
late
hose
night
rode
toe
note
own
ice
gone
son
nice
dip
light
save

Longo's secret message reads: ______________

Well, blow me over!

© School Zone Publishing Company

LONG U SOUND: silent e, ui, ew, ue

Draw a line from the long u word to the right picture. Then write the word next to the picture.

tube

suit

cube

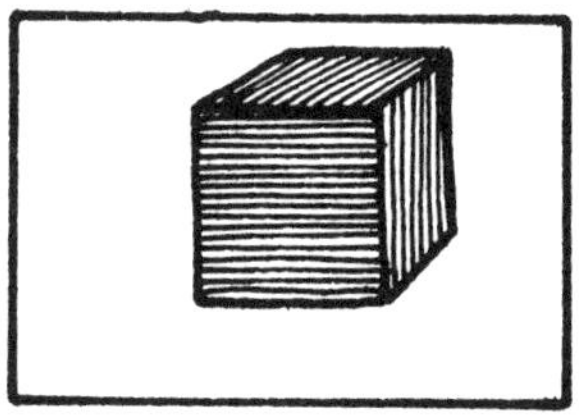

fuel

glue

mule

screw

© School Zone Publishing Company

LONG U SOUND: REVIEW

The Great Longo has made up some riddles. Each riddle can be answered by a long u word! The words are at the bottom of the page. Write the correct word on each line.

1. If there aren't many, there are ______________.

2. Standing on a mountain top, you have a nice ______________.

3. An elephant is a ______________ animal.

4. I thought that baby was very ______________.

5. I heard the kitten ______________.

6. When you work with something, you ______________ it.

mew	huge	few	view	cute	use

© School Zone Publishing Company

LONG VOWEL SOUNDS: GENERAL REVIEW

Circle the word in each row that has the same long vowel sound as the first word in the row.

If it isn't long, it doesn't belong.

mule	lip	fuel	hot
go	clam	nut	post
chief	milk	me	fun
five	sky	stick	gift
cane	way	fan	end
leave	step	key	miss
know	fast	float	dock
rice	mile	trick	dish

© School Zone Publishing Company

LONG VOWEL SOUNDS: GENERAL REVIEW

Let's color Longo! Use the sound key to color the big picture of Longo.

Long a - - black
Long e - - red
Long i - - brown
Long o - - green
Long u - - blue

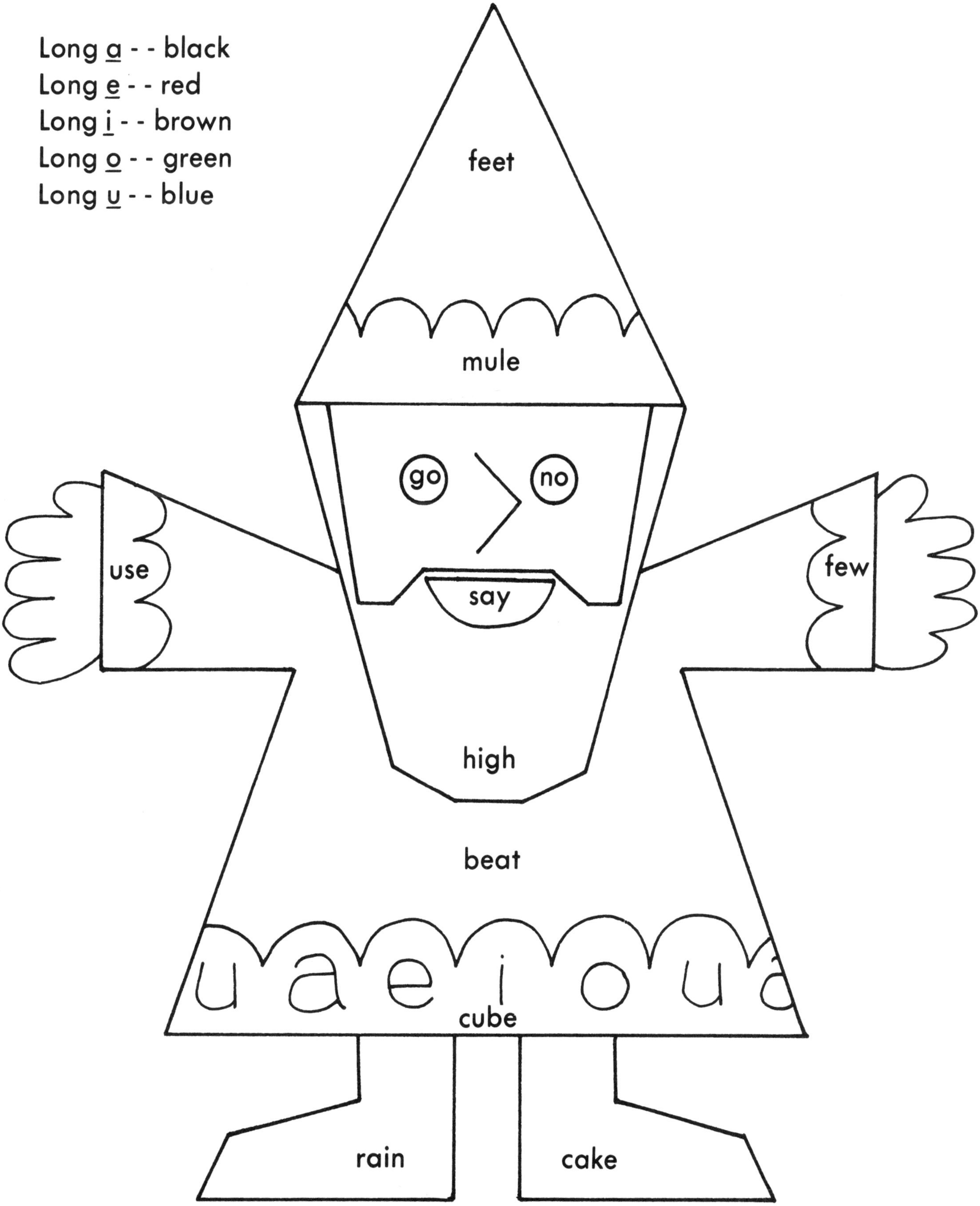

© School Zone Publishing Company

LONG VOWEL SOUNDS: GENERAL REVIEW

The Great Longo likes to play Long Vowel Opposites. You can play, too! Look at each word. Next to it, write a long vowel word that means the opposite! Use the words from the bottom of the page.

1. dirty ______
2. hot _____
3. sour ______
4. you __
5. black ______
6. under ____
7. day ______
8. wake ______
9. come __
10. sun _____
11. wet ___
12. high ___

Is the opposite of Longo... Shorto?
a e i o u

sleep	clean	dry	cold	white	night
rain	go	over	low	sweet	me

© School Zone Publishing Company

LONG VOWEL SOUNDS: GENERAL REVIEW

Look at each word. Say it out loud. Draw a line from the word to the long vowel sound you hear.

sheep

eight

gold

few

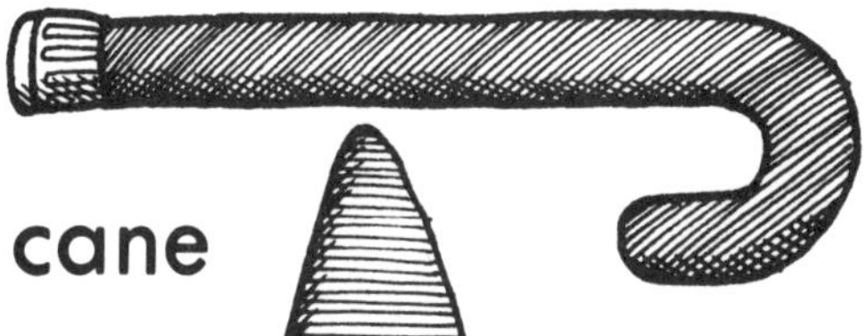

try

chief

LONG A

LONG E

LONG I

LONG O

LONG U

goat

cube

wild

cane

The longer, the better!

© School Zone Publishing Company

LONG VOWEL SOUNDS: GENERAL REVIEW

Color all the long vowel words green. Then read Longo's secret message to you.

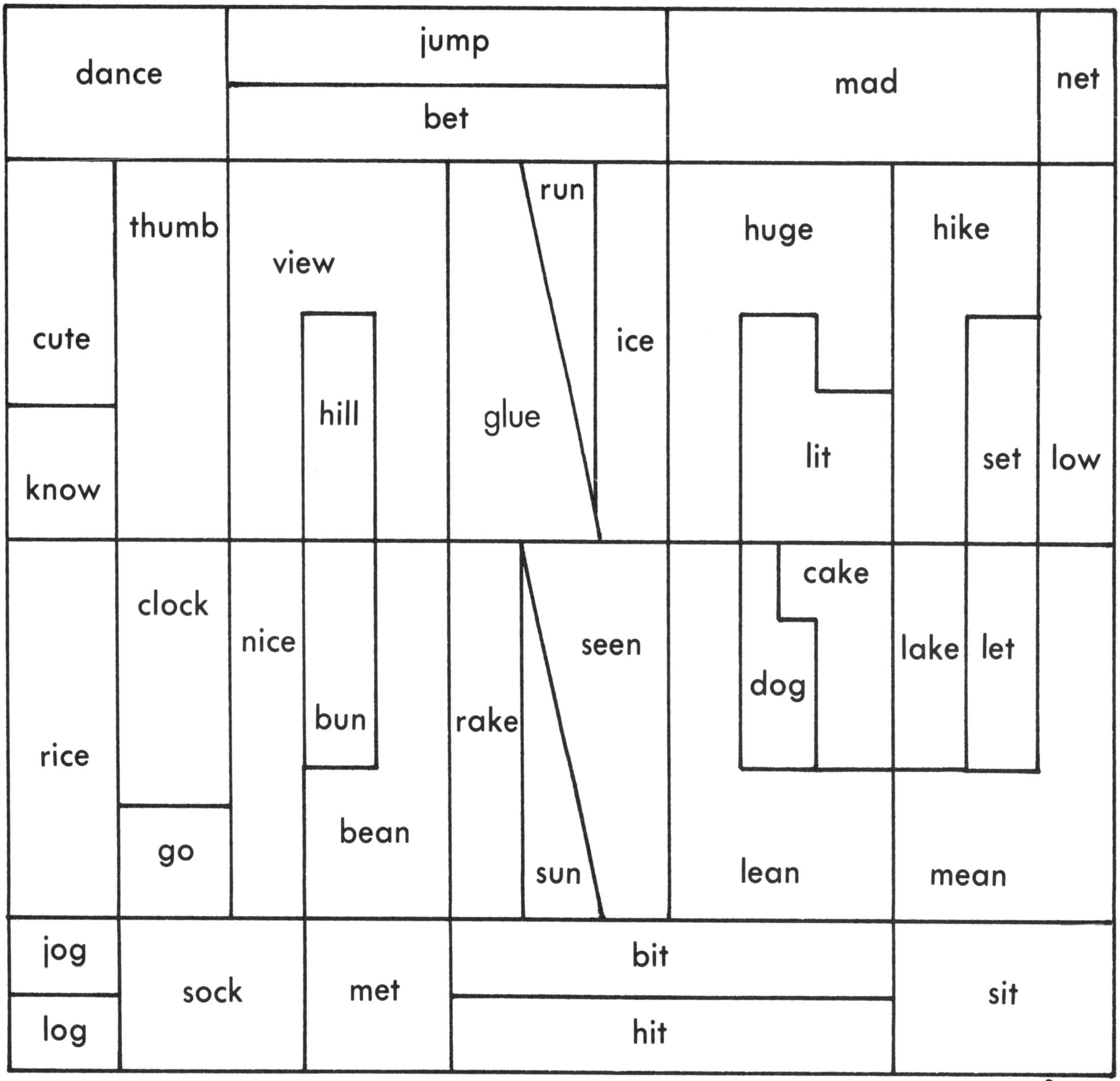
dance
jump
bet
mad
net
cute
know
thumb
view
hill
glue
run
ice
huge
hike
lit
set
low
rice
clock
go
nice
bun
bean
rake
seen
sun
cake
dog
lake
let
lean
mean
jog
log
sock
met
bit
hit
sit

Longo's secret message reads: ______________

Way to go!

© School Zone Publishing Company

Page 129
train snail rain
sail tail pail

Page 130
hay spray pray crayon
tray jay May

Page 131
1. eight
2. weigh
3. weight
4. freight
5. eight

Page 132
Automatic fill-in.

Page 133
1. hate
2. pane
3. cane
4. pale
5. plane

Page 134
play
tail
plane
cake
weigh
cane
train
say
eight
pail

Page 135
stay
rain
made
take
day
bake
pail
gray

Page 136
Automatic fill-in.

Page 137
meat leaf seal
peanut eagle wheat
beak sea seat

Page 138
Automatic fill-in.

Page 139
cookie
chief
she
field
he
priest
thief

Page 140
Automatic fill-in.

Page 141
thief, yes sheep, yes bed, no
peach, yes net, no feet, yes
men, no bee, yes monkey, yes

Page 142
fly, sky
spy, sly
my, shy
lie, die
pie, tie
try, cry

Page 143
light
high
fright
knight
night
thigh
fight

Page 144
1. wild
2. child
3. mind
4. blind
5. find
6. kind

Page 145
Automatic fill-in.

Page 146
bike
lie
write
might
fire
sky
wife
sight
pie
ice

Page 147
fly
pie
bike
tire
pipe
dime
knight
five

Page 148
toe hoe doe
road coat toast
boat goat toad

Page 149
1. go
2. bowl
3. snow
4. gold
5. ghost
6. crow
7. no
8. old

Page 150
nose
rose
rope
notes
hole
pole
bone
home

Page 151
globe
know
told
rode
row
rope
note
goat
home
toe

Page 152
old hoe
go roll
hose bowl
no note
own goat
toe rode
so globe
blow (hello)
low
row

Page 153
Automatic fill-in.

Page 154
1. few
2. view
3. huge
4. cute
5. mew
6. use

Page 155
fuel
post
me
sky
way
key
float
mile

Page 156
Automatic fill-in.

Page 157
1. clean
2. cold
3. sweet
4. me
5. white
6. over
7. night
8. sleep
9. go
10. rain
11. dry
12. low

Page 158
Long a – eight, cane
Long e – sheep, chief
Long i – try, wild
Long o – gold, goat
Long u – cube, few

Page 159
cute nice rake mean
know bean lean low
rice glue cake huge
go ice hike (Longo)
view seen lake

© School Zone Publishing Company

<u>m</u>ouse

BEGINNING SOUNDS

DIRECTIONS: Look at the picture. Say the word.
Write in the first sound.
Write the whole word on the line.

<u>p</u>encil

____oon

____

____ig

____

____an

____

____an

____

Now color the pictures.

© School Zone Publishing Company

BEGINNING SOUNDS

milk

DIRECTIONS: Look at the picture. Say the word.
Write in the first sound.
Write the whole word on the line.

pipe

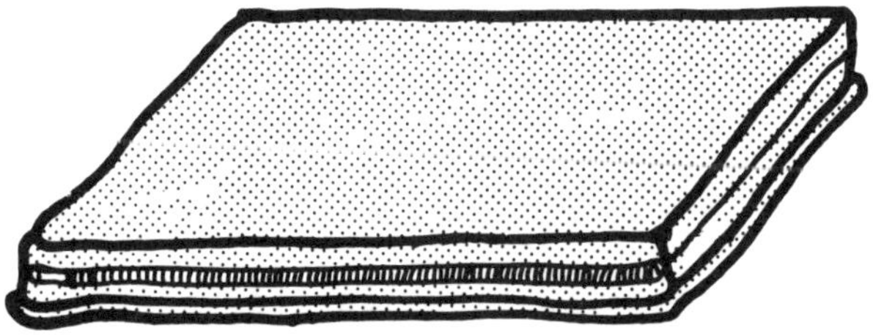

____at

____

____op

____

____op

____

____en

____

Now read this page to a friend.

© School Zone Publishing Company

BEGINNING SOUNDS

DIRECTIONS: Look at the picture. Say the word.
Write in the first sound.
Write the whole word on the line.

turtle **numbers**

____op

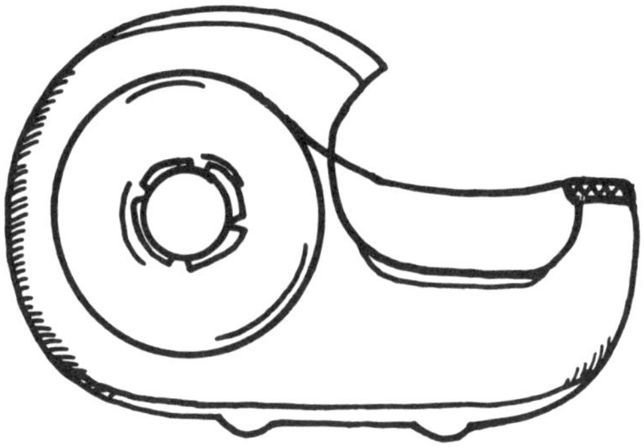

____ape

____est

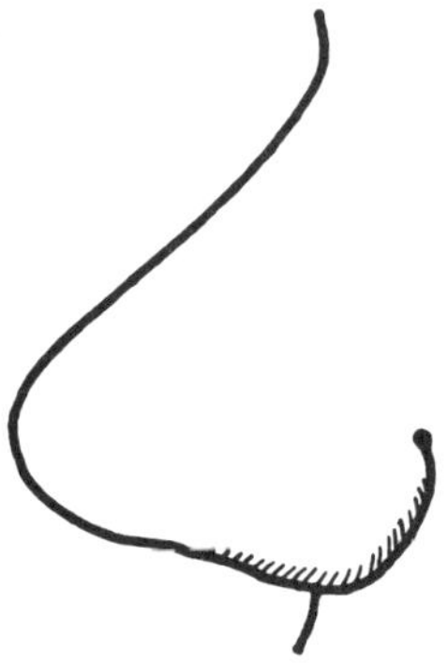

____ose

Now color the pictures.

© School Zone Publishing Company

BEGINNING SOUNDS

DIRECTIONS: Look at the picture. Say the word.
Write in the first sound.
Write the whole word on the line.

Chris
Dave
Brad

tennis **names**

 ____ut ____________	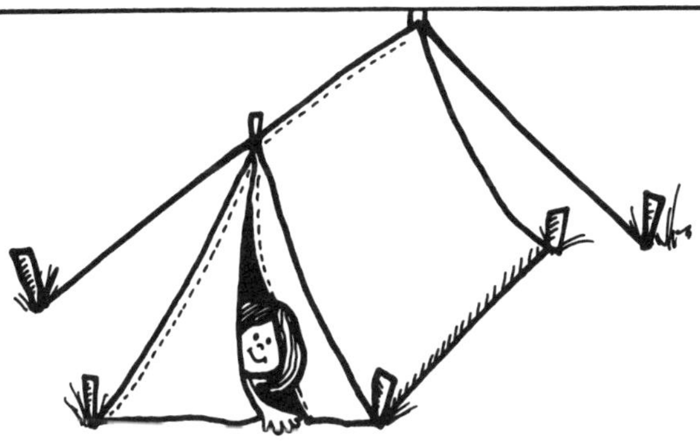 ____ent ____________
 ____en ____________	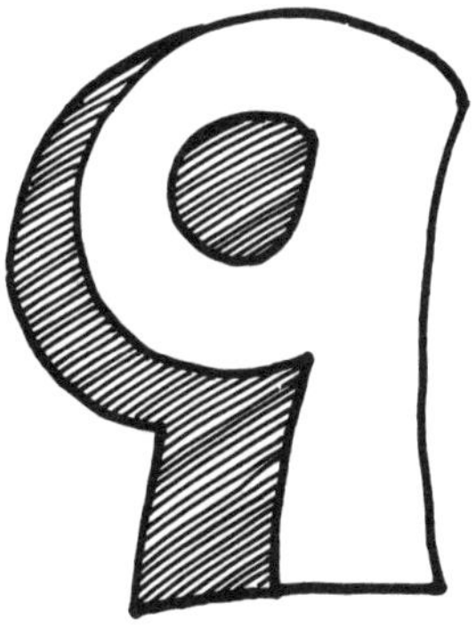 ____ine ____________

Now read this page to a friend.

© School Zone Publishing Company

BEGINNING SOUNDS

DIRECTIONS: Look at the picture. Say the word.
Write in the first sound.
Write the whole word on the line.

button

donkey

____og

____

____ed

____

____oor

____

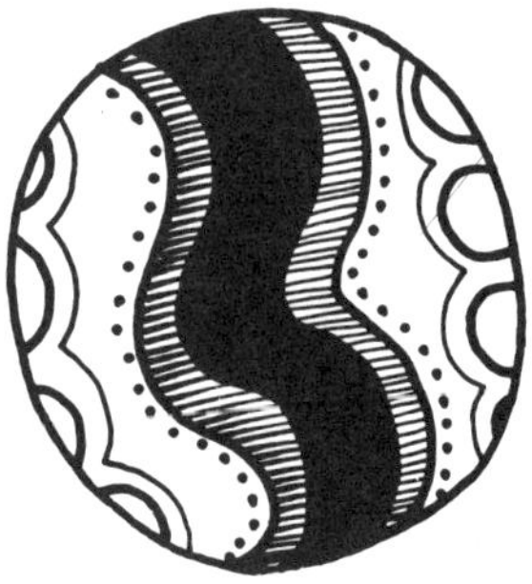

____all

____

Now color the pictures.

© School Zone Publishing Company

BEGINNING SOUNDS

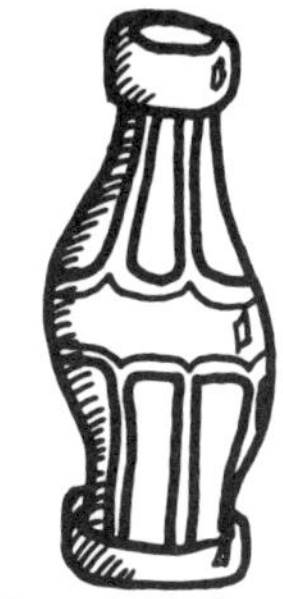

DIRECTIONS: Look at the picture. Say the word.
Write in the first sound.
Write the whole word on the line.

bottle

dollar

 ____aby ________________	 ____oll ________________
 ____eer ________________	 ____ird ________________

Now read this page to a friend.

© School Zone Publishing Company

BEGINNING SOUNDS

DIRECTIONS: Look at the picture. Say the word.
Write in the first sound.
Write the whole word on the line.

sail

rug

 ___at ________________	 ___ing ________________
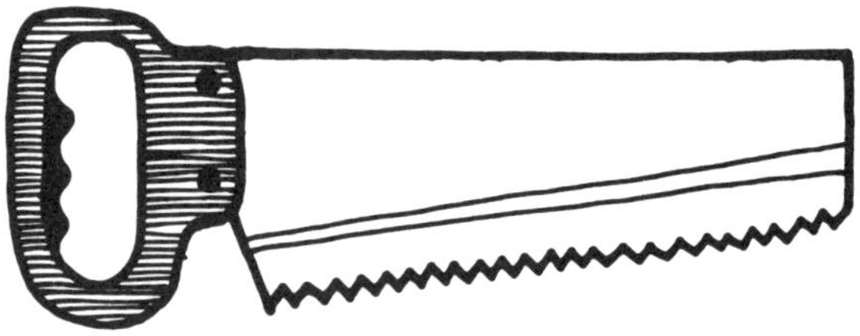 ___aw ________________	 ___ock ________________

Now color the pictures.

© School Zone Publishing Company

BEGINNING SOUNDS

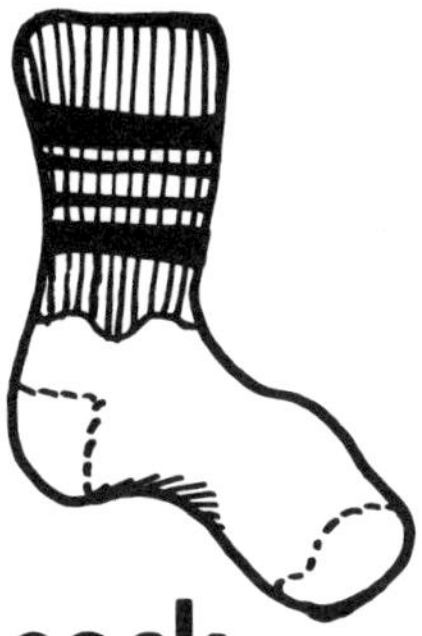

sock

DIRECTIONS: Look at the picture. Say the word.
Write in the first sound.
Write the whole word on the line.

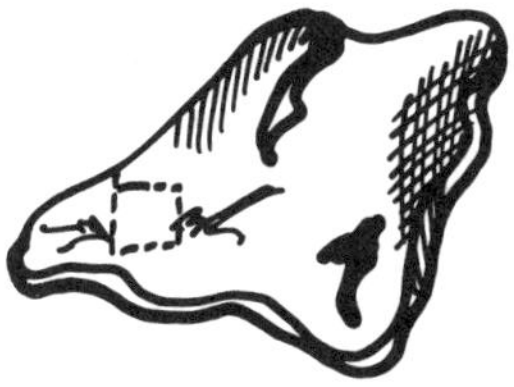

rag

____ink

____

____ope

____

____ain

____

____oap

____

Now read this page to a friend.

© School Zone Publishing Company

BEGINNING SOUNDS

farm

DIRECTIONS: Look at the picture. Say the word.
Write in the first sound.
Write the whole word on the line.

candle

____an

____

____at

____

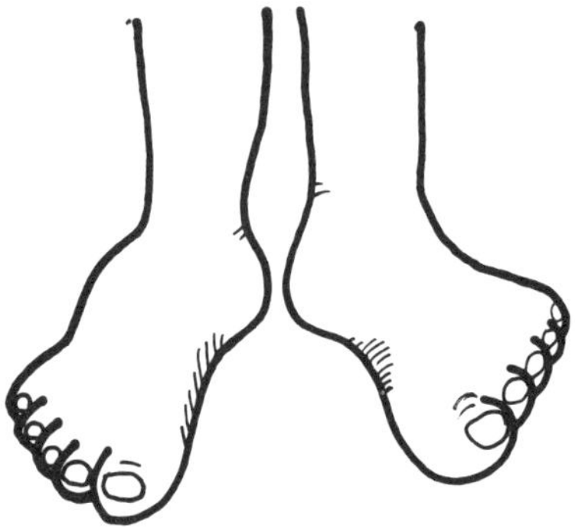

____eet

____

____ar

____

Now color the pictures.

© School Zone Publishing Company

BEGINNING SOUNDS

DIRECTIONS: Look at the picture. Say the word.
Write in the first sound.
Write the whole word on the line.

fox

camera

____ake

____

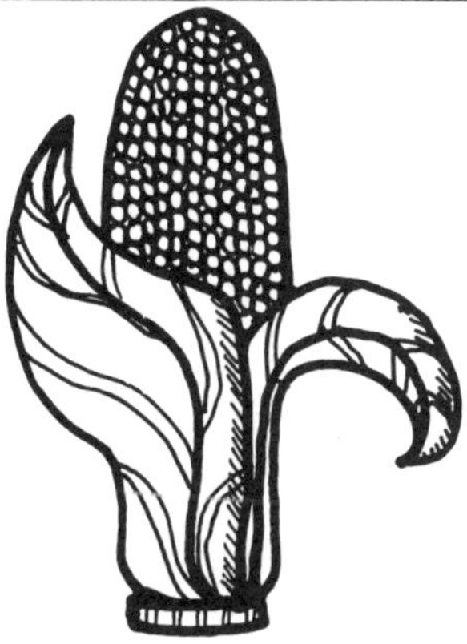

____orn

____

____ive

____

____ish

____

Now read this page to a friend.

© School Zone Publishing Company

BEGINNING SOUNDS

DIRECTIONS: Look at the picture. Say the word.
Write in the first sound.
Write the whole word on the line.

gas

lamb

___irl

____

___eg

____

___amp

____

___ate

____

Now color the pictures.

© School Zone Publishing Company

garden

BEGINNING SOUNDS

DIRECTIONS: Look at the picture. Say the word.
Write in the first sound.
Write the whole word on the line.

lantern

____ock

____

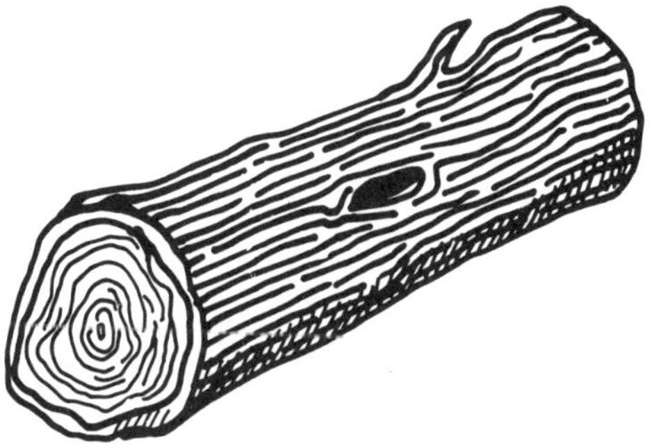

____og

____

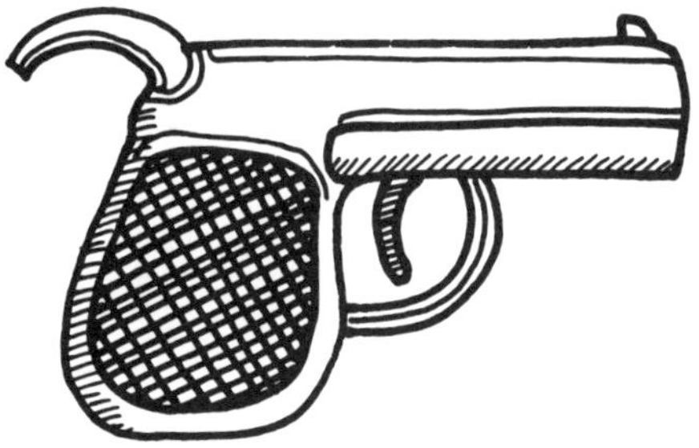

____un

____

____oat

____

Now read this page to a friend.

© School Zone Publishing Company

BEGINNING SOUNDS

DIRECTIONS: Look at the picture. Say the word.
Write in the first sound.
Write the whole word on the line.

kiss

hamster

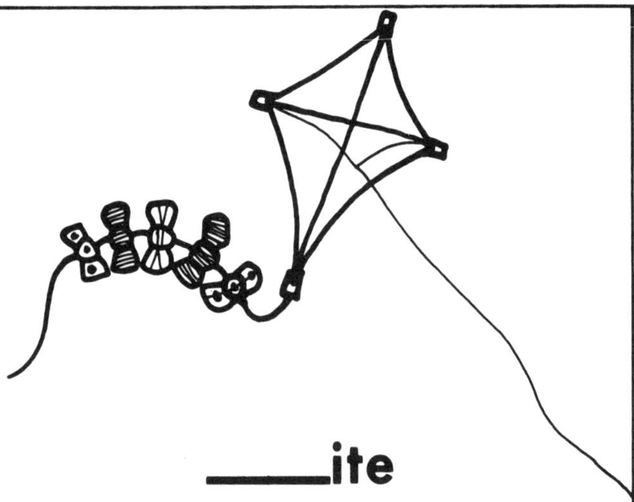

___ite

____

___at

____

___ing

____

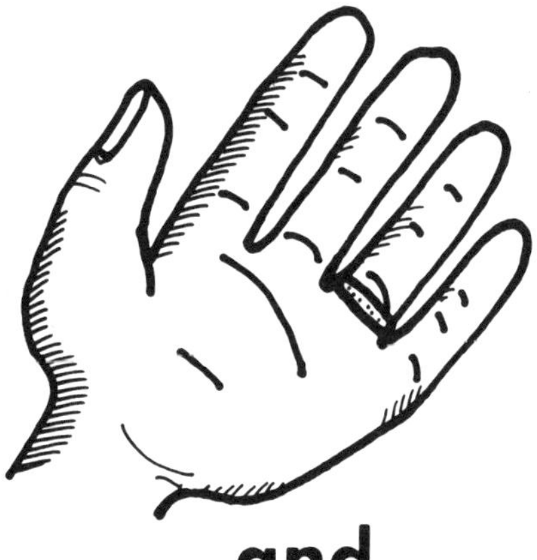

___and

____

Now color the pictures.

© School Zone Publishing Company

BEGINNING SOUNDS

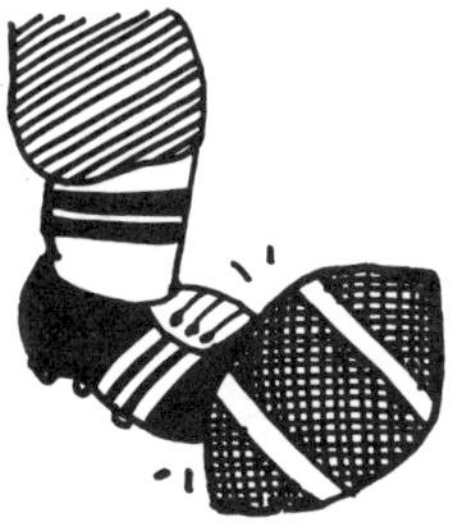

DIRECTIONS: Look at the picture. Say the word.
Write in the first sound.
Write the whole word on the line.

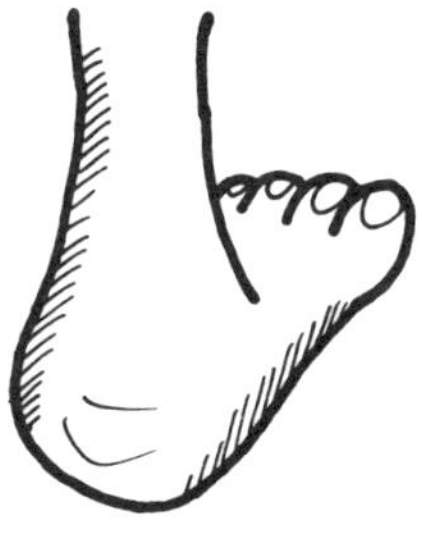

kick **heel**

____ouse

____

____orse

____

____itten

____

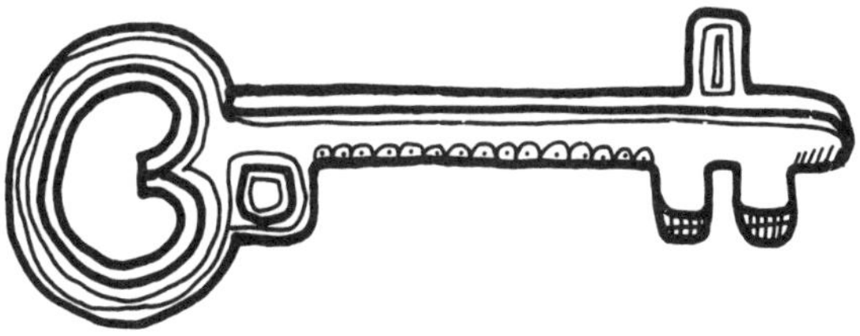

____ey

____

Now read this page to a friend.

© School Zone Publishing Company

jacket

BEGINNING SOUNDS

DIRECTIONS: Look at the picture. Say the word.
Write in the first sound.
Write the whole word on the line.

violin

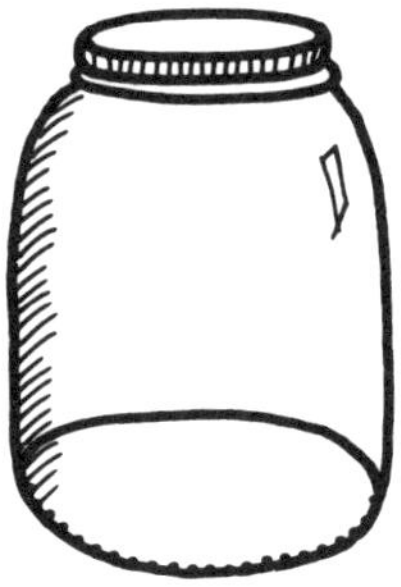

____ar

____

____an

____

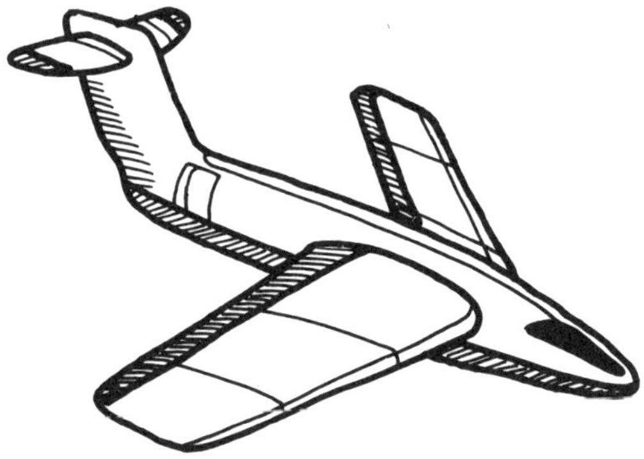

____et

____

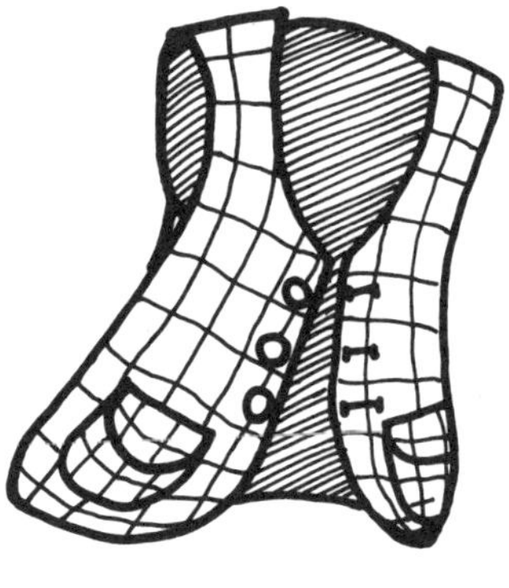

____est

____

Now color the pictures.

© School Zone Publishing Company

jail

BEGINNING SOUNDS

DIRECTIONS: Look at the picture. Say the word.
Write in the first sound.
Write the whole word on the line.

vegetables

____ase

____

____ine

____

____og

____

____ump

____

Now read this page to a friend.

© School Zone Publishing Company

BEGINNING SOUNDS

DIRECTIONS: Look at the picture. Say the word.
Write in the first sound.
Write the whole word on the line.

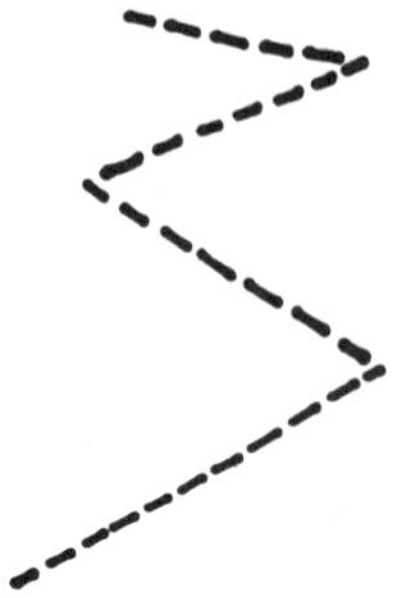

wig

zigzag

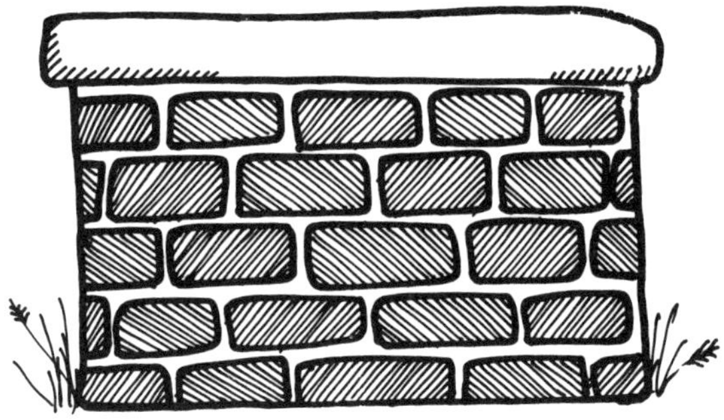 ____all ______________	 ____ing ______________
 ____ebra ______________	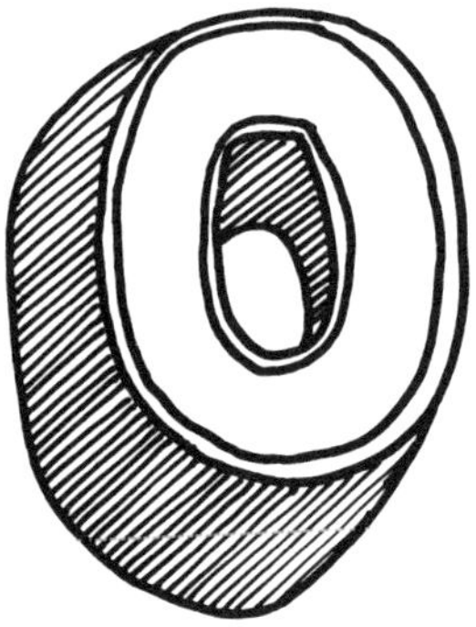 ____ero ______________

Now color the pictures.

© School Zone Publishing Company

window

BEGINNING SOUNDS

DIRECTIONS: Look at the picture. Say the word.
Write in the first sound.
Write the whole word on the line.

zipper

____ip

____

____eb

____

____agon

____

____oo

____

Now read this page to a friend.

© School Zone Publishing Company

ENDING SOUNDS

cent

DIRECTIONS: Look at the picture. Say the word.
Write in the last sound.
Write the whole word on the line.

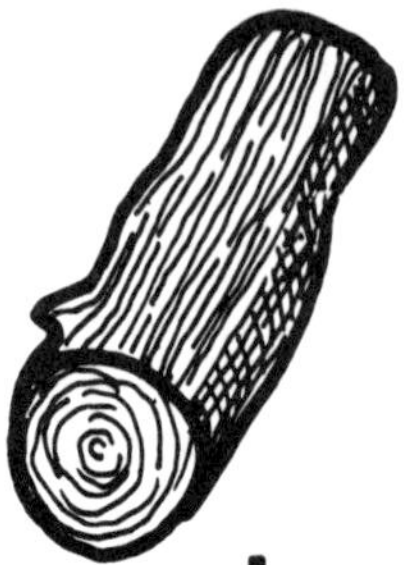

log

ho____

____

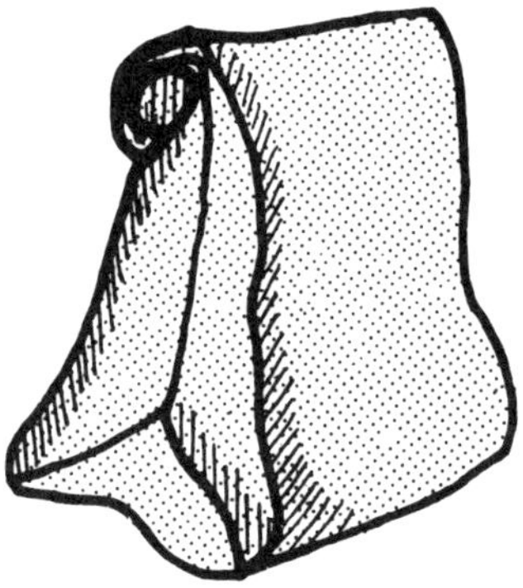

ba____

____

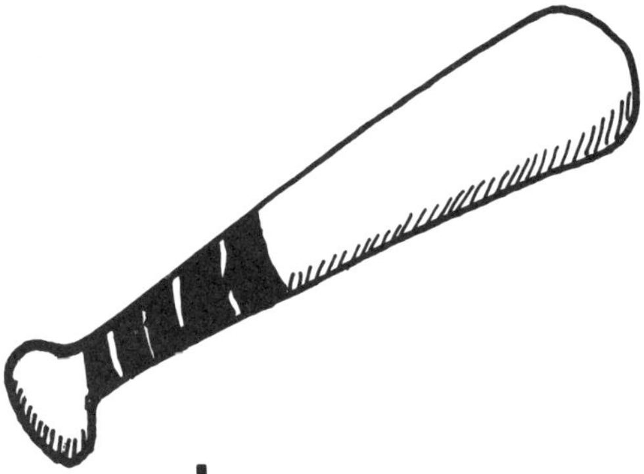

ba____

____

an____

____

Now color the pictures.

© School Zone Publishing Company

ENDING SOUNDS

DIRECTIONS: Look at the picture. Say the word.
Write in the last sound.
Write the whole word on the line.

rabbit **tag**

boa____

____

bu____

____

do____

____

ca____

____

Now read this page to a friend.

© School Zone Publishing Company

ENDING SOUNDS

DIRECTIONS: Look at the picture. Say the word.
Write in the last sound.
Write the whole word on the line.

wor<u>m</u>

lio<u>n</u>

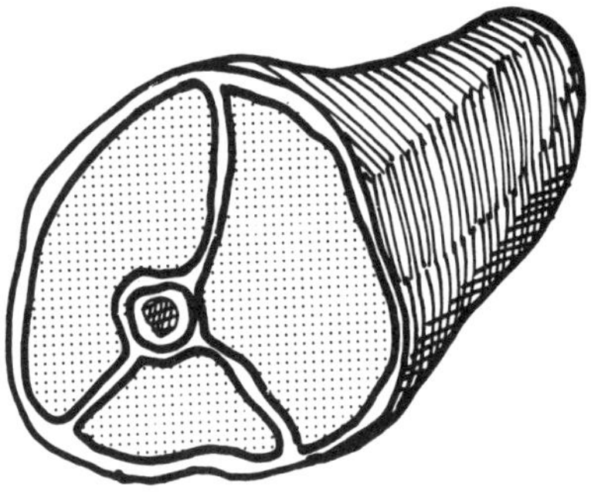

ha___

____

gu___

____

ca___

____

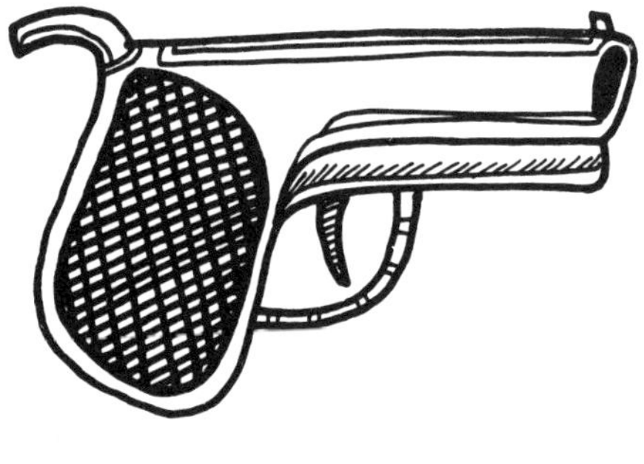

gu___

____

Now color the pictures.

© School Zone Publishing Company

ENDING SOUNDS

foam

DIRECTIONS: Look at the picture. Say the word.
Write in the last sound.
Write the whole word on the line.

robin

fa___

____

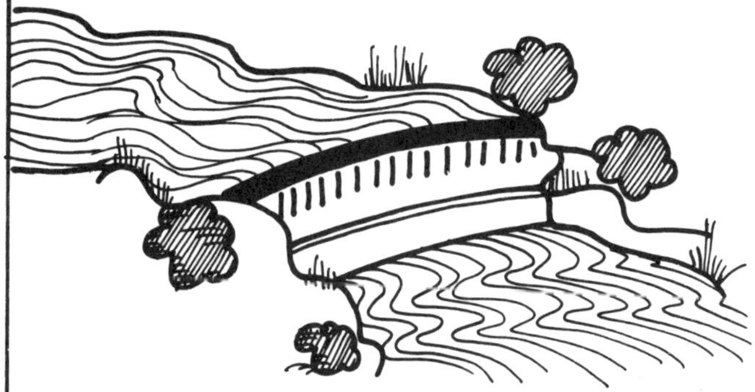

da___

____

ja___

____

su___

____

Now read this page to a friend.

© School Zone Publishing Company

ENDING SOUNDS

DIRECTIONS: Look at the picture. Say the word.
Write in the last sound.
Write the whole word on the line.

jee<u>p</u> **clu<u>b</u>**

 **cu____** ________________	 **tu____** ________________
 **bi____** ________________	 **ca____** ________________

Now color the pictures.

© School Zone Publishing Company

lamp

ENDING SOUNDS

DIRECTIONS: Look at the picture. Say the word.
Write in the last sound.
Write the whole word on the line.

sob

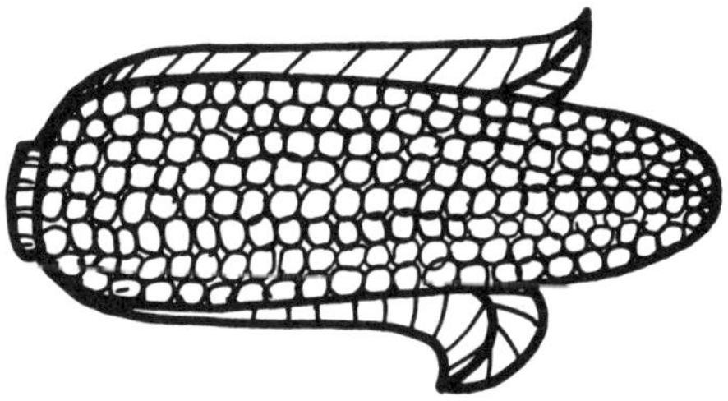

co____

____

ca____

____

mo____

____

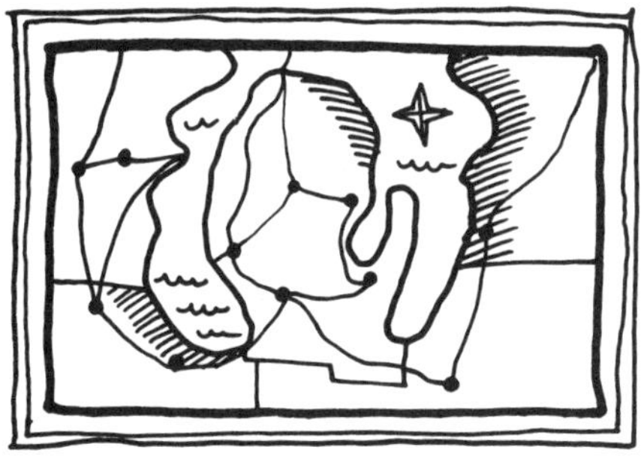

ma____

____

Now read this page to a friend.

© School Zone Publishing Company

ENDING SOUNDS

DIRECTIONS: Look at the picture. Say the word.
Write in the last sound.
Write the whole word on the line.

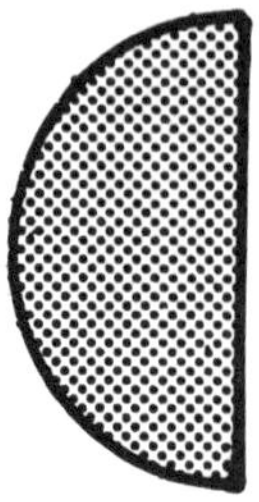

kid **half**

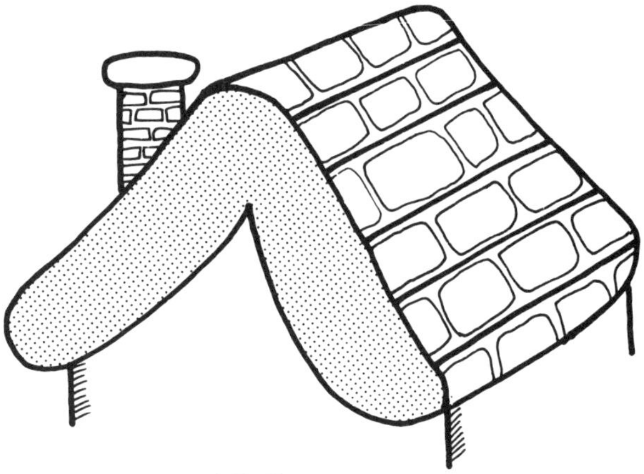

roo____

____

lea____

____

sa____

____

ma____

____

Now color the pictures.

© School Zone Publishing Company

ENDING SOUNDS

DIRECTIONS: Look at the picture. Say the word.
Write in the last sound.
Write the whole word on the line.

head

calf

la____

____

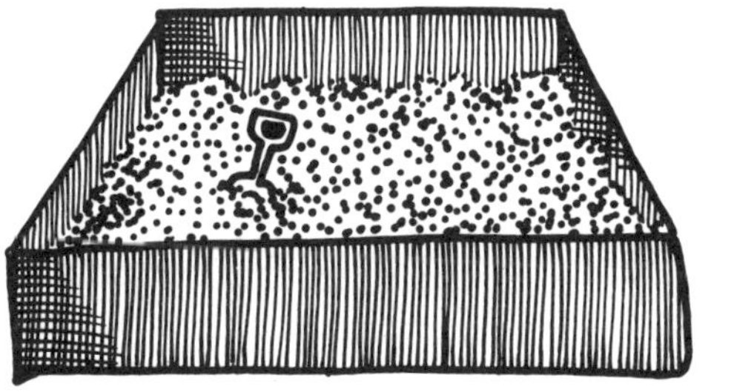

san____

____

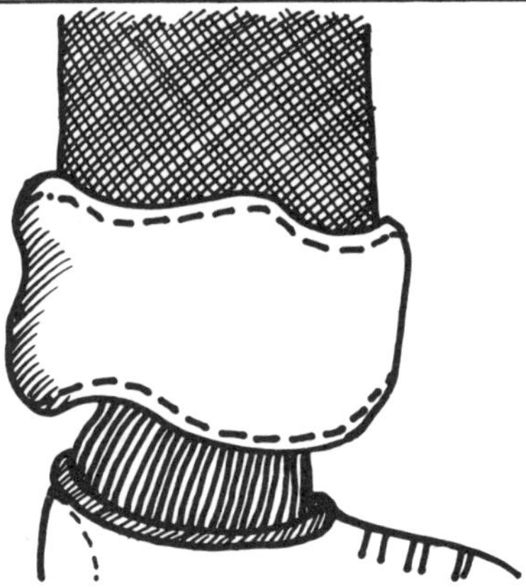

cu__ __

____

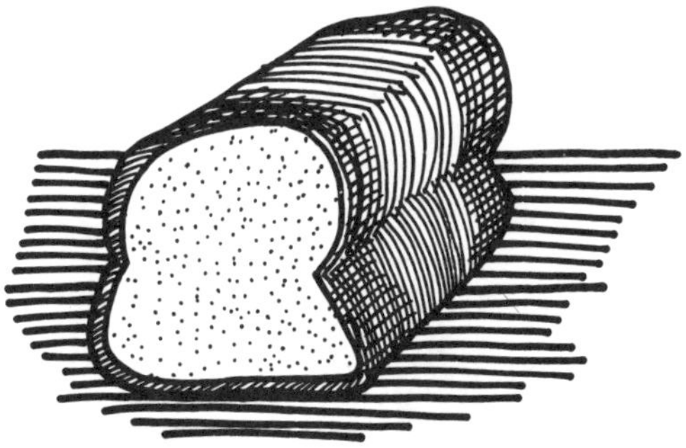

loa____

____

Now read this page to a friend.

© School Zone Publishing Company

ENDING SOUNDS

DIRECTIONS: Look at the picture. Say the word.
Write in the last sound.
Write the whole word on the line.

gir<u>l</u>

apple<u>s</u>

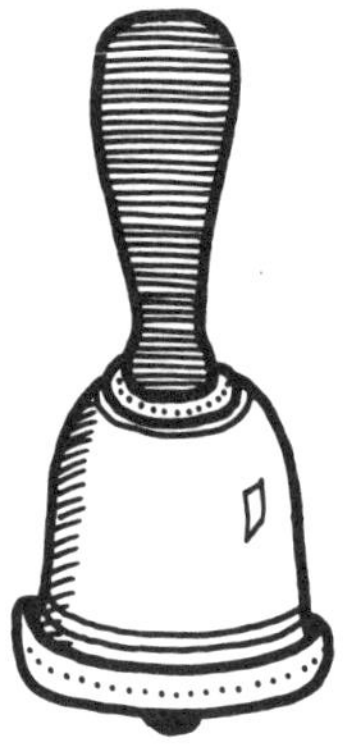

be__ __

____

boot____

____

sea____

____

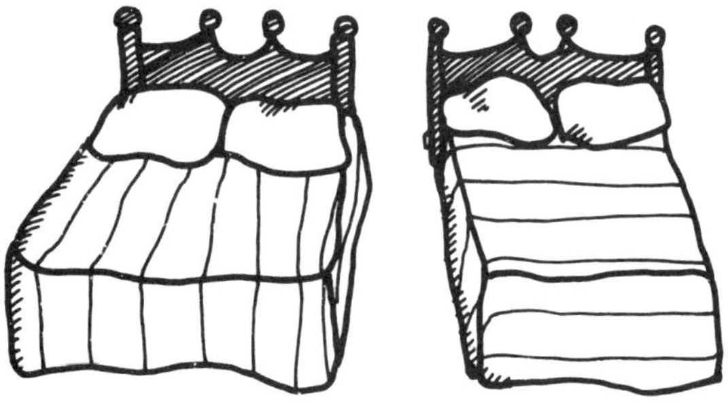

bed____

____

Now color the pictures.

© School Zone Publishing Company

ENDING SOUNDS

DIRECTIONS: Look at the picture. Say the word.
Write in the last sound.
Write the whole word on the line.

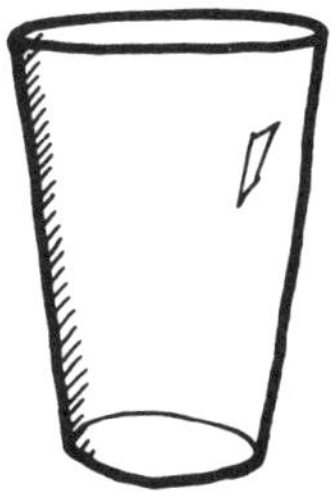

bill **glass**

dre__ __

____

ba__ __

____

hi__ __

____

boy____

____

Now read this page to a friend.

© School Zone Publishing Company

ENDING SOUNDS

truck

DIRECTIONS: Look at the picture. Say the word.
Write in the last sound.
Write the whole word on the line.

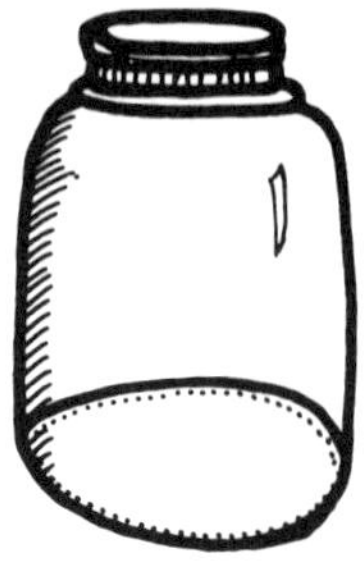

jar

hoo____

____

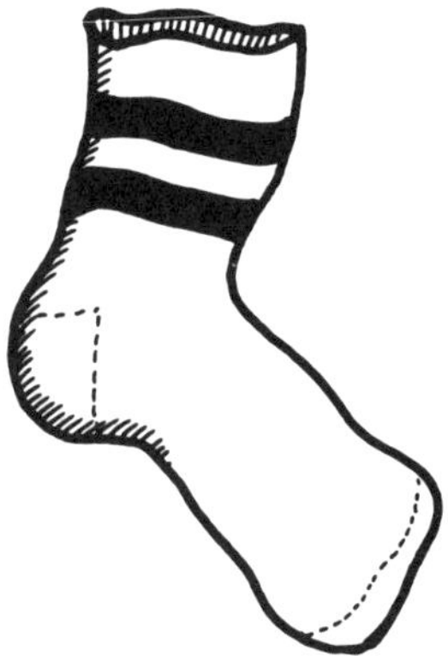

soc____

____

sta____

____

fou____

____

Now color the pictures.

© School Zone Publishing Company

ENDING SOUNDS

DIRECTIONS: Look at the picture. Say the word.
Write in the last sound.
Write the whole word on the line.

clock **hair**

ea____

____

ca____

____

duc____

____

for____

____

Now read this page to a friend.

© School Zone Publishing Company

Put in the right beginning and ending letter to name these things you'll find around your house.

© School Zone Publishing Company

Page 161
1. moon
2. pig
3. pan
4. man

Page 162
1. mat
2. mop
3. pop
4. pen

Page 163
1. top
2. tape
3. nest
4. nose

Page 164
1. nut
2. tent
3. ten
4. nine

Page 165
1. dog
2. bed
3. door
4. ball

Page 166
1. baby
2. doll
3. deer
4. bird

Page 167
1. rat
2. ring
3. saw
4. sock

Page 168
1. sink
2. rope
3. rain
4. soap

Page 169
1. fan
2. cat
3. feet
4. car

Page 170
1. cake
2. corn
3. five
4. fish

Page 171
1. girl
2. leg
3. lamp
4. gate

Page 172
1. lock
2. log
3. gun
4. goat

Page 173
1. kite
2. hat
3. king
4. hand

Page 174
1. house
2. horse
3. kitten
4. key

Page 175
1. jar
2. van
3. jet
4. vest

Page 176
1. vase
2. vine
3. jog
4. jump

Page 177
1. wall
2. wing
3. zebra
4. zero

Page 178
1. zip
2. web
3. wagon
4. zoo

Page 179
1. hog
2. bag
3. bat
4. ant

Page 180
1. boat
2. bug
3. dog
4. cat

Page 181
1. ham
2. gum
3. can
4. gun

Page 182
1. fan
2. dam
3. jam
4. sun

Page 183
1. cup
2. tub
3. bib
4. cap

Page 184
1. cob
2. cab
3. mop
4. map

Page 185
1. roof
2. leaf
3. sad
4. mad

Page 186
1. lad
2. sand
3. cuff
4. loaf

Page 187
1. bell
2. boots
3. seal
4. beds

Page 188
1. dress
2. ball
3. hill
4. boys

Page 189
1. hook
2. sock
3. star
4. four

Page 190
1. ear
2. car
3. duck
4. fork

Page 191
1. bird
2. grass
3. kitten
4. flower
5. kids
6. door
7. table
8. chair
9. jet
10. sun
11. cloud
12. tree
13. barn
14. dog
15. nest
16. kite

© School Zone Publishing Company

Read each sentence.
Circle the picture that goes with it.

The dog has a birthday.

Dad paints the house.

Here comes the train.

Mother jumps.

Cold Cat rides a bike.

I see two fish.

This car is little.

© School Zone Publishing Company

Read each sentence.
Circle the picture that goes with it.

See the big boat.

We like to run.

The bird is wet.

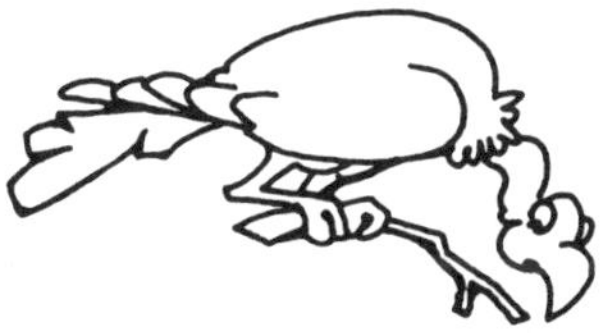

Cold Cat plays ball.

The goat ate a hat.

Thank you for the book.

They are happy.

© School Zone Publishing Company

Circle the correct word for each sentence.

Amy is my **(brother sister)**.

I have a red **(dress hat)**.

Stop that **(bus car)**.

There is **(word water)** in the wagon.

We must **(hide help)** Cold Cat.

Give the **(did dog)** some water.

Let's go to the **(zoo zebra)**.

© School Zone Publishing Company

Circle the correct word for each sentence.

The (**duck** **dark**) can swim.

I hear the dog (**book** **bark**).

We like to eat (**food** **from**).

See the (**moon** **make**) in the sky.

Look at the (**dish** **dress**).

The girl rides a (**house** **horse**).

Cold Cat likes to (**soon** **sleep**).

© School Zone Publishing Company

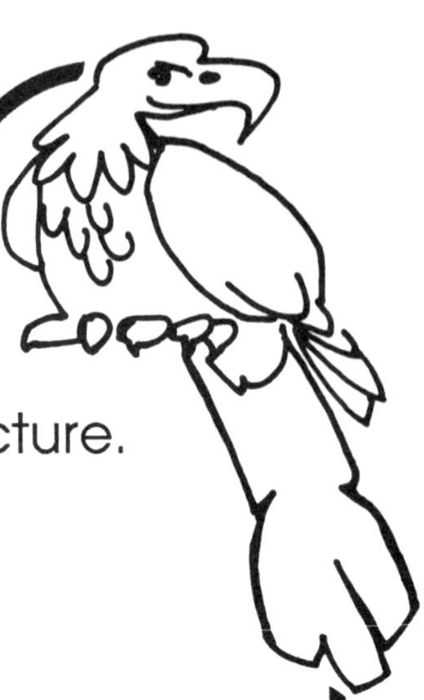

Draw a line from each sentence to the correct picture.

It lives in the water.

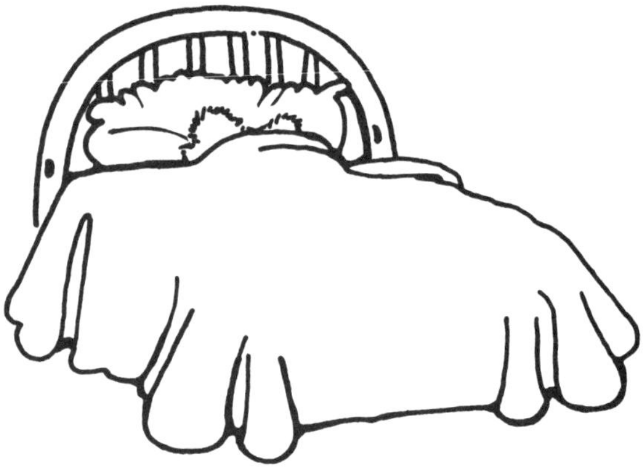

This is big and yellow.

It can fly.

This animal is cold.

You can ride on this.

This animal is wet.

You can sleep in it.

© School Zone Publishing Company

Draw a line from each sentence to the correct picture.

There are four of these.

Children go here.

It lives in a barn.

Please do not cry.

There are five of these.

It lives in a nest.

It has two very big feet.

Read each sentence.
Do what it says.

Color Cold Cat **orange**.
Color his cap **purple**.
Color the dog **black** and the car **red**.
Color the house **yellow**.
Color the pig **pink** and her coat **green**.

© School Zone Publishing Company

Read each sentence.
Do what it says.

Write **1** next to the rabbit.
Write **2** next to the horse.
Write **3** next to the rocket.
Draw an **O** around the men.
Write **C** on Cold Cat.
Write **X** on the box.
Draw a ✓ on the balloon.

© School Zone Publishing Company

Circle **Yes** if the sentence is true.
Circle **No** if it is not true.

Yes	**No**	You can eat a boot.
Yes	**No**	Cold Cat can bark.
Yes	**No**	A book will bite.
Yes	**No**	**Three** comes after **two**.
Yes	**No**	A mouse is small.
Yes	**No**	Elephants are green.
Yes	**No**	**Four** comes before **five**.
Yes	**No**	A kitten is a baby cat.

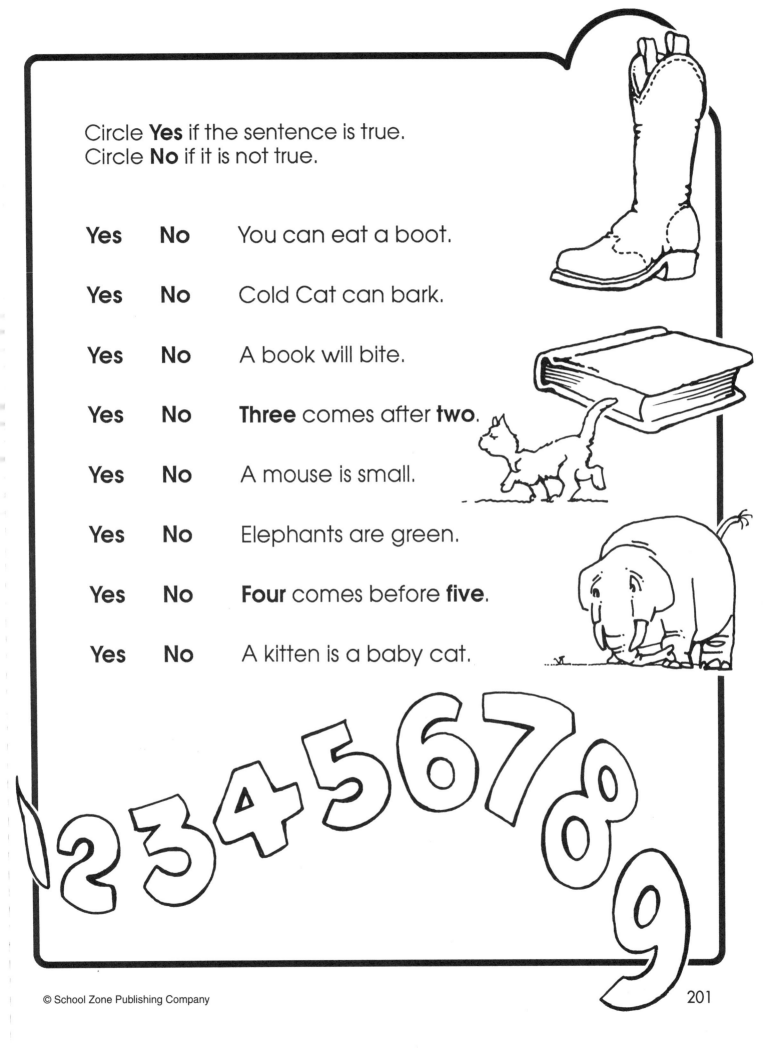

© School Zone Publishing Company

Circle **Yes** if the sentence is true.
Circle **No** if it is not true.

Yes	**No**	Snow is white.
Yes	**No**	It is dark at night.
Yes	**No**	A penny is not round.
Yes	**No**	Cars go on streets.
Yes	**No**	A boy can walk up a hill.
Yes	**No**	A girl can walk down a hill.
Yes	**No**	Fire is cold.
Yes	**No**	Cold Cat has a tail.

© School Zone Publishing Company

Words that rhyme have the same last sound.
Who, zoo, blue, and **you** all rhyme.

Read each sentence.
Write the word that **rhymes** with the bold word on each line.

sun **sat** **big** **you** **fan** **train** **red**

The **man** holds a fan.

Did it **rain** on the ____________?

Bob will **run** in the ____________.

Who will give the ball to ____________?

Lee will paint the **bed** ____________.

Cold **Cat** ____________.

That **pig** is very ____________.

© School Zone Publishing Company

Read each sentence.
Write the word that **rhymes** with the bold word on each line.

pie   away   cake   too   dish   tree   book

Will you go ____________________ to **play**?

Stop! Don't you **see** the ____________________?

Cold Cat **took** the ____________________.

This is **my** apple ____________________.

Please **take** the ____________________.

The **fish** jumped out of the ____________________!

This hat is ____________________ **blue**.

© School Zone Publishing Company

Circle the sentence that goes with each picture.

Run up the hill!
Here we go down the hill.

That duck has three boots.
That duck has four boots.

Two birds sit in a cage.
Two birds sit on a cow.

I read at school.
I read at home.

Cold Cat sits by the fire.
Cold Cat puts out the fire.

Stop that horse!
Help that horse!

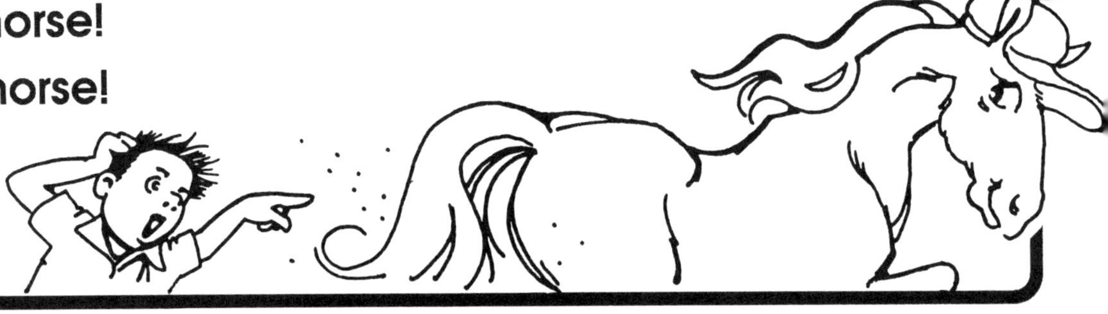

© School Zone Publishing Company

Circle the sentence that goes with each picture.

This bear is too small.
This bear is too big.

Cold Cat will fly the plane.
Cold Cat will ride the train.

Where are my boots?
Where are my mittens?

The coat is on the boy.
The goat is in the pen.

The baby is on the box.
The box is on the baby.

The pony and pig race.
The pony wins.

© School Zone Publishing Company

Circle the sentence that goes with each picture.

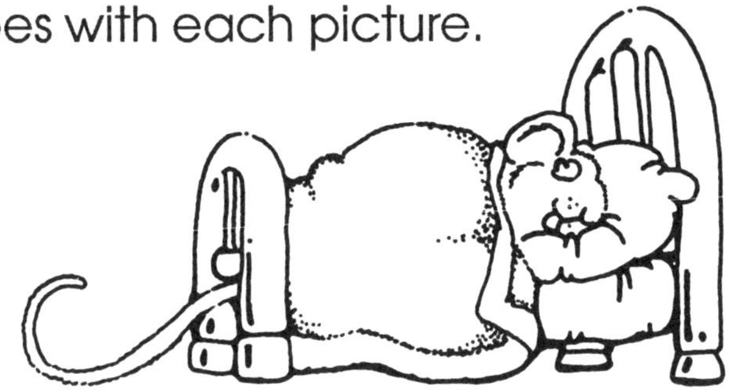

It is morning!
Please go to sleep.

Say hello to the duck.
Say goodbye to the bird.

My friend lives on a farm.
My friend plays a game with me.

Cold Cat has five feet.
Cold Cat sings a song.

I see three toy trucks.
I see three toy cars.

Amy hurt her leg.
Amy helps her mother.

© School Zone Publishing Company

Look at each picture and sentence.
Write the correct word on the line.

truck ice baby light pan walks three

The baby_____ sleeps.

The ____________ is very clean.

Two eggs are in the ____________.

Please turn off the ____________.

Cold Cat is happy when he ____________.

We like to skate on ____________.

Ann has ____________ brothers.

© School Zone Publishing Company

Look at each picture and sentence.
Write the correct word on the line.

turtle Five name cut behind Children pocket

He will ______________ the cake.

The dog is ______________ the big tree.

______________ like to play.

Your mittens are in your ______________ .

______________ ducks fly away.

My ______________ is Jim.

Cold Cat finds a ______________ .

© School Zone Publishing Company

Look at each picture and sentence.
Write the correct word on the line.

four hair under girl hold letter party

The ________________ gave me a picture.

This ________________ is for me!

Please ________________ this box for me.

Cold Cat is ________________ the bed.

________________ men were in the water.

Jenny has a birthday ________________ .

Her ________________ is very long.

© School Zone Publishing Company

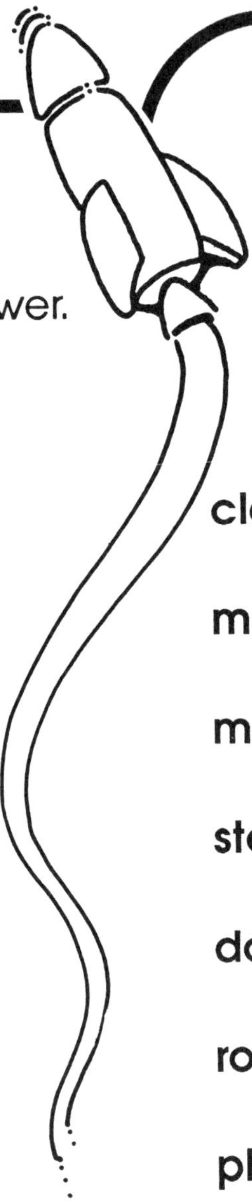

Draw a line from each sentence to the answer.

You can go up these or down them.	**clock**
This animal barks at cars.	**mouse**
It goes up, up, up into the sky.	**money**
You use it to buy things.	**steps**
It is a very small animal.	**dog**
You say **Hello** on it.	**rocket**
It tells you the time.	**phone**

© School Zone Publishing Company

Draw a line from each sentence to the answer.

Cold Cat might read you one.	**airplane**
You can do this to a picture.	**hit**
It's the day after today.	**story**
A kangaroo can do this.	**color**
You hear this.	**tomorrow**
You might see one in the sky.	**sound**
Cold Cat might do this to a ball.	**hop**

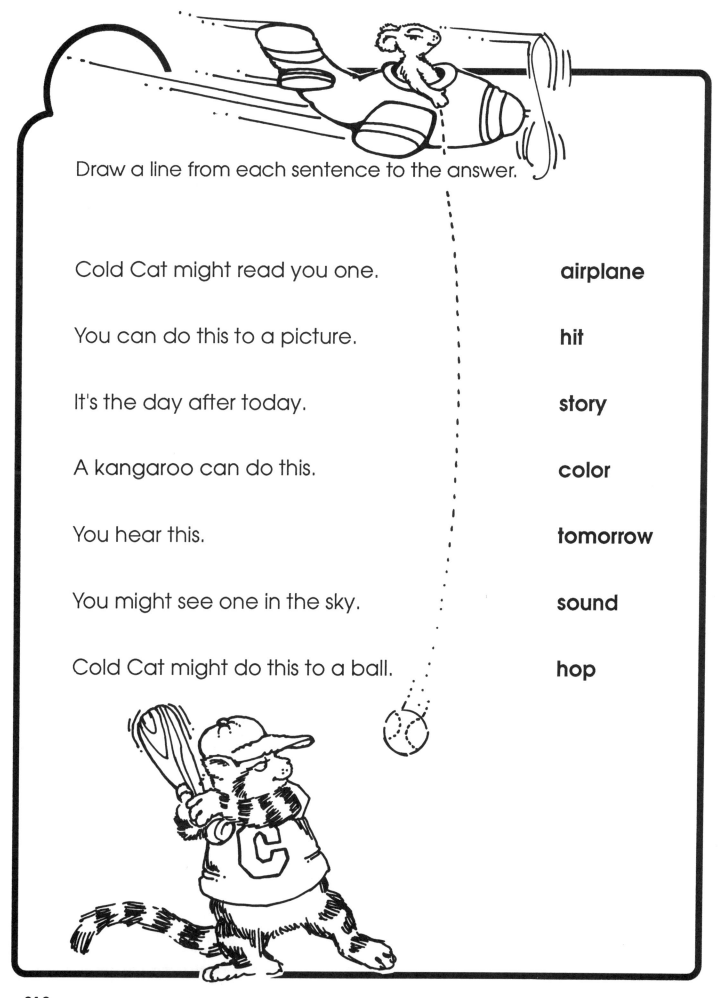

© School Zone Publishing Company

Draw a line from each sentence to the answer.

This is money.	**hurry**
Grass is this color.	**yellow**
Cold Cat cooks fish in one.	**pony**
You do this when you walk fast.	**pan**
This animal is a small horse.	**goat**
The sun is this color.	**penny**
This animal has horns.	**green**

© School Zone Publishing Company

Read each sentence.
Do what it says.

Two birds are the same. **Circle** them.

Two birds are different. Draw a **box** around them.

Color Cold Cat **yellow**.

Color the mouse **red**.

Write **L** next to the long snake.

Write **S** next to the short snake.

Draw a **box** around Cold Cat and the mouse.

© School Zone Publishing Company

Read each sentence.
Do what it says.

Draw an **X** by the real Cold Cat.

Draw a big **C** on his shirt.

Draw a **happy face** on the girl.

Draw a **sad face** on the boy.

Two caps are the same. Draw a **box** around them.

Two caps are different. Draw a **circle** around them.

Which duck is bigger? Color it **green** and **brown**.

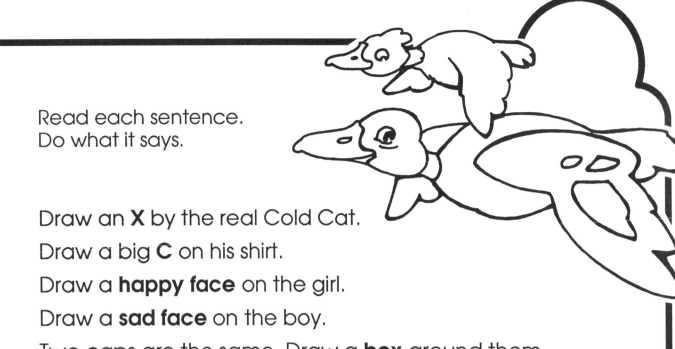

© School Zone Publishing Company

Read each sentence.
Do what it says.

Draw a **line** under the wagon.

Draw **two lines** over the dragon.

Draw **two circles** around Cold Cat.

Write **L** on Cold Cat's left hand.

Write **R** on Cold Cat's right hand.

Two mittens go together. Color them **red** and **blue.**

Two mittens do not go together. Draw a **box** around them.

© School Zone Publishing Company

Circle **Yes** if the sentence is true.
Circle **No** if it is not true.

Yes **No** Two boots can sing a song.

Yes **No** A cat might be cold.

Yes **No** Rabbits can hop.

Yes **No** A brother is a girl.

Yes **No** A big yellow bus has four feet.

Yes **No** Children can go to school.

Yes **No** **Six** comes after **ten**.

Yes **No** Fire trucks eat fish.

© School Zone Publishing Company

Circle **Yes** if the sentence is true.
Circle **No** if it is not true.

Yes	**No**	A **mother** is a **mom**.
Yes	**No**	You can look out of a window.
Yes	**No**	There are no animals in a zoo.
Yes	**No**	You can carry things in a basket.
Yes	**No**	A penny is something to wear.
Yes	**No**	**D** comes after **C**.
Yes	**No**	A cat can have kittens.
Yes	**No**	A cupcake is something to eat.

© School Zone Publishing Company

Circle **Yes** if the sentence is true.
Circle **No** if it is not true.

Yes	**No**	All elephants are very little.
Yes	**No**	Apples and cookies are food.
Yes	**No**	A box is always round.
Yes	**No**	You can buy eggs in a store.
Yes	**No**	A cat has four tails.
Yes	**No**	**Stop** is not the same as **go**.
Yes	**No**	**Four** comes before **five**.
Yes	**No**	A book is something to read.

© School Zone Publishing Company

Read the first sentence in each group.
Then read the next two sentences.
Write an **X** next to the one that **rhymes** with the first sentence.

Cold Cat stops the train.

______ Cold Cat has no car.

__X__ Cold Cat has no brain.

Cold Cat goes to bed.

______ Cold Cat hides his head.

______ Cold Cat says good night.

Mother, Mother, take my book.

______ Put it on the table.

______ Put it in the pot to cook.

Cold Cat paints a sled.

______ Every day he paints it black.

______ Every day he paints it red.

© School Zone Publishing Company

Read the first sentence in each group.
Then read the next two sentences.
Write an **X** next to the one that **rhymes** with the first sentence.

Cold Cat paints his shoe.

______ Cold Cat paints it blue.

______ Cold Cat paints it green.

Linda saw the box and made a guess.

______ In the box was a glass.

______ In the box was a dress.

Mom can cook and Mom can bake.

______ Mom gives me a big cupcake.

______ Mom gives me a good cookie.

In the chair sat a dog.

______ On the ground sat a cat.

______ On the ground sat a frog.

© School Zone Publishing Company

Read the first sentence in each group.
Then read the next two sentences.
Write an **X** next to the one that **rhymes** with the first sentence.

Listen to what Grandma said.

______ Never paint a tiger red.

______ Never paint a tiger green.

Cold Cat finds some money.

______ Cold Cat buys a mouse.

______ Cold Cat thinks it's funny.

I see something in a chair.

______ Can it be a cat?

______ Can it be a bear?

What a very funny pen.

______ I will give it to the hen.

______ I will give it to the man.

© School Zone Publishing Company

Color the picture.
Then write a story about Cold Cat.

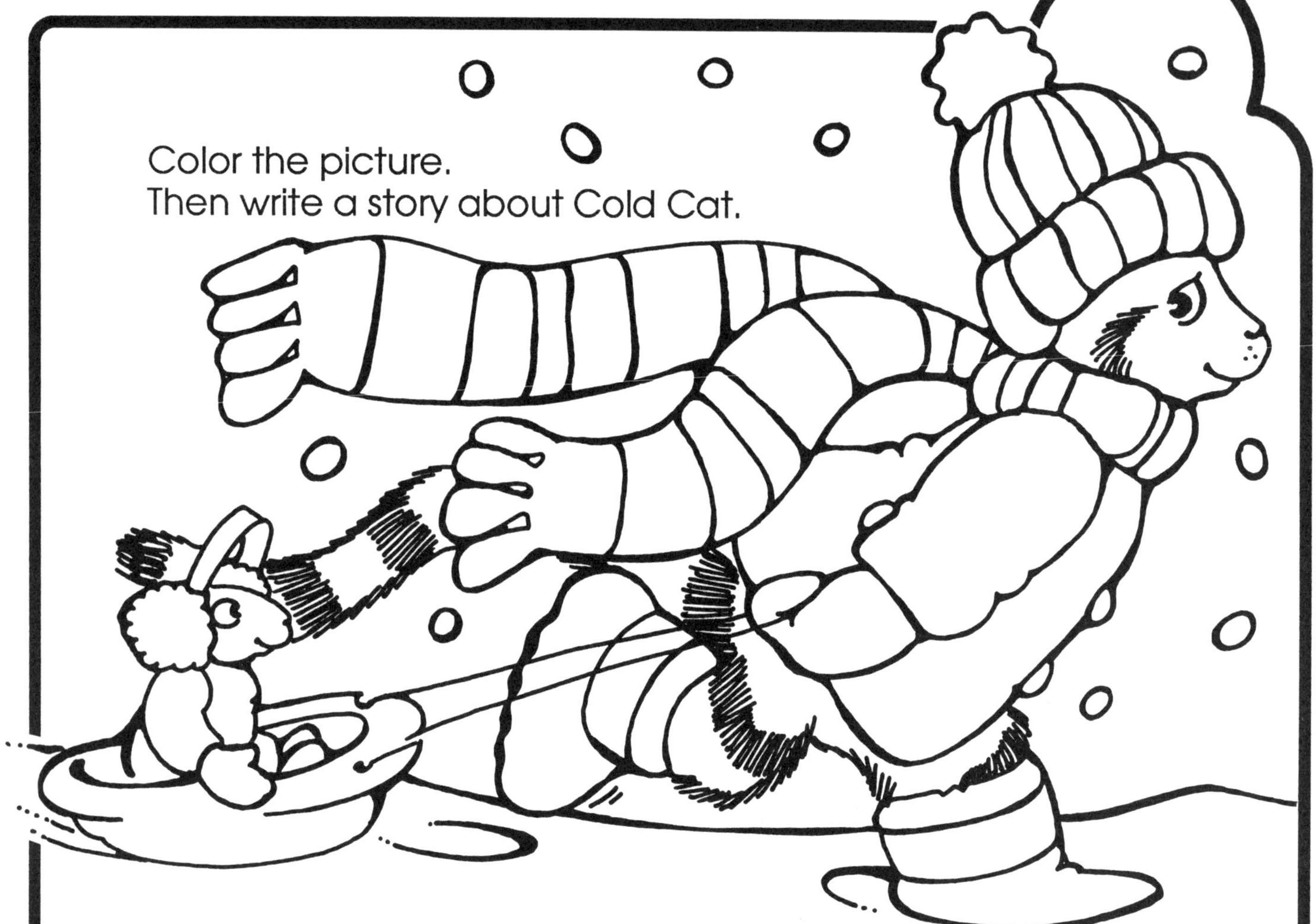

© School Zone Publishing Company

Page 195
sister
dress
bus
water
help
dog
zoo

Page 196
duck
bark
food
moon
dish
horse
sleep

Page 201
No
No
No
Yes
Yes
No
Yes
Yes

Page 202
Yes
Yes
No
Yes
Yes
Yes
No
Yes

Page 203
fan
train
sun
you
red
sat
big

Page 204
away
tree
book
pie
cake
dish
too

Page 205
Run up the hill!
That duck has four boots.
Two birds sit on a cow.
I read at home.
Cold Cat sits by the fire.
Stop that horse!

Page 206
This bear is too big.
Cold Cat will ride the train.
Where are my boots?
The goat is in the pen.
The baby is on the box.
The pony wins.

Page 207
It is morning!
Say goodbye to the bird.
My friend plays a game with me.
Cold Cat sings a song.
I see three toy cars.
Amy hurt her leg.

Page 208
baby
truck
pan
light
walks
ice
three

Page 209
cut
behind
Children
pocket
Five
name
turtle

Page 210
girl
letter
hold
under
Four
party
hair

Page 211
steps
dog
rocket
money
mouse
phone
clock

Page 212
story
color
tomorrow
hop
sound
airplane
hit

Page 213
penny
green
pan
hurry
pony
yellow
goat

Page 217
No
Yes
Yes
No
No
Yes
No
No

Page 218
Yes
Yes
No
Yes
No
Yes
Yes
Yes

Page 219
No
Yes
No
Yes
No
Yes
Yes
Yes

Page 220
Cold Cat has no brain.
Cold Cat hides his head.
Put it in the pot to cook.
Every day he paints it red.

Page 221
Cold Cat paints it blue.
In the box was a dress.
Mom gives me a big cupcake.
On the ground sat a frog.

Page 222
Never paint a tiger red.
Cold Cat thinks it's funny.
Can it be a bear?
I will give it to the hen.

© School Zone Publishing Company

Cold Cat Jumps

Cold Cat saw a dog.
The dog was big.
"Go away," said Cold Cat to the dog.
But the dog did not go away.
So Cold Cat jumped.
Cold Cat jumped over the dog.

Read each question. Then read the story again.
Circle the answer.
Write a sentence to answer the last question.

What did Cold Cat see?

cat dog ball

Did the dog go away?

why yes no

Why did Cold Cat jump over the dog?

____

© School Zone Publishing Company

The Red Cake

Scott likes cars. And Scott likes the color red.

It is Scott's birthday.

Scott gets a big cake.

The cake looks like a car! It looks like a big red car.

Read each question. Then read the story again.
Circle the answer.
Write a sentence to answer the last question.

What does Scott like?

trucks   cakes   cars

What color does Scott like?

blue   red   yellow

What does the cake look like?

____

© School Zone Publishing Company

Where Is Cold Cat?

The big dog got up. Then the big dog ran after Cold Cat.

Cold Cat ran away.

"Help!" said Cold Cat.

Cold Cat saw a house. Cold Cat ran into the house. Then Cold Cat locked the door.

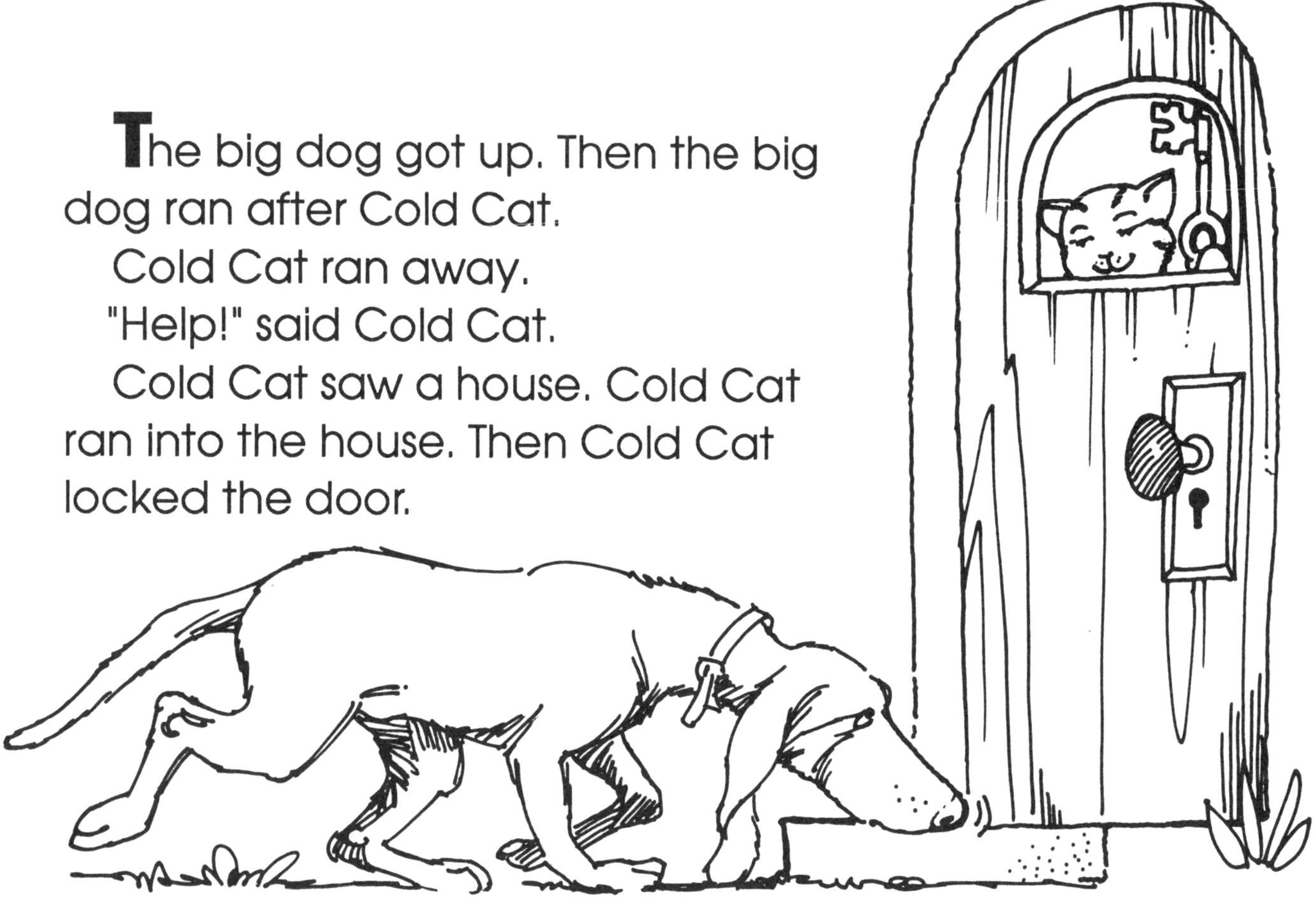

Read the sentences below. Then read the story again. Number the sentences in story order. Number them **1**, **2**, **3**, and **4**.

_______ **The big dog ran after Cold Cat.**

_______ **Cold Cat locked the door.**

_______ **Cold Cat ran into the house.**

_______ **The big dog got up.**

© School Zone Publishing Company

Bit Likes to Eat

Ann has a pet goat. The name of her goat is Bit.

Bit likes to eat. One day he ate the dog's food.

One day he ate Ann's cake.

Bit likes to eat grass, too. Ann likes it when Bit eats grass.

Read each question. Then read the story again.
Circle the answer.
Write a sentence to answer the last question.

Who is Bit?

goat dog cake

What does Bit like to do?

run play eat

Why does Ann like it when Bit eats grass?

___

© School Zone Publishing Company

Hello, Dog

Cold Cat looked at the dog.

"Hello," said the dog. "My name is Hot Dog. I am always hot."

"Hello," said Cold Cat. "My name is Cold Cat. I am always cold."

"Come out and play," said Hot Dog.

So that is what Cold Cat did.

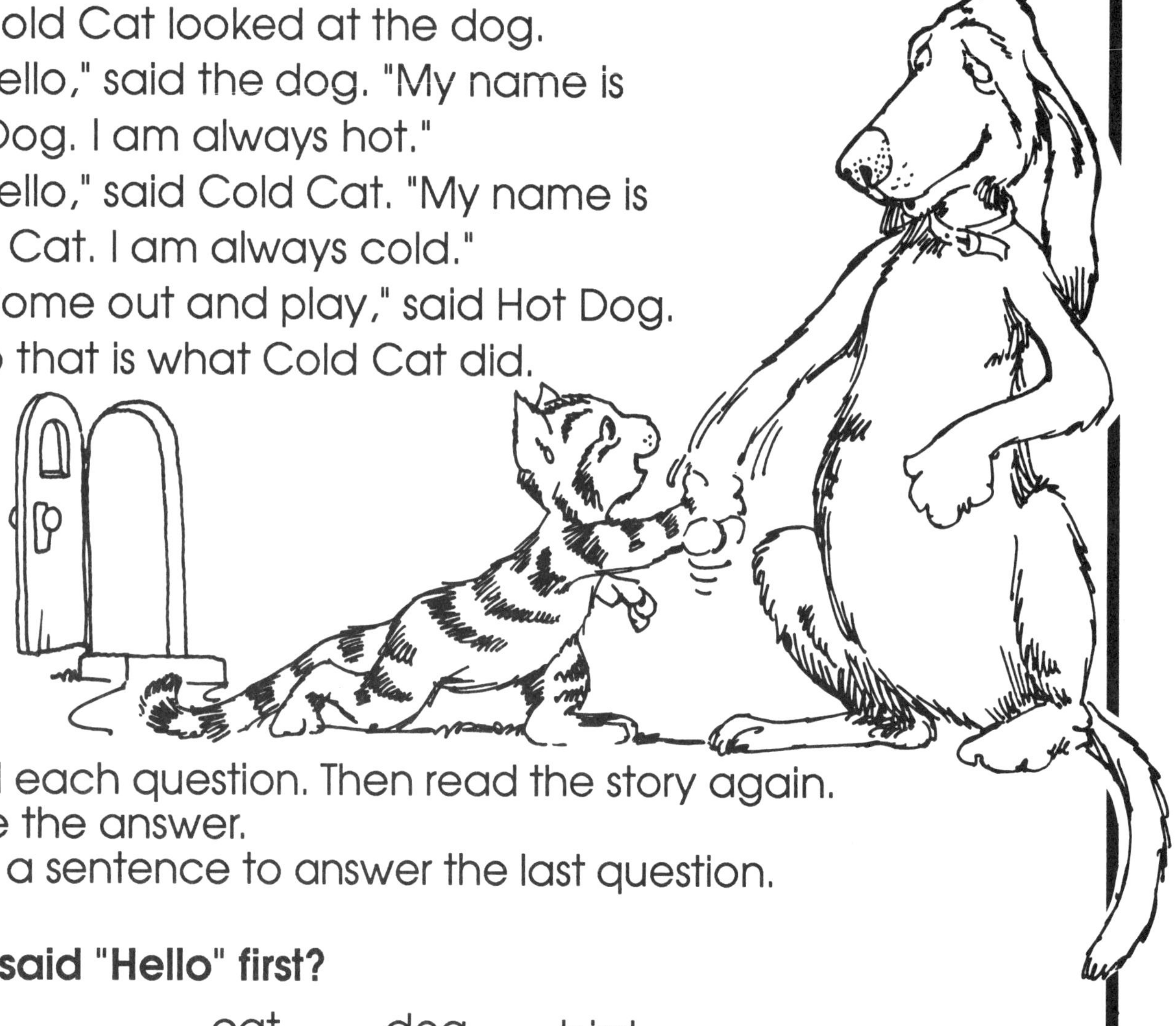

Read each question. Then read the story again.
Circle the answer.
Write a sentence to answer the last question.

Who said "Hello" first?

cat dog bird

Who is always hot?

dog goat cat

Why is Cold Cat called Cold Cat?

____

Who Took My Book?

Father and I like to fish. We like to read, too.

We read and we fish. Father reads a big book.

I read a book, too. My book is little.

But I can not find my book. Who took my book? Who is reading my book?

Read each question. Then read the story again.
Circle the answer.
Write a sentence to answer the last question.

Who reads a big book?

boy   fish   father

Who can not find his book?

boy   father   fish

Who reads the little book now?

____

© School Zone Publishing Company

The First Pink Pig

Once there were three pink pigs.

The first pink pig said, "I will make a house."

"I will make a pink house," she said. "I will make my house out of balloons."

So the first pink pig made a house. She made it out of pink balloons. She was very happy.

Read the words. Then read the story again. Write each word on the correct line.

first **balloon** **pink**

This is a color. It is ______________________.

This comes before the second. It comes ______________.

This is a toy. It is a ______________________.

© School Zone Publishing Company

Cold Kitten

"I am a cold cat," said the little cat.

"No," said Cold Cat. "You are Cold Kitten. When you are little, you are a kitten."

Cold Kitten saw two dogs. One was big and one was little. "There is a dog and a kitten," said Cold Kitten.

"No, no!" said Cold Cat. "A little dog is a puppy. Only a little cat is a kitten."

Read the words. Then read the story again.
Write each word on the correct line.

puppy **kitten** **little**

A little cat is a ______________________.

A kitten is ______________________.

A little dog is a ______________________.

© School Zone Publishing Company

Ann's Pet

Ann has a pet. The pet's name is Bit. Ann could not find her pet. She looked in the yard. But Bit was not in the yard.

So Ann looked in the house. Bit was not in the house.

Then Ann looked in the car. There was Bit! Bit was in the car.

Read the sentences below. Then read the story again.
Number the sentences in story order.
Number them **1**, **2**, **3**, and **4**.

_______ **She found Bit in the car.**

_______ **Ann looked in the yard.**

_______ **She looked in the house.**

_______ **Ann could not find her pet.**

© School Zone Publishing Company

See the Kid

Cold Kitten saw a little goat. "There is a puppy," she said.

"No, no!" said Cold Cat. "There is a kid, not a puppy. A little goat is called a kid."

Cold Kitten saw a boy. "There is a kid," she said.

"Yes," said Cold Cat. "There is a kid."

Read each question. Then read the story again.
Circle the answer.
Write a sentence to answer the last question.

What is a little goat called?

puppy kitten kid

Who did Cold Kitten talk to?

Hot Dog Cold Cat Big Boy

What is a boy or girl called?

____

© School Zone Publishing Company

How to Feed Your Dog

Do you have a dog? Then you must feed your dog. Here is how.

First find the dog dish. Put the dish down.

Then get the bag of dog food. Put some dog food in the dish.

Now move away! Let your dog eat!

Read the sentences below. Then read the story again.
Number the sentences in story order.
Number them **1**, **2**, **3**, and **4**.

_______ **Let your dog eat.**

_______ **Get the bag of dog food.**

_______ **Find the dog dish.**

_______ **Put some food in the dish.**

© School Zone Publishing Company

The Second Pink Pig

The first pink pig made a house. She made it out of pink balloons.

The second pink pig looked at the balloons. The second pink pig said, "I will make a house, too. I will make a pink house."

So the second pink pig made a house. She made it out of pink gum.

"There," said the second pink pig. "A gum house is better."

Read the sentences below. Then read the story again. Number the sentences in story order. Number them **1**, **2**, **3**, and **4**.

_______ **The first pink pig made a balloon house.**

_______ **The second pig said, "A gum house is better."**

_______ **The second pig made a pink gum house.**

_______ **The second pig looked at the balloon house.**

© School Zone Publishing Company

Up, Up, Up

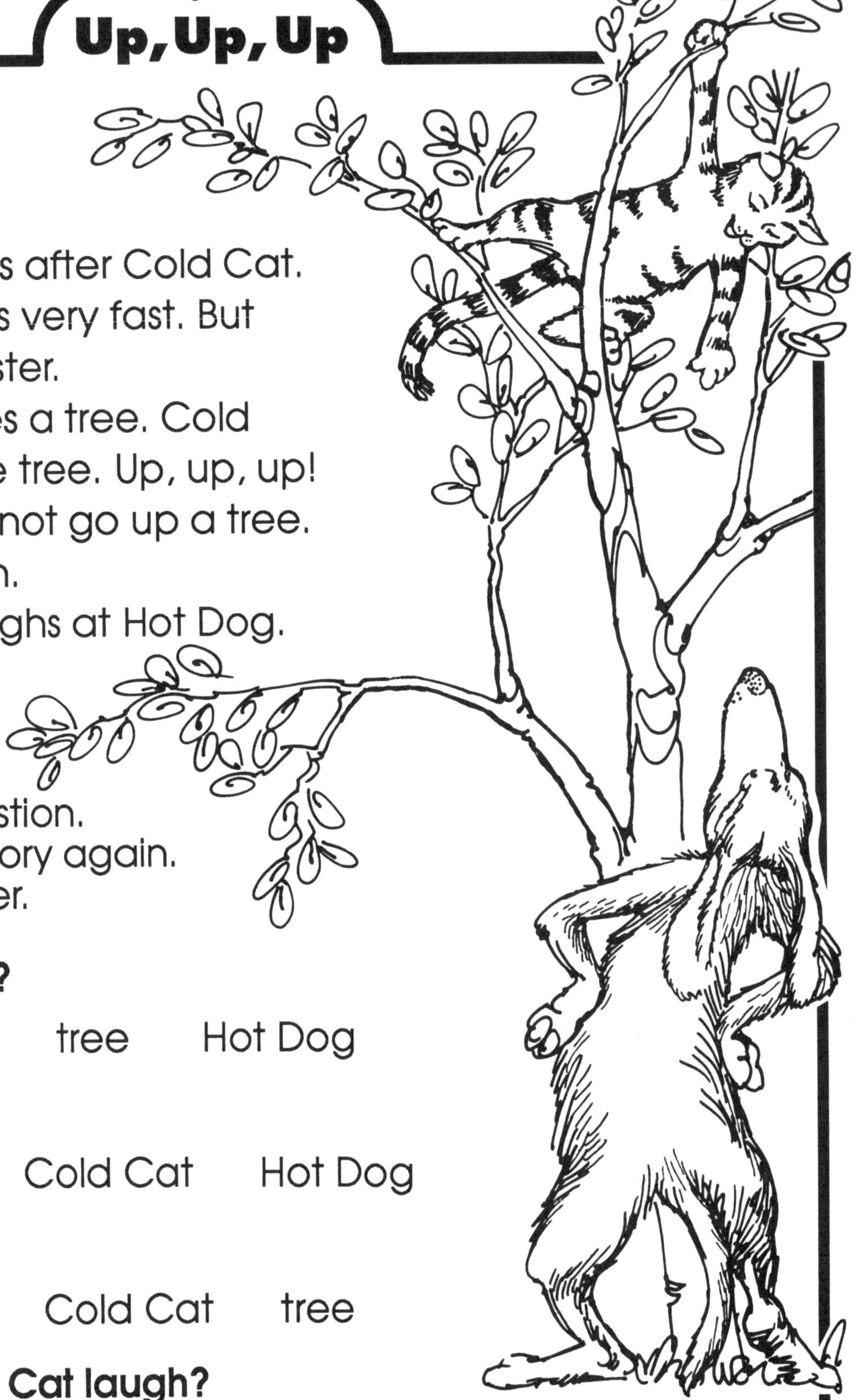

Hot Dog runs after Cold Cat. Cold Cat runs very fast. But Hot Dog runs faster.

Cold Cat sees a tree. Cold Cat goes up the tree. Up, up, up!

Hot Dog cannot go up a tree. Hot Dog is down.

Cold Cat laughs at Hot Dog.

Read each question.
Then read the story again.
Circle the answer.

Who runs faster?

Cold Cat tree Hot Dog

Who is up?

faster Cold Cat Hot Dog

Who is down?

Hot Dog Cold Cat tree

Why does Cold Cat laugh?

____

© School Zone Publishing Company

The Goat in the Coat

The goat put on a coat. Then the goat went out.

A wolf looked at the goat. "You are a big goat," said the wolf. "I will not run after you."

The goat went to the store. The goat got a hat.

Then the goat went home. The goat took off the coat. It was a big, big coat. The coat was big, but the goat was not.

Read each question. Then read the story again. Circle the answer.

Who would not run after the goat?

coat wolf store

Where did the goat go?

store school up

What did the goat buy?

coat wolf hat

Why did the goat have on a big, big coat?

____

© School Zone Publishing Company

The Third Pink Pig

"I will make a house," said the third pink pig. "I will make a pink house. It will be the best pink house."

So the third pink pig got in her truck. She took the truck to town. Then she came back. She came back with many bricks.

The third pink pig made a house. She made her house out of pink bricks.

Read the words. Then read the story again. Write each word on the correct line.

truck **third** **bricks**

It was not first or second, but ____________________.

You can build with ____________________.

A ______________ is like a car but bigger.

© School Zone Publishing Company

At the Zoo

Mom took Jason and Sara to the zoo.

Jason wanted to see the tigers. So they all went to see the tigers.

Sara wanted to see the bears. So they all went to see the bears.

Mom wanted to see the zebras. So they all went to see the zebras.

Then they all went home.

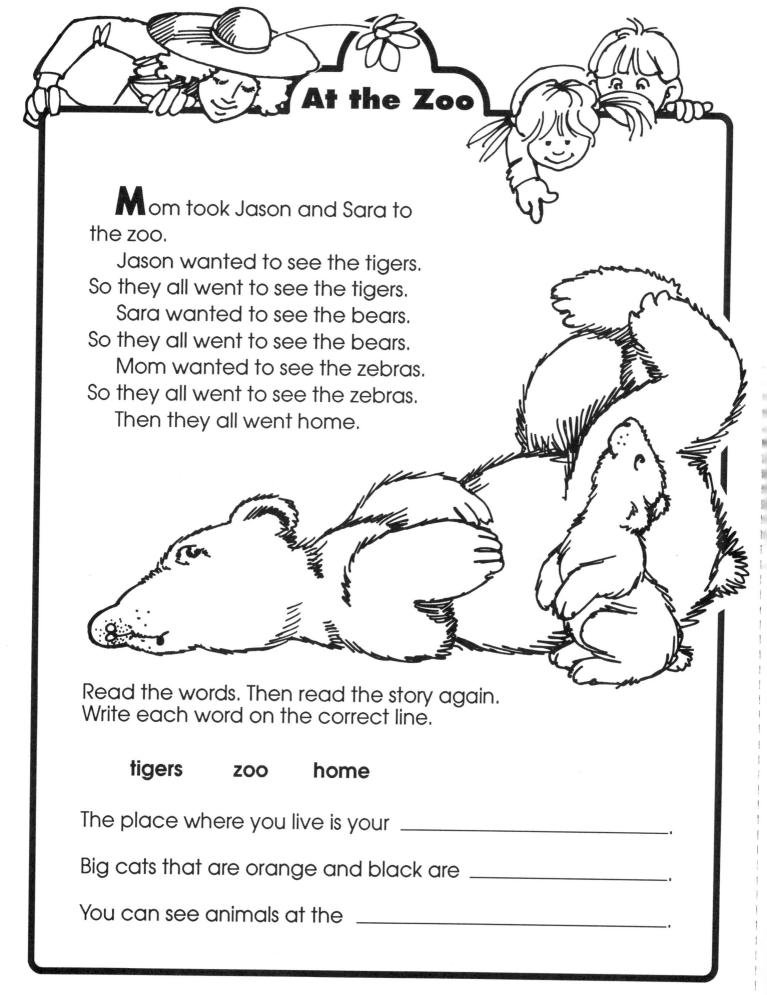

Read the words. Then read the story again.
Write each word on the correct line.

tigers　　**zoo**　　**home**

The place where you live is your ____________________.

Big cats that are orange and black are ____________________.

You can see animals at the ____________________.

© School Zone Publishing Company

Hot Dog

Hot Dog was hot. Yes, hot!

"I do not want to be hot," said Hot Dog. "I want to be cold."

Hot Dog got a box. Then he got cold water. He put the cold water in the box.

Hot Dog sat in the box of cold water. At last, Hot Dog was not hot.

Read each question. Then read the story again.
Write a sentence to answer each question.

What did Hot Dog do first?

____

What did Hot Dog do second?

____

Why was Hot Dog not hot at last?

____

© School Zone Publishing Company

Show and Tell

The children were in school. It was time to show and tell.

First Ann told about her goat. Her goat was named Bit. Ann showed what Bit looked like. Ann said that Bit liked to eat things.

Then Scott told about his car. Scott showed what the car looked like. It was a red car. Scott told the children all about his car.

Read each question. Then read the story again.
Write a sentence to answer each question.

Who told about a car?______________________________

Who told first?___________________________________

Who told about something red? ________________________

Who told about a goat?_____________________________

© School Zone Publishing Company

Which Is Best?

The three pink pigs looked. They looked at the three houses.

"My house is best," said the first pink pig. "My house is best because it is made of pink balloons."

"No," said the second pink pig. "My house is best. It is best because it is made of pink gum."

The third pink pig said, "No, my house is best. It is best because it is made of pink bricks."

This story is called **Which Is Best?**
Which Is Best? helps tell what the story is about.
Circle two other titles that help tell what the story is about.

The Three Pink Pigs | **A Day at School**

The Big Bad Wolf | **Three Pink Houses**

Write your own title for this story.

____

© School Zone Publishing Company

Walking to Town

Cold Cat and Cold Kitten walked to town.

As they walked, rain came down. Down, down, down.

"We are walking in the rain," said Cold Kitten.

"Yes," said Cold Cat. "We are walking in the rain. But we are not wet."

This story is called **Walking to Town.**
Walking to Town helps tell what the story is about.
Circle two other titles that help tell what the story is about.

Cold Cat Goes Home **We Are Not Wet**

Walking in the Rain **Cold Kitten Is Hot**

© School Zone Publishing Company

Give Me Boots

"I need boots," said Sara. "I do not want my feet to get wet."

Jason said, "I need boots, too. I want yellow boots for the rain."

So Dad took Jason and Sara to the store. "You will get rain boots," said Dad. "And you will get snow boots, too."

Sara got red boots and blue boots.

Jason got yellow boots and green boots.

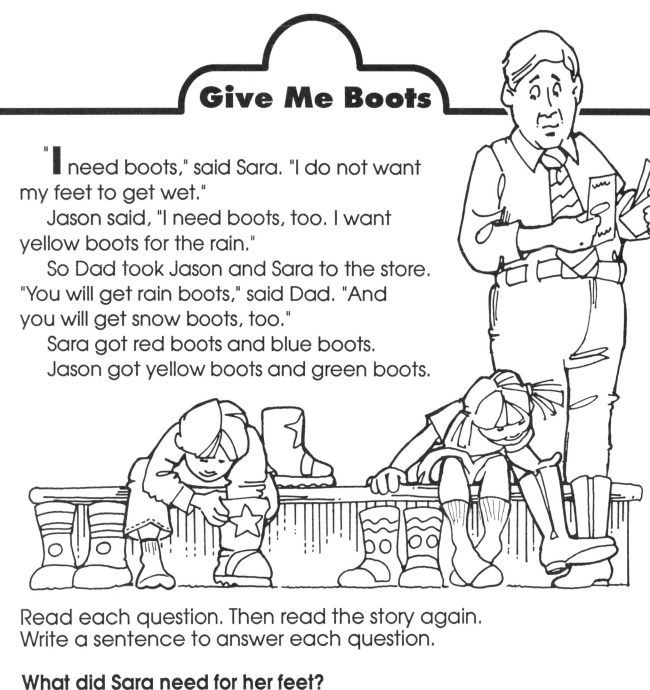

Read each question. Then read the story again.
Write a sentence to answer each question.

What did Sara need for her feet?

____

What color boots did Jason want?

____

Why did Dad buy Sara and Jason both rain boots and snow boots?

____

© School Zone Publishing Company

The Big Sad Wolf

"My house is best," said the first pink pig. "No, mine is best," said the second pink pig. "No, my house is best," the third pink pig said.

Just then, the three pigs saw a wolf. He was a big wolf. He was a sad wolf. He was a big sad wolf.

"Why are you sad?" asked the three pink pigs.

"I don't know," said the big sad wolf. "I am sad, but I don't know why."

Read each question. Then read the story again.
Circle the answer.
Write a sentence to answer the last question.

Who did the three pink pigs see?

best   wolf   house

Was the wolf happy?

yes   no   best

Why was the wolf sad?

____

© School Zone Publishing Company

Up or Down?

Some things can go up. Birds can go up. They fly up into the sky.

Some balloons can go up. If you let go, the balloon goes up!

Kites can go up, too. You can fly a kite in the sky.

Some things do not go up. A car does not go up. A dog does not go up. And a truck does not go up.

Read the words. Then read the story again. Write each word where it belongs.

kite **truck** **car** **bird**

They Go Up	**They Do Not Go Up**
________________	________________
________________	________________

© School Zone Publishing Company

Is It Round?

Some things are round. A ball is round. A ball is very, very round!

A dish can be round, too. So can a cake. A cake can be round.

Some things are not round. Bricks are not round. No, a brick is never round.

Most books are not round. And a house is not round.

Read the words. Then read the story again. Write each word where it belongs.

brick **dish** **cake** **book**

They Are Round	**They Are Not Round**
______________________	______________________
______________________	______________________

© School Zone Publishing Company

Cold Cat Finds a Penny

Cold Cat walked along. He looked up and down as he walked. He looked up and saw the sky. Then he looked down and saw a penny.

"A penny," said Cold Cat. "I will pick it up." So he picked up the penny.

Soon Cold Cat saw another penny. He picked up the second penny, too.

Then Cold Cat had two pennies.

Read each question. Then read the story again. Write a sentence to answer each question.

What did Cold Cat see when he looked up?

___

What did Cold Cat see when he looked down?

___

How many pennies did Cold Cat pick up?

___

What do you think Cold Cat will do with the pennies?

___

© School Zone Publishing Company

Come into My House

The third pink pig looked at the big sad wolf. "Do not be sad," said the third pink pig.

"Come into my house," said the third pink pig. "My house is made of pink bricks. My house will make you happy."

So the big sad wolf went into the brick house.

But it did not make him happy. "This house is too hard," said the big sad wolf. "It is so hard it makes me sad."

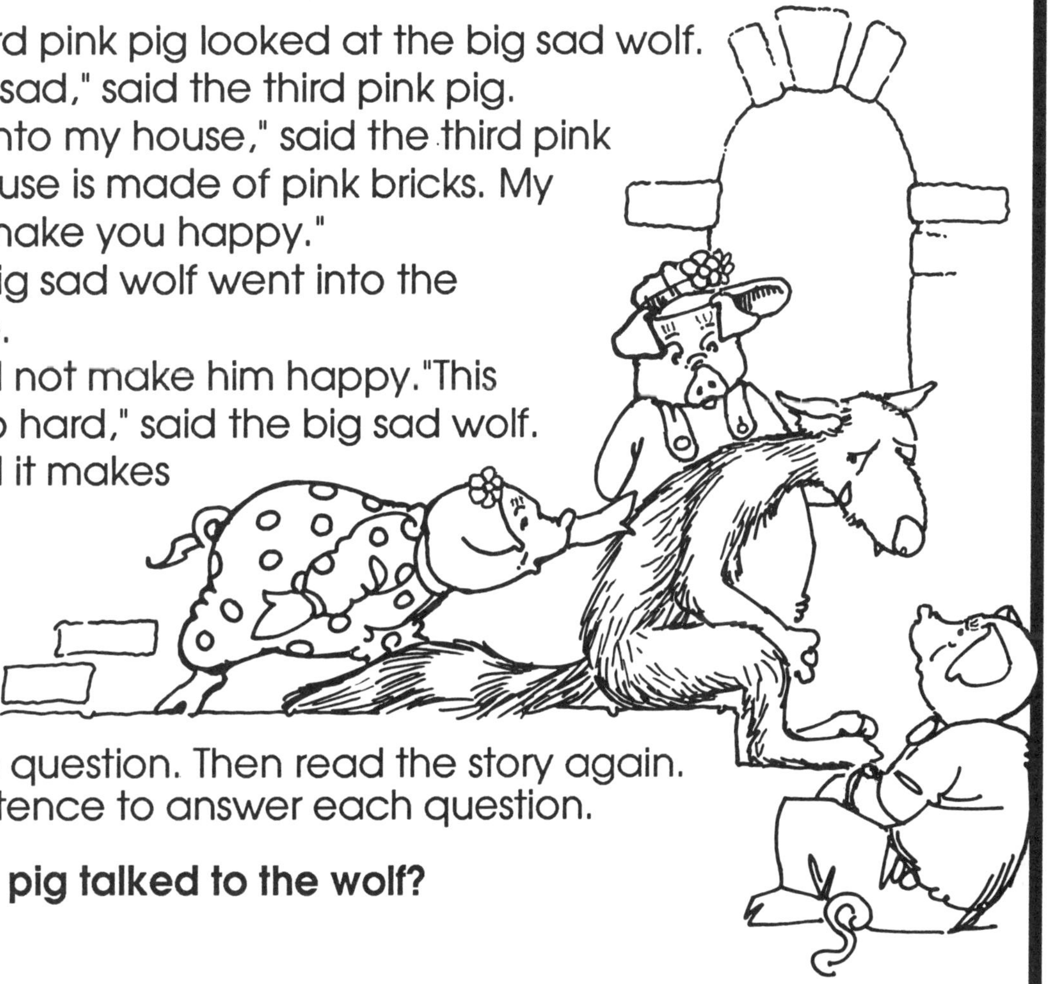

Read each question. Then read the story again. Write a sentence to answer each question.

Which pink pig talked to the wolf?

Who said, "Come into my house?"

What kind of house was it?

Why didn't this house make the wolf happy?

© School Zone Publishing Company

The Gum House

"Come into my house," said the second pink pig. "My house is made of pink gum. My house will make you happy."

So the wolf went into the gum house.

Just then, rain came down. A lot of rain came down. The rain came into the gum house.

"This house is too wet," said the big sad wolf. "It is so wet it makes me sad. I am still a big sad wolf."

This story is called **The Gum House.**
The Gum House helps tell what the story is about.
Circle two other titles that help tell what the story is about.

Wolf Is Happy	**The Wet House**
The First Pink Pig	**Wolf Is Still Sad**

Write your own title for this story.

____

© School Zone Publishing Company

Looking for Pennies

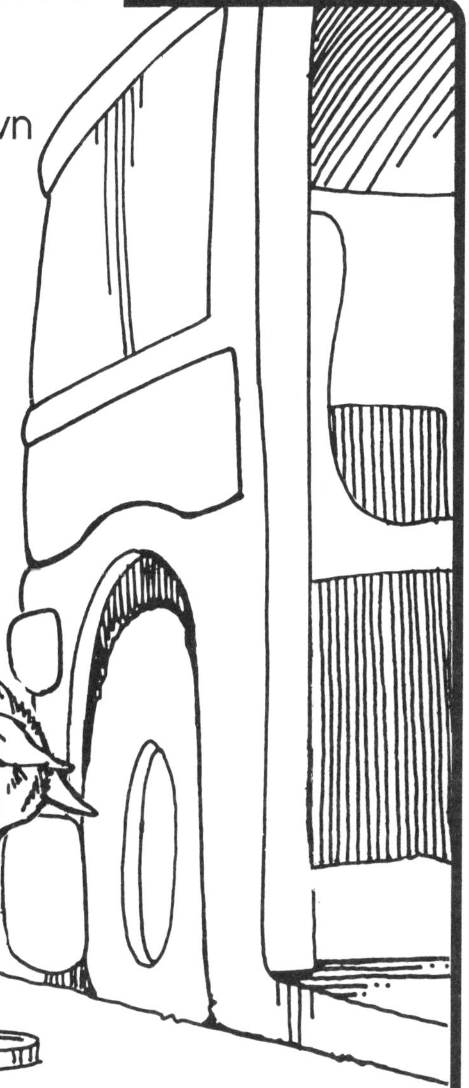

Cold Cat walked along. He looked down and saw a third penny. So he picked it up.

Now Cold Cat had three pennies.

Then he found another penny. Now he had four pennies!

Cold cat walked and looked. He looked down, not up.

Cold Cat walked right into a bus. The doors closed. The bus went away.

"Oh, oh," said Cold Cat. "Where am going?"

This story is called **Looking for Pennies.**
Looking for Pennies helps tell what the story is about.
Circle two other titles that help tell what the story is about.

Look Up, Cold Cat **Cold Cat Is Hot**

Five Pennies **Where Is Cold Cat Going?**

Write your own title for this story.

____

© School Zone Publishing Company

Up, Up, and Away!

The big sad wolf was still sad.
"Come into my house," said the first pink pig. "It is made of pink balloons."

So the big sad wolf went into the balloon house.

Just then, the wind blew. The wind blew and blew. It blew the house into the sky!

The big wolf looked down at the trees. "What fun!" said the big wolf. "I love this house! I love being in the sky! I am a very happy wolf."

Read each question. Then read the story again. Write a sentence to answer each question.

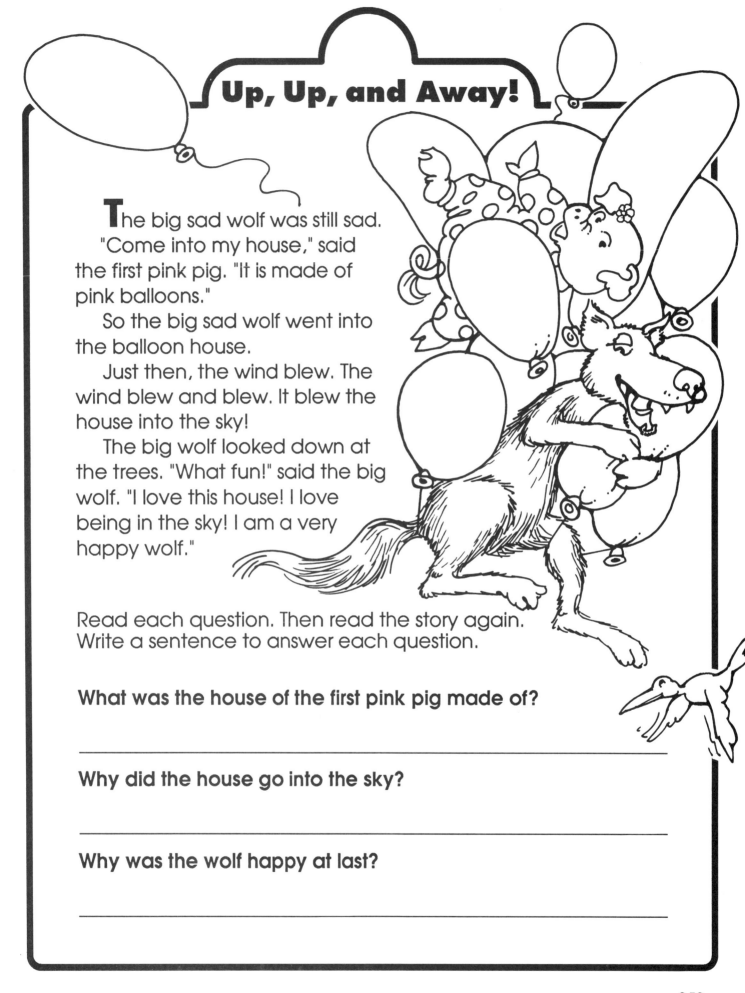

What was the house of the first pink pig made of?

____

Why did the house go into the sky?

____

Why was the wolf happy at last?

____

© School Zone Publishing Company

The Animals

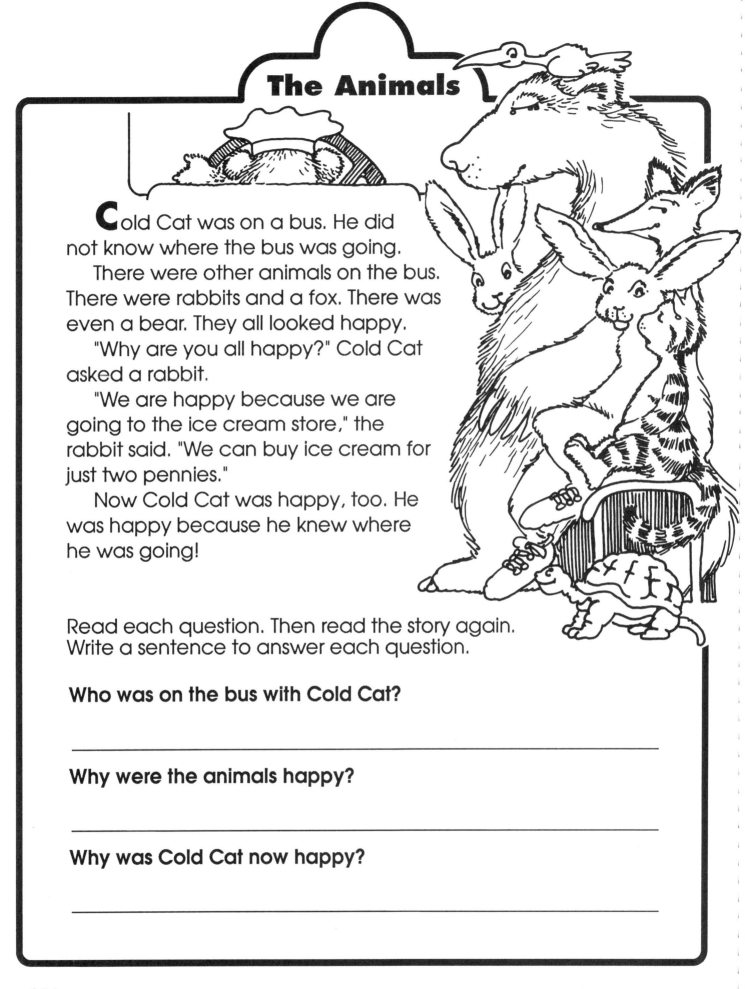

Cold Cat was on a bus. He did not know where the bus was going.

There were other animals on the bus. There were rabbits and a fox. There was even a bear. They all looked happy.

"Why are you all happy?" Cold Cat asked a rabbit.

"We are happy because we are going to the ice cream store," the rabbit said. "We can buy ice cream for just two pennies."

Now Cold Cat was happy, too. He was happy because he knew where he was going!

Read each question. Then read the story again. Write a sentence to answer each question.

Who was on the bus with Cold Cat?

____

Why were the animals happy?

____

Why was Cold Cat now happy?

____

© School Zone Publishing Company

Two Ice Creams

Cold Cat looked all around the bus. He saw Hot Dog. But Hot Dog did not look happy. Hot Dog looked sad.

"Why are you sad?" asked Cold Cat. "Don't you like ice cream?"

"I love ice cream," said Hot Dog. "But I lost my pennies. I had four pennies, but I lost them. Now I can't buy ice cream."

"Yes, you can," said Cold Cat. "I found your pennies." Cold Cat gave the four pennies to Hot Dog.

The bus stopped at the ice cream store.

"Come on," said Hot Dog. "I will buy two ice creams. One for you and one for me." And so he did.

Read each question. Then read the story again. Write a sentence to answer each question.

Why was Hot Dog sad?

____

Why did Cold Cat give the pennies to Hot Dog?

____

Why was Cold Cat a good friend?

____

© School Zone Publishing Company

Page 225
dog
no
The dog did not go away.

Page 226
cars
red
The cake looks like a car.

Page 227
2
4
3
1

Page 228
goat
eat
That is what goats should eat.

Page 229
dog
dog
Cold Cat is always cold.

Page 230
father
boy
A fish reads the book.

Page 231
pink
first
balloon

Page 232
kitten
little
puppy

Page 233
4
2
3
1

Page 234
kid
Cold Cat
A boy or girl is called a kid.

Page 235
4
2
1
3

Page 236
1
4
3
2

Page 237
Hot Dog
Cold Cat
Hot Dog
Hot Dog cannot go up a tree.

Page 238
wolf
store
hat
He wanted to look big.

Page 239
third
bricks
truck

Page 240
home
tigers
zoo

Page 241
Hot Dog got a box.
He put cold water in the box.
Hot Dog sat in the cold water.

Page 242
Scott
Ann
Scott
Ann

Page 243
The Three Pink Pigs
Three Pink Houses
Answers will vary.

Page 244
Walking in the Rain
We Are Not Wet

Page 245
Sara needed boots.
Jason wanted yellow boots.
He did not want their feet to get wet.

Page 246
wolf
no
The wolf did not know why.

Page 247
They Go Up
kite
bird
They Do Not Go up
truck
car

Page 248
They Are Round
dish
cake
They Are Not Round
brick
book

Page 249
Cold Cat saw the sky.
He saw a penny.
He picked up two pennies.
Answers will vary.

Page 250
The third pink pig talked to the wolf.
The third pink pig said it.
It was a brick house.
The house was too hard.

Page 251
The Wet House
Wolf Is Still Sad
Answers will vary.

Page 252
Look up, Cold Cat
Where is Cold Cat Going?
Answers will vary.

Page 253
It was made of balloons.
The wind blew the house into the sky.
The wolf liked being in the sky.

Page 254
There were other animals on the bus.
They were going to the ice cream store.
He knew where he was going.

Page 255
Hot Dog lost his pennies.
They were Hot Dog's pennies.
He gave Hot Dog the pennies he found.

Note:
Children's sentences will vary from these in the answer key.
Accept the answer when it is in correct sentence form and answers the question.

© School Zone Publishing Company

LET'S COUNT

Write the numbers in order from 0-9.

0, 1, 2, 3, 4,

5, 6, 7, 8, 9

______ ______ ______ ______ ______

______ ______ ______ ______ ______

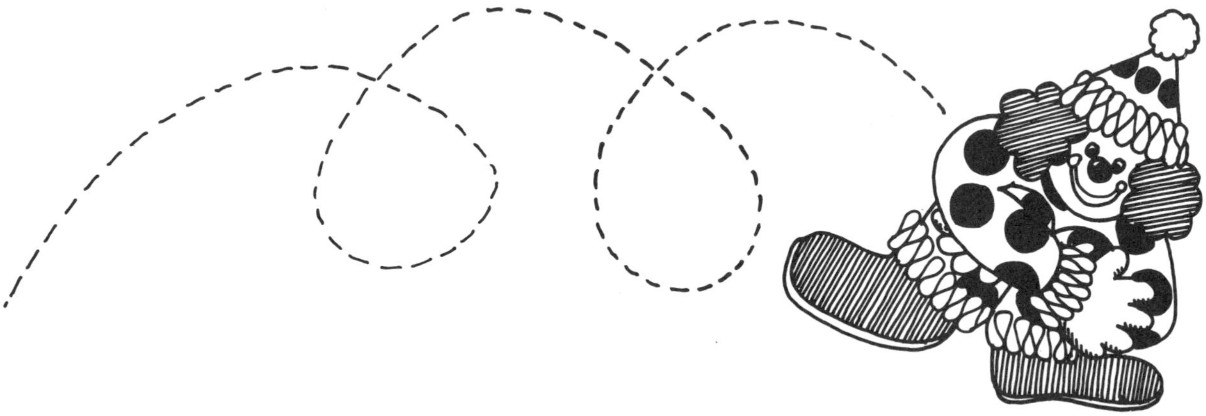

© School Zone Publishing Company

BEFORE AND AFTER

Write the number that comes before and after.

0 1 2 3 4 5 6 7 8 9

1.

2.

3.

4.

5.

© School Zone Publishing Company

MATCH THE SET

Draw a line from each set to the correct number.

0

1

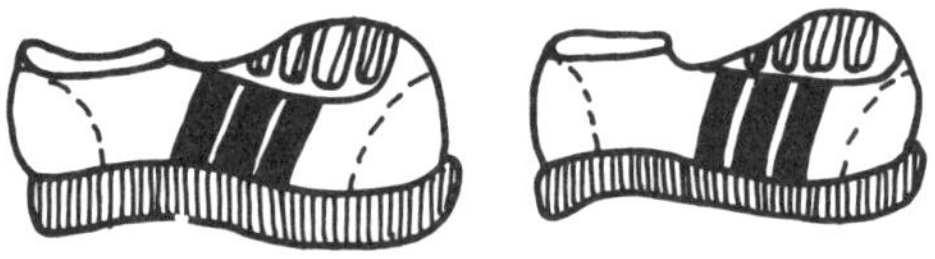

2

3

4

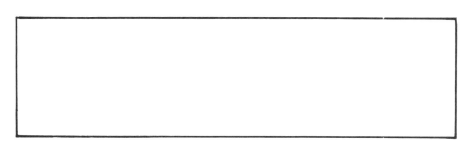

5

© School Zone Publishing Company

MATCH AGAIN!

Draw a line from each set to the correct number.

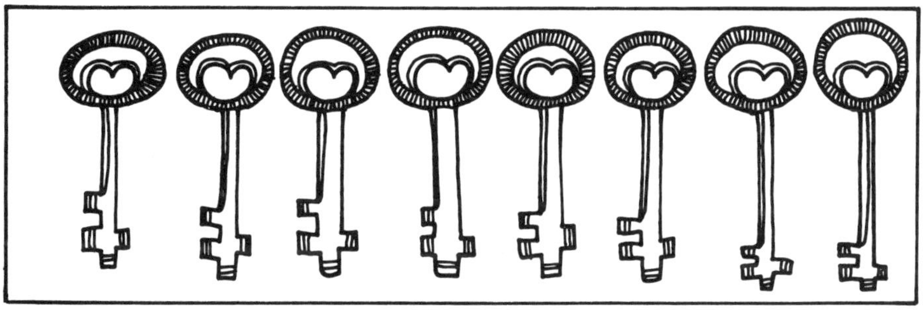

5

6

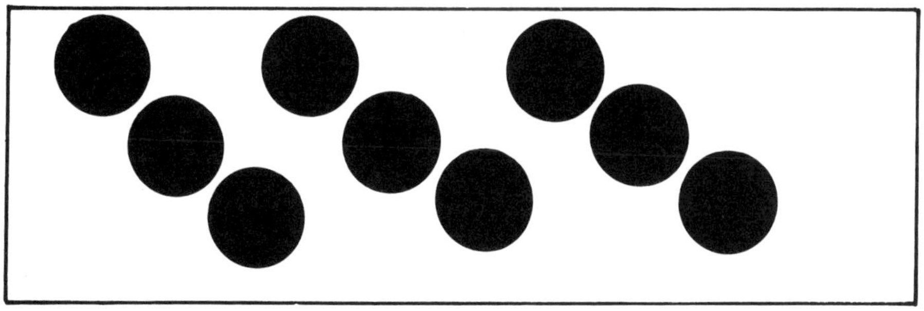

7

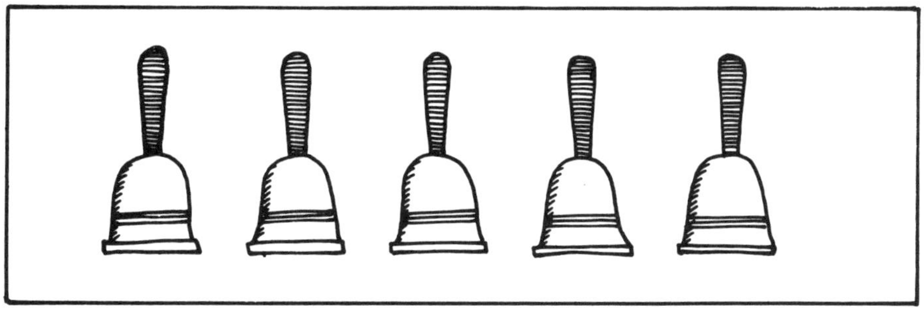

8

9

© School Zone Publishing Company

PICK TEN

Circle ten objects in each set.

= 10

1. 

2. 

3. 

4. 

5. 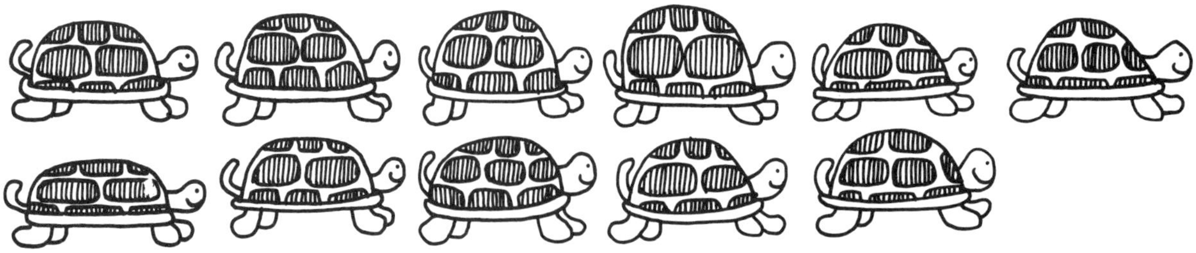

© School Zone Publishing Company

SETS OF TEN

How many tens?

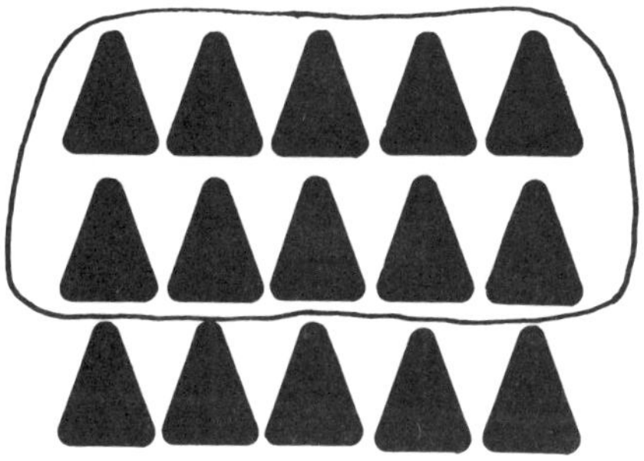

How many sets of ten?

1 ______

1. 

How many sets of ten?

______

2. 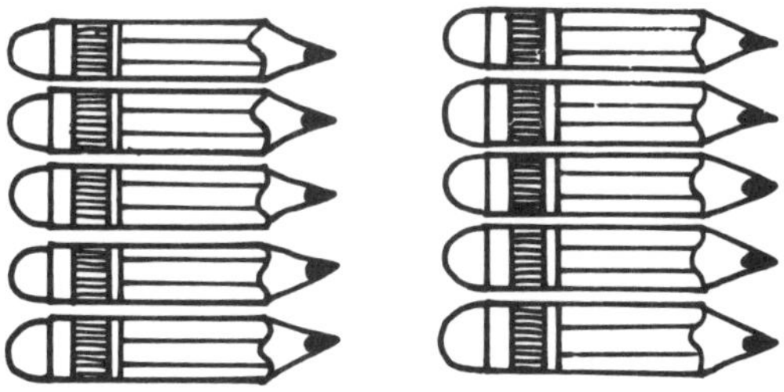

How many sets of ten?

______

3. 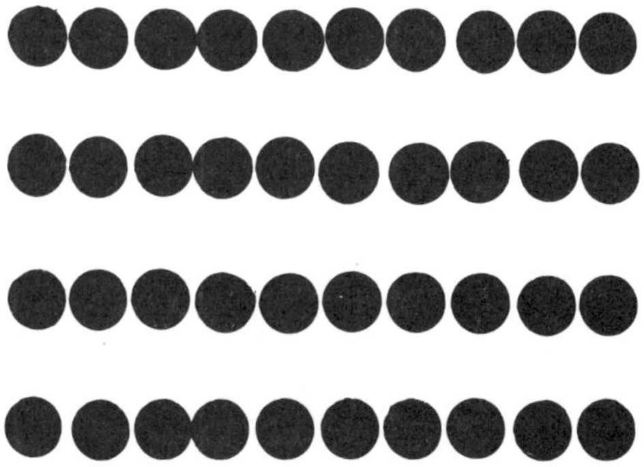

How many sets of ten?

______

© School Zone Publishing Company

TEN COUNT DOWN

Count the objects by sets of ten.
Write the number on the line.

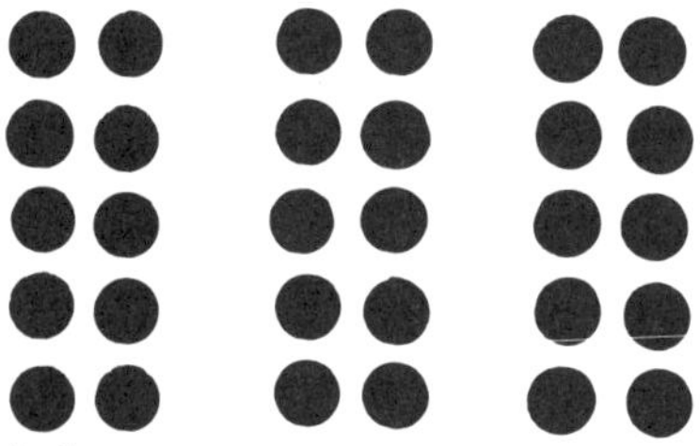

__30__ balls

How many?

1.

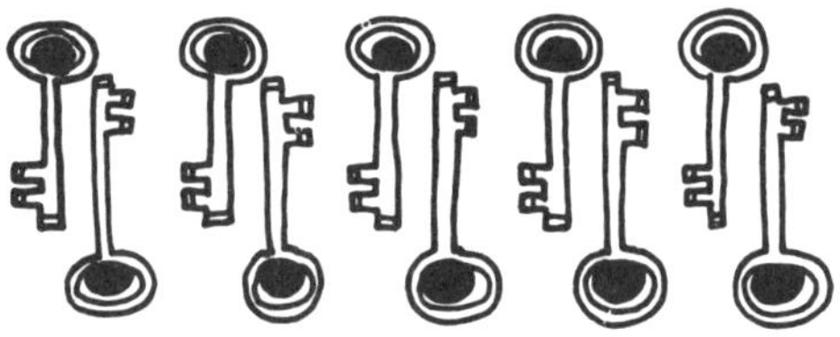

________ keys

2.

________ hats

3.

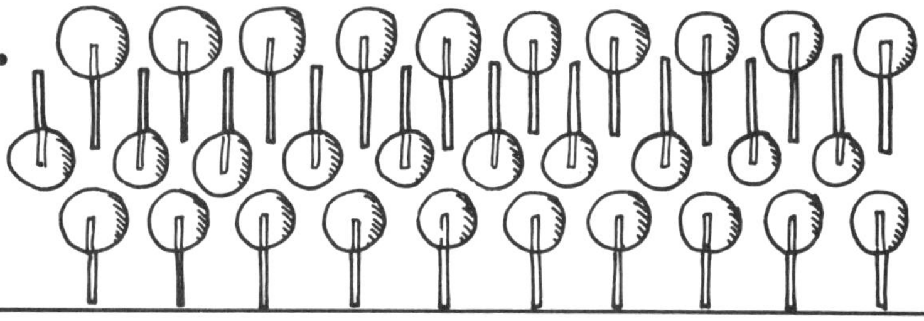

________ lollipops

4.

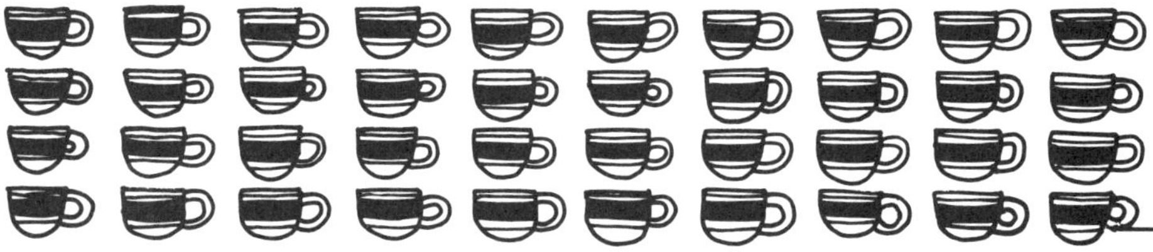

________ cups

5.

________ stars

© School Zone Publishing Company

COUNT BY TEN

Practice counting by 10's.

10, 20, 30, 40, 50, 60, 70, 80, 90, 100

Write the numbers in order.

______ ______ ______ ______ ______

______ ______ ______ ______ ______

© School Zone Publishing Company

WHAT IS THE WORD?

Draw a line from the number to the number word.

0	two
1	nine
2	eight
3	six
4	seven
5	four
6	ten
7	three
8	zero
9	five
10	one

© School Zone Publishing Company

UNSCRAMBLE THE TEN'S

Write the numbers in order.

© School Zone Publishing Company

COUNTING SQUARES TO 100

Write the numbers 0-100 in order.

0	1	2	3	4	5	6	7	8	9
10									
20									
30									
40									
50									
60									
70									
80									
90									
100									

© School Zone Publishing Company

MAKE A SET

Make a set.

8

Make a set of 8 balls.

12	Make a set of 12 kites.
21	Make a set of 21 circles.
45	Make a set of 45 lollipops.

© School Zone Publishing Company

TEN AND MORE

Count the sets of 10.
Count the ones left over.

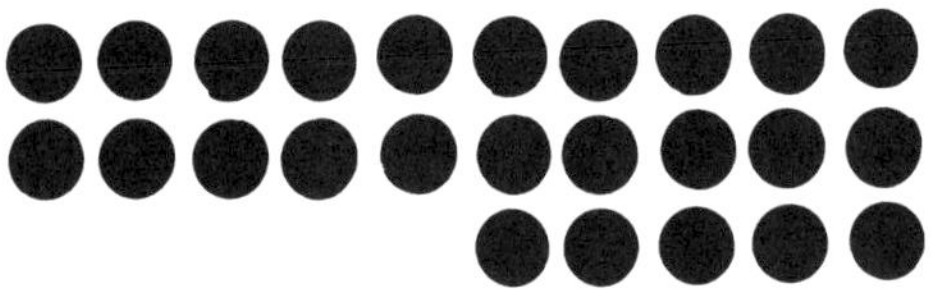

2 tens 5 ones

How many in all? 25

1.

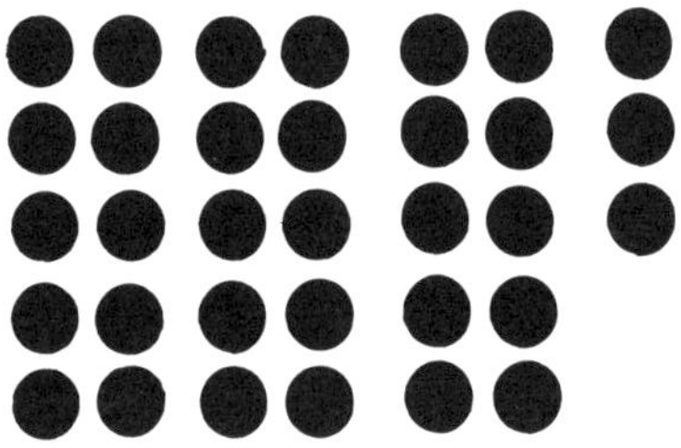

_____ tens _____ ones

How many in all? _____

2.

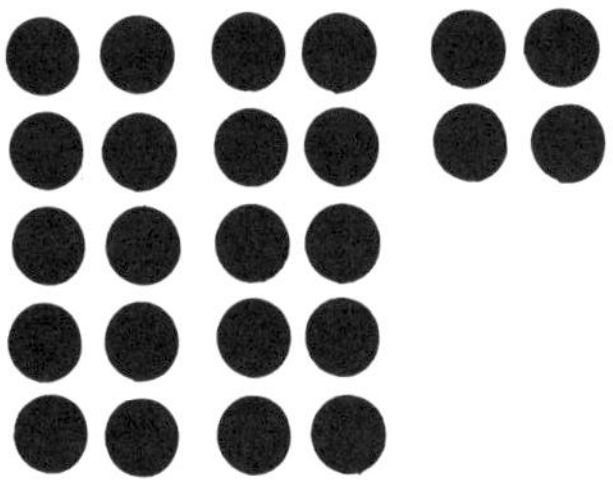

_____ tens _____ ones

How many in all? _____

3.

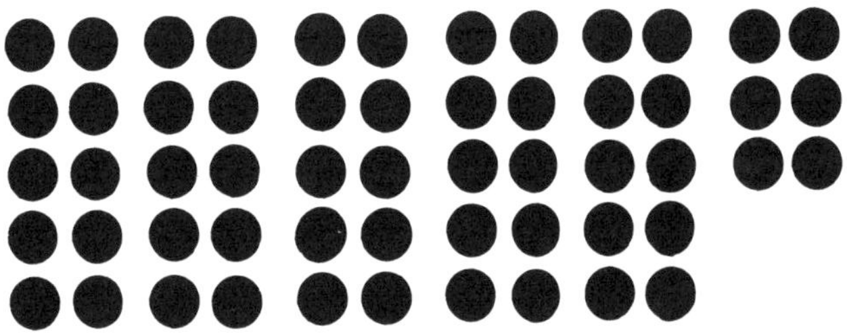

_____ tens _____ ones

How many in all? _____

© School Zone Publishing Company

MORE–TEN AND MORE

Count the sets of 10.
Count the ones left over.

1. 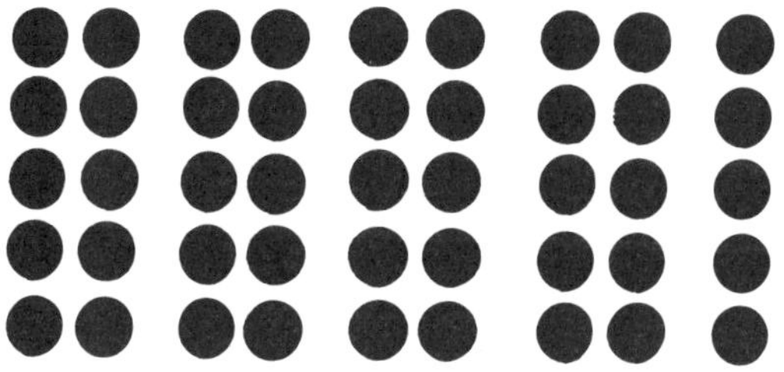

_____ tens _____ ones

How many in all? _____

2. 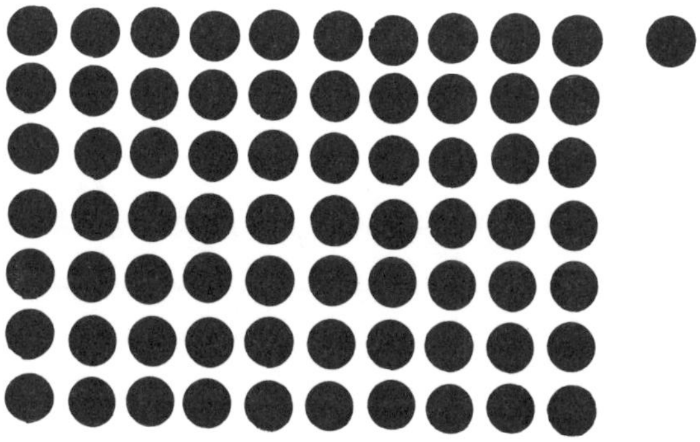

_____ tens _____ ones

How many in all? _____

3. 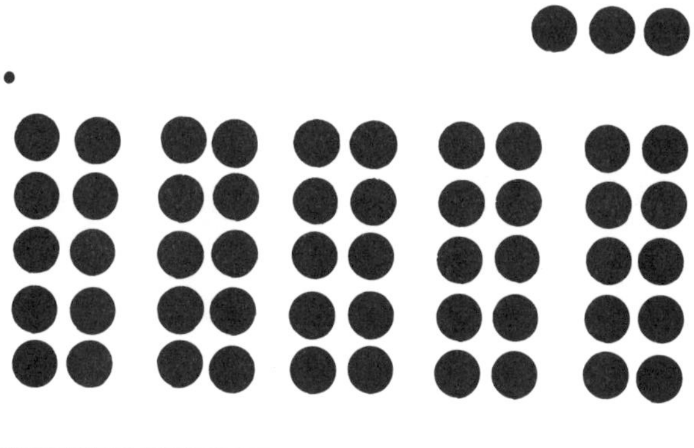

_____ tens _____ ones

How many in all? _____

4. 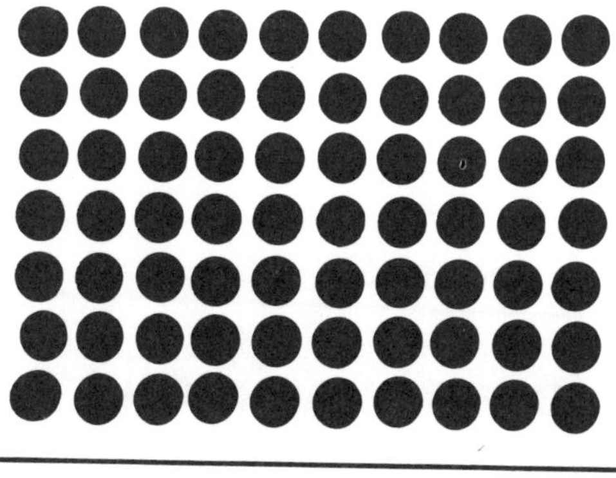

_____ tens _____ ones

How many in all? _____

© School Zone Publishing Company

BEFORE AND AFTER

Circle the number that comes before and after.

Circle the number that comes before and after 6.

1 2 3 4 (5) 6 (7) 8 9 10

1.

Circle the number that comes before and after 36.

30 31 32 33 34 35 36 37 38 39

2.

Circle the number that comes before and after 14.

10 11 12 13 14 15 16 17 18 19

3.

Circle the number that comes before and after 52.

50 51 52 53 54 55 56 57 58 59

4.

Circle the number that comes before and after 28.

20 21 22 23 24 25 26 27 28 29

© School Zone Publishing Company

GREATER THAN

The sign > means "greater than."

27 is greater than **25**

27 > 25

The opening of the sign is always next to the "greater than" number.

Circle the number that is greater.

1. 23 14	2. 25 27
3. 17 12	4. 21 19
5. 30 27	6. 12 21
7. 18 10	8. 40 52

© School Zone Publishing Company

GREATER THAN

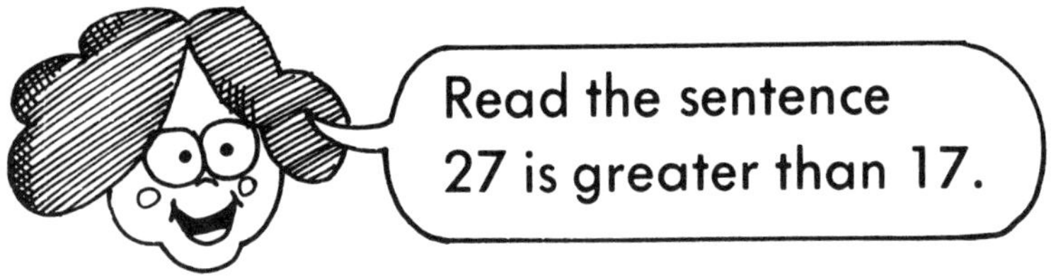
Read the sentence
27 is greater than 17.

Use the sign.

27 > 17

The opening goes toward the greater number.

1. 15 ____ 12	2. 25 ____ 16
3. 27 ____ 24	4. 12 ____ 10
5. 21 ____ 19	6. 17 ____ 13
7. 30 ____ 24	8. 19 ____ 11

© School Zone Publishing Company

LESS THAN

The sign < means "less than."

13 is less than **20**

13 < 20

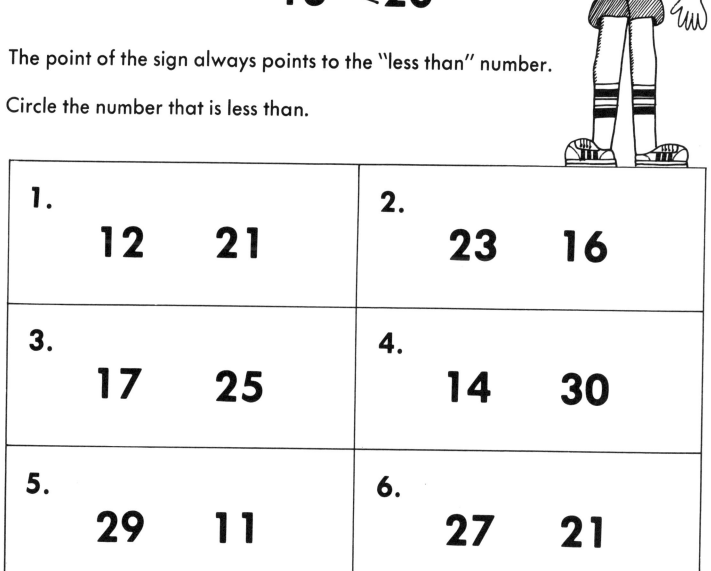

The point of the sign always points to the "less than" number.

Circle the number that is less than.

1. 12 21	2. 23 16
3. 17 25	4. 14 30
5. 29 11	6. 27 21
7. 24 30	8. 40 23

© School Zone Publishing Company

LESS THAN

Read the sentence
17 is less than 21.

Use the sign.

$17 < 21$

The point always goes toward the lesser number.

1. 12 ______ 15	2. 14 ______ 17
3. 21 ______ 27	4. 22 ______ 28
5. 11 ______ 30	6. 16 ______ 29
7. 24 ______ 28	8. 40 ______ 50

© School Zone Publishing Company

GREATER OR LESS

Remember!

> means greater than.
The opening goes toward the greater number.

< means less than.
The point goes toward the lesser number.

1. 21 ______ 28	2. 16 ______ 12
3. 14 ______ 17	4. 24 ______ 11
5. 20 ______ 30	6. 26 ______ 22
7. 40 ______ 60	8. 25 ______ 21

© School Zone Publishing Company

WHAT'S IN A DOZEN?

Here are a dozen balls.

How many? 12

A dozen is the same as 12.

Put an "X" on the sets with a dozen.

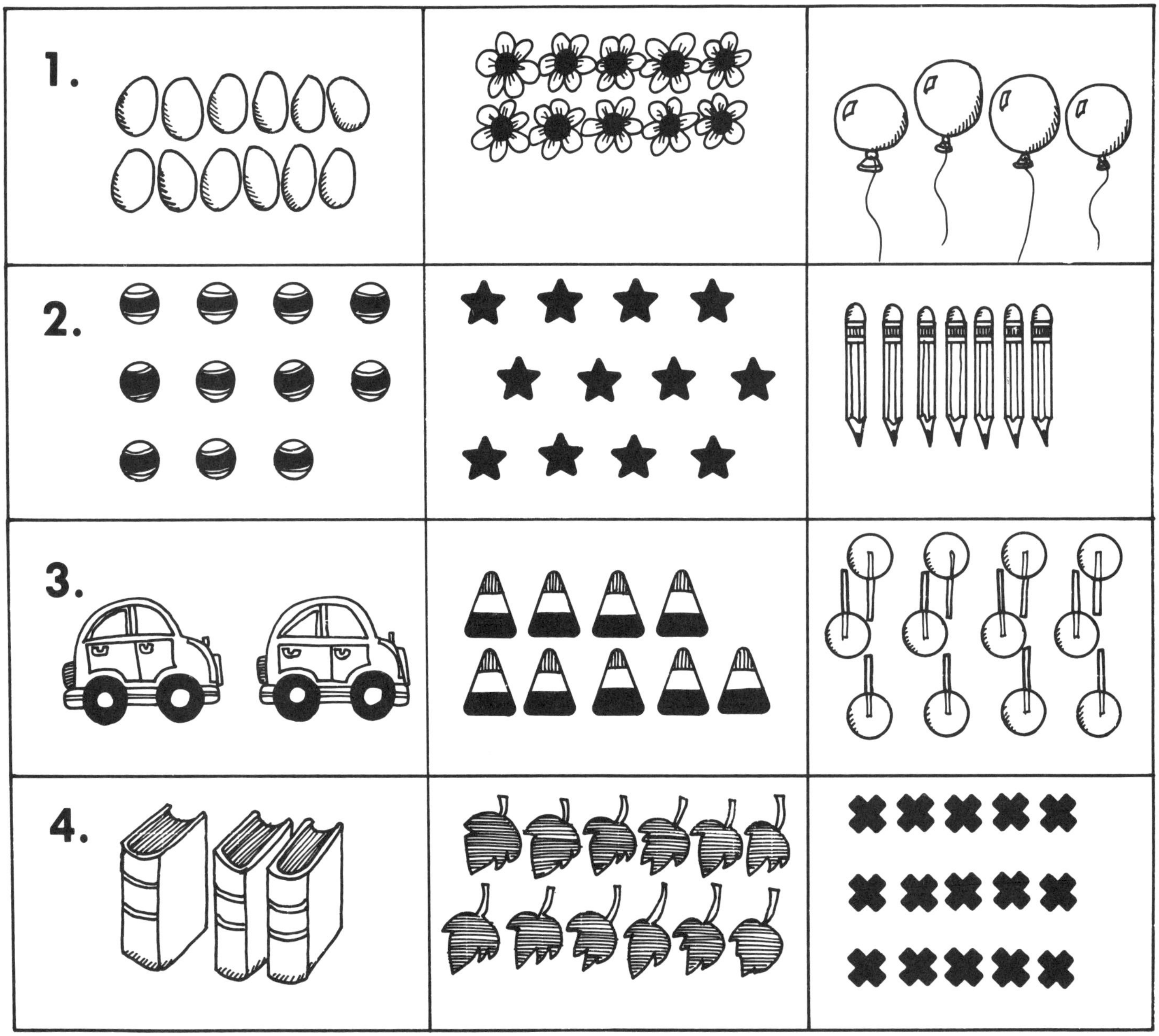

© School Zone Publishing Company

FIND THE SUM

The sum tells how many when you add numbers.

3 + 4 = 7

Write the correct sum.

1. 

2 + 6 = ________

2. 

5 + 2 = ________

3. 

7 + 3 = ________

4. 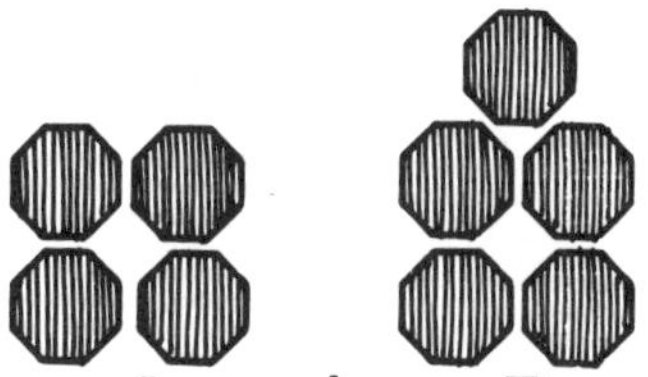

4 + 5 = ________

5. 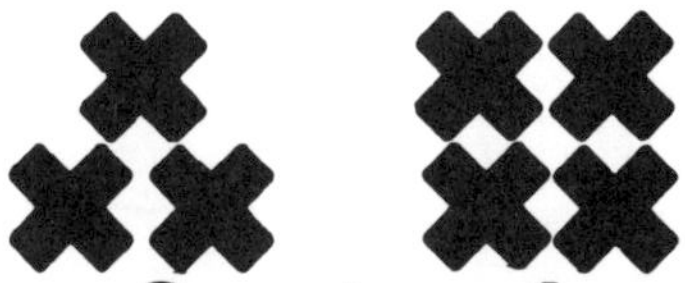

3 + 4 = ________

© School Zone Publishing Company

DOT TO DOT

Find the sum.
Start with number 1.
What is the shape?
Have fun coloring it.

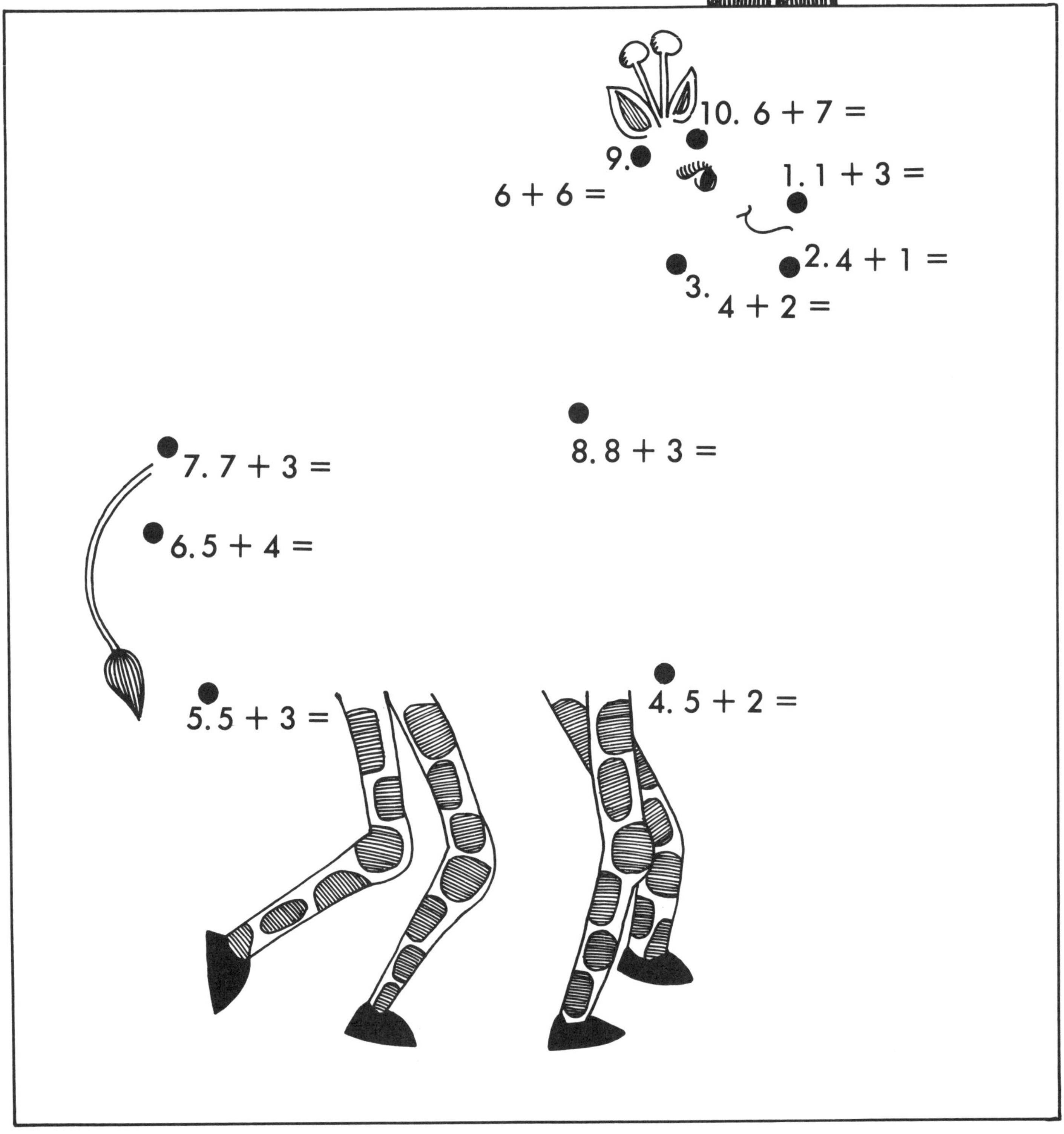

© School Zone Publishing Company

LET'S ADD

Add the numbers.

Write the correct sum. $8 + 6 = 14$

1. $6 + 4 =$ ____

2. $9 + 4 =$ ____

3. $6 + 7 =$ ____

4. $8 + 9 =$ ____

5. $9 + 9 =$ ____

6. $5 + 7 =$ ____

7. $3 + 5 =$ ____

8. $7 + 3 =$ ____

© School Zone Publishing Company

LET'S ADD SOME MORE

Find the sum.

$$\begin{array}{r} 4 \\ +4 \\ \hline 8 \end{array}$$

1.	$\begin{array}{r} 2 \\ +2 \\ \hline \end{array}$	$\begin{array}{r} 3 \\ +2 \\ \hline \end{array}$	$\begin{array}{r} 6 \\ +1 \\ \hline \end{array}$	$\begin{array}{r} 5 \\ +0 \\ \hline \end{array}$	$\begin{array}{r} 4 \\ +4 \\ \hline \end{array}$
2.	$\begin{array}{r} 6 \\ +7 \\ \hline \end{array}$	$\begin{array}{r} 8 \\ +8 \\ \hline \end{array}$	$\begin{array}{r} 7 \\ +2 \\ \hline \end{array}$	$\begin{array}{r} 6 \\ +6 \\ \hline \end{array}$	$\begin{array}{r} 1 \\ +1 \\ \hline \end{array}$
3.	$\begin{array}{r} 4 \\ +8 \\ \hline \end{array}$	$\begin{array}{r} 1 \\ +3 \\ \hline \end{array}$	$\begin{array}{r} 5 \\ +5 \\ \hline \end{array}$	$\begin{array}{r} 8 \\ +0 \\ \hline \end{array}$	$\begin{array}{r} 6 \\ +2 \\ \hline \end{array}$
4.	$\begin{array}{r} 7 \\ +4 \\ \hline \end{array}$	$\begin{array}{r} 3 \\ +5 \\ \hline \end{array}$	$\begin{array}{r} 5 \\ +1 \\ \hline \end{array}$	$\begin{array}{r} 7 \\ +7 \\ \hline \end{array}$	$\begin{array}{r} 8 \\ +2 \\ \hline \end{array}$
5.	$\begin{array}{r} 1 \\ +8 \\ \hline \end{array}$	$\begin{array}{r} 2 \\ +9 \\ \hline \end{array}$	$\begin{array}{r} 4 \\ +5 \\ \hline \end{array}$	$\begin{array}{r} 6 \\ +5 \\ \hline \end{array}$	$\begin{array}{r} 9 \\ +3 \\ \hline \end{array}$
6.	$\begin{array}{r} 3 \\ +8 \\ \hline \end{array}$	$\begin{array}{r} 8 \\ +5 \\ \hline \end{array}$	$\begin{array}{r} 5 \\ +9 \\ \hline \end{array}$	$\begin{array}{r} 7 \\ +1 \\ \hline \end{array}$	$\begin{array}{r} 9 \\ +9 \\ \hline \end{array}$

© School Zone Publishing Company

DIFFERENCE

The difference tells how many are left when you subtract numbers.

8 − 3 = 5 

Subtract and find the difference.

1.

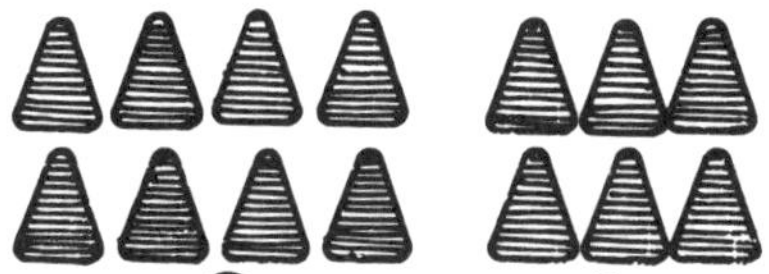

8 − 6 = ______

2.

10 − 7 = ______

3.

9 − 5 = ______

4.

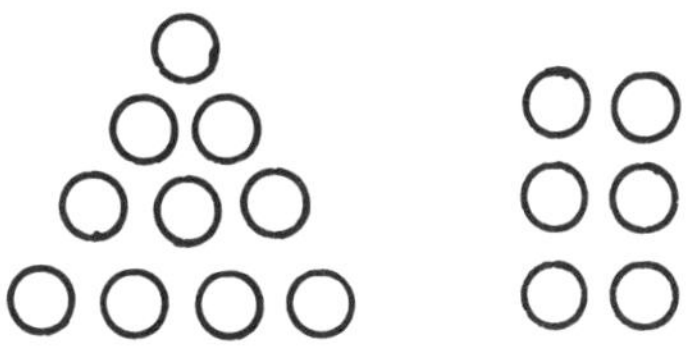

10 − 6 = ______

5.

7 − 5 = ______

© School Zone Publishing Company

FIND THE DIFFERENCE

Subtract and find the difference.

$$\begin{array}{r} 9 \\ -3 \\ \hline 6 \end{array}$$

1.

$$\begin{array}{r} 8 \\ -4 \\ \hline \end{array} \quad \begin{array}{r} 7 \\ -3 \\ \hline \end{array} \quad \begin{array}{r} 6 \\ -5 \\ \hline \end{array} \quad \begin{array}{r} 10 \\ -4 \\ \hline \end{array} \quad \begin{array}{r} 5 \\ -3 \\ \hline \end{array}$$

2.

$$\begin{array}{r} 3 \\ -2 \\ \hline \end{array} \quad \begin{array}{r} 6 \\ -4 \\ \hline \end{array} \quad \begin{array}{r} 4 \\ -3 \\ \hline \end{array} \quad \begin{array}{r} 8 \\ -5 \\ \hline \end{array} \quad \begin{array}{r} 9 \\ -8 \\ \hline \end{array}$$

3.

$$\begin{array}{r} 11 \\ -7 \\ \hline \end{array} \quad \begin{array}{r} 14 \\ -7 \\ \hline \end{array} \quad \begin{array}{r} 10 \\ -5 \\ \hline \end{array} \quad \begin{array}{r} 9 \\ -3 \\ \hline \end{array} \quad \begin{array}{r} 8 \\ -2 \\ \hline \end{array}$$

4.

$$\begin{array}{r} 7 \\ -6 \\ \hline \end{array} \quad \begin{array}{r} 5 \\ -4 \\ \hline \end{array} \quad \begin{array}{r} 13 \\ -3 \\ \hline \end{array} \quad \begin{array}{r} 4 \\ -2 \\ \hline \end{array} \quad \begin{array}{r} 7 \\ -4 \\ \hline \end{array}$$

© School Zone Publishing Company

THE HIDDEN DIFFERENCES

Work the problems.
Find the differences hidden in the jungle.
Circle the answer.
Have fun coloring the picture.

1. 5 - 2 = ____

2. 9 - 7 = ____

3. 7 - 2 = ____

4. 9 - 2 = ____

5. 8 - 4 = ____

6. 9 -8 ____

7. 9 -0 ____

8. 8 -2 ____

9. 10 -2 ____

10. 9 -2 ____

© School Zone Publishing Company

TICK TOCK TIME

The small hand tells the hour.
Read the problems.
Write the correct letter on the line.

1. Pam goes to school at eight o'clock.
Which clock shows what time Pam goes to school? ________

2. Pam eats lunch at twelve o'clock.
Which clock shows what time Pam eats lunch? ________

3. Mother calls Pam for dinner. Pam looks at the clock.
It says 6 o'clock.
Which clock shows 6 o'clock? ________

4. It is 9 o'clock. It is time for Pam to go to bed.
Which clock shows 9 o'clock? ________

© School Zone Publishing Company

HOW MUCH?

MONEY

 **PENNY**  **NICKEL**  **DIME**

When we count pennies, we count by ones . . .  = 1¢

When we count nickels, we count by fives . . .  = 5¢

When we count dimes, we count by tens . . .  = 10¢

Draw a line to the correct amount.

1.  3¢

2.  10¢

3.  26¢

4.  15¢

5.  7¢

© School Zone Publishing Company

Page 257
0, 1, 2, 3, 4, 5, 6, 7, 8, 9

Page 258
1. 4, 6
2. 3, 5
3. 6, 8
4. 2, 4
5. 5, 7

Page 259
1. 5 balloons – 5
2. 4 cats – 4
3. 2 shoes – 2
4. 1 dog – 1
5. empty set – 0
6. 3 baseballs – 3

Page 260
1. 8 keys – 8
2. 7 ice cream cones – 7
3. 9 balls – 9
4. 5 bells – 5
5. 6 fish – 6

Page 261
1. 10 – 2 left
2. 10 – 4 left
3. 10 – 3 left
4. 10 – 5 left
5. 10 – 1 left

Page 262
1. 2 sets of ten
2. 1 set of ten
3. 4 sets of ten

Page 263
1. 10 keys
2. 20 hats
3. 30 lollipops
4. 40 cups
5. 50 stars

Page 264
10
20
30
40
50
60
70
80
90
100

Page 265
0 – zero
1 – one
2 – two
3 – three
4 – four
5 – five
6 – six
7 – seven
8 – eight
9 – nine
10 – ten

Page 266
10
20
30
40
50
60
70
80
90
100

Page 267
Automatic fill-in.

Page 268
Automatic fill-in.

Page 269
1. 3 tens, 3 ones, 33
2. 2 tens, 4 ones, 24
3. 5 tens, 6 ones, 56

Page 270
1. 4 tens, 5 ones, 45
2. 7 tens, 1 one, 71
3. 5 tens, 3 ones, 53
4. 8 tens, 7 ones, 87

Page 271
1. 35, 37
2. 13, 15
3. 51, 53
4. 27, 29

Page 272
1. 23
2. 27
3. 17
4. 21
5. 30
6. 21
7. 18
8. 52

Page 273
1. 15 > 12
2. 25 > 16
3. 27 > 24
4. 12 > 10
5. 21 > 19
6. 17 > 13
7. 30 > 24
8. 19 > 11

Page 274
1. 12
2. 16
3. 17
4. 14
5. 11
6. 21
7. 24
8. 23

© School Zone Publishing Company

Page 275
1. 12 < 15
2. 14 < 17
3. 21 < 27
4. 22 < 28
5. 11 < 30
6. 16 < 29
7. 24 < 28
8. 40 < 50

Page 276
1. 21 < 28
2. 16 > 12
3. 14 < 17
4. 24 > 11
5. 20 < 30
6. 26 > 22
7. 40 < 60
8. 25 > 21

Page 277
1. 12 eggs
2. 12 stars
3. 12 lollipops
4. 12 leaves

Page 278
1. 8
2. 7
3. 10
4. 9
5. 7

Page 279
1. 4
2. 5
3. 6
4. 7
5. 8
6. 9
7. 10
8. 11
9. 12
10. 13

Page 280
1. 10
2. 13
3. 13
4. 17
5. 18
6. 12
7. 8
8. 10

Page 281
1. 4,5,7,5,8
2. 13,16,9,12,2
3. 12,4,10,8,8
4. 11,8,6,14,10
5. 9,11,9,11,12
6. 11,13,14,8,18

Page 282
1. 2
2. 3
3. 4
4. 4
5. 2

Page 283
1. 4,4,1,6,2
2. 1,2,1,3,1
3. 4,7,5,6,6
4. 1,1,10,2,3

Page 284
1. 3
2. 2
3. 5
4. 7
5. 4
6. 1
7. 9
8. 6
9. 8
10. 7

Page 285
1. D
2. A
3. B
4. C

Page 286
1. 10¢
2. 26¢
3. 7¢
4. 3¢
5. 15¢

© School Zone Publishing Company

BEGINNING TO ADD

The answer you get is called the SUM.

Example: 

Write the equation (problem).

4 + 2 = 6

You try it . . . ________________

Write the equations for the problems below.

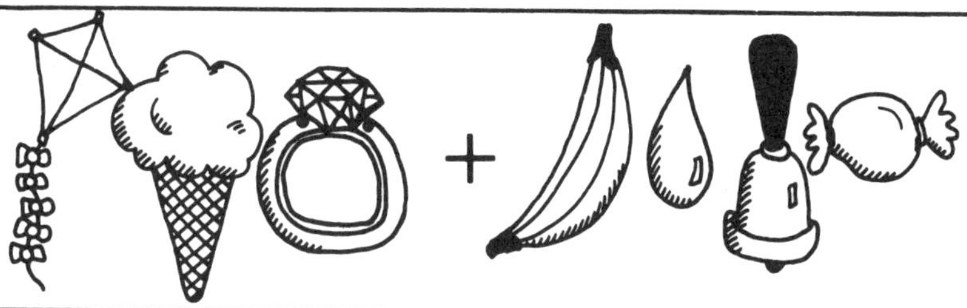

___ + ___ = ___

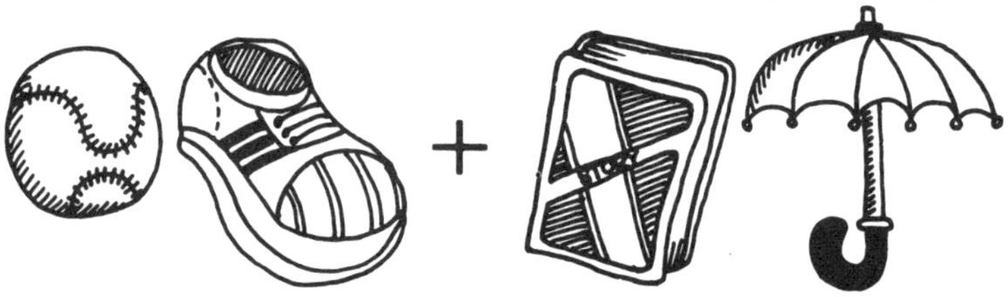

___ + ___ = ___

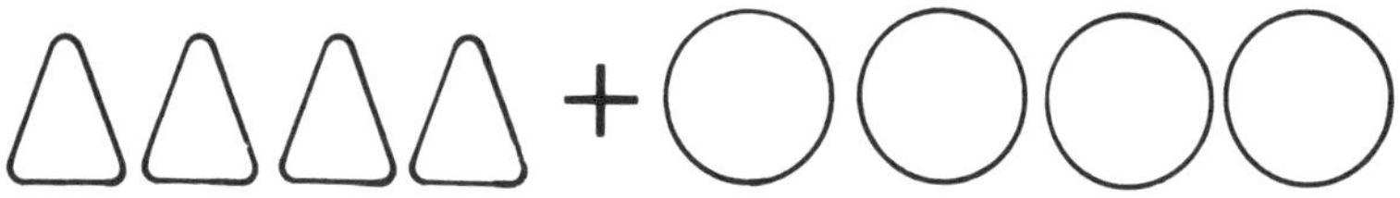

___ + ___ = ___

___ + ___ = ___

© School Zone Publishing Company

FIND THE SUMS

Horizontally

1. 2 + 3 = ______
2. 6 + 1 = ______
3. 4 + 3 = ______
4. 1 + 5 = ______
5. 8 + 2 = ______
6. 7 + 2 = ______

Vertically

7. $\begin{array}{r} 9 \\ +1 \\ \hline \end{array}$
8. $\begin{array}{r} 3 \\ +2 \\ \hline \end{array}$
9. $\begin{array}{r} 6 \\ +3 \\ \hline \end{array}$
10. $\begin{array}{r} 1 \\ +7 \\ \hline \end{array}$
11. $\begin{array}{r} 5 \\ +3 \\ \hline \end{array}$
12. $\begin{array}{r} 2 \\ +4 \\ \hline \end{array}$

Let's mix them

13. 8 + 2 = _____
14. $\begin{array}{r} 1 \\ +8 \\ \hline \end{array}$
15. 5 + 5 = _____
16. $\begin{array}{r} 6 \\ +4 \\ \hline \end{array}$
17. 3 + 2 = _____
18. $\begin{array}{r} 2 \\ +6 \\ \hline \end{array}$
19. 1 + 1 = _____
20. $\begin{array}{r} 2 \\ +1 \\ \hline \end{array}$
21. 4 + 4 = _____
22. $\begin{array}{r} 3 \\ +1 \\ \hline \end{array}$
23. 2 + 2 = _____
24. $\begin{array}{r} 3 \\ +3 \\ \hline \end{array}$

Your score ________

© School Zone Publishing Company

FUN WITH ADDITION

Find the sums.

Example:

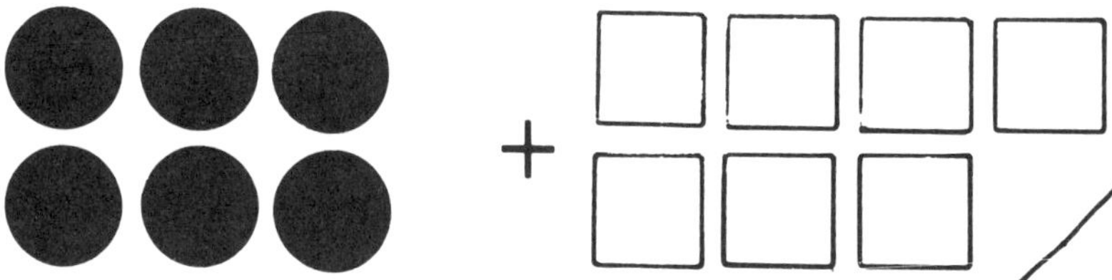

6 + 7 = 13

1. 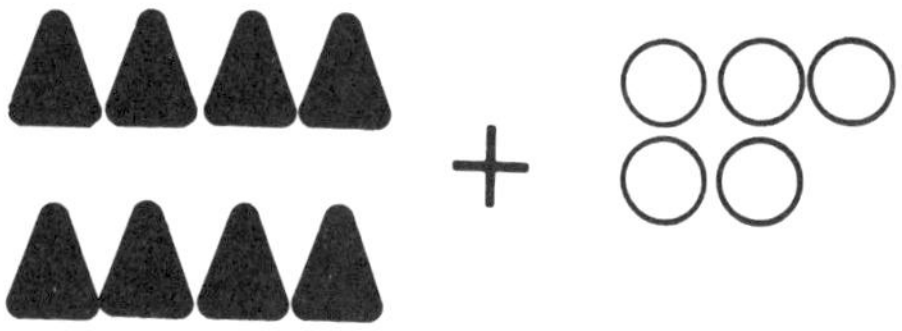

___ + ___ = _____

2. 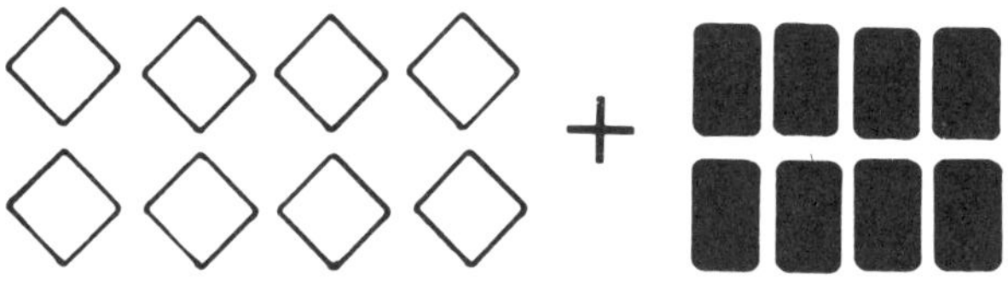

___ + ___ = _____

3. 

___ + ___ = _____

4. 

___ + ___ = _____

5. 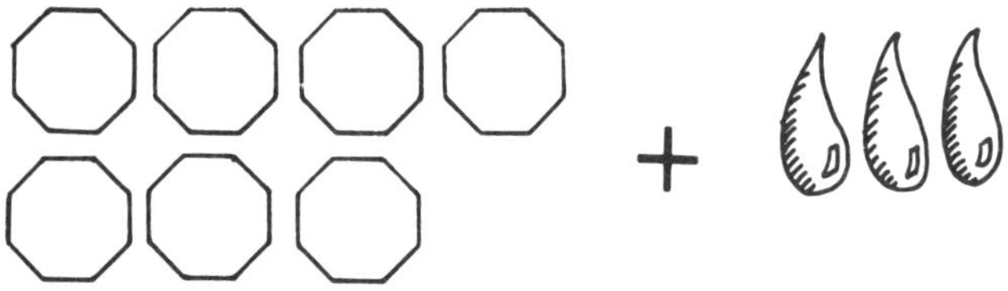

___ + ___ = _____

6. 

___ + ___ = _____

© School Zone Publishing Company

ADD NUMBERS UP TO TWENTY

Find the sum:

1. 8 + 4 = ______
2. 6 + 6 = ______
3. 9 + 10 = ______
4. 7 + 5 = ______
5. 5 + 9 = ______
6. 10 + 7 = ______

---

7. 8 + 8 = _____

8. $\begin{array}{r} 7 \\ +7 \\ \hline \end{array}$

9. 9 + 9 = _____

10. $\begin{array}{r} 6 \\ +7 \\ \hline \end{array}$

11. 8 + 5 = _____

12. $\begin{array}{r} 9 \\ +7 \\ \hline \end{array}$

13. 5 + 6 = _____

14. $\begin{array}{r} 4 \\ +8 \\ \hline \end{array}$

---

15. $\begin{array}{r} 9 \\ +3 \\ \hline \end{array}$

16. $\begin{array}{r} 7 \\ +8 \\ \hline \end{array}$

17. $\begin{array}{r} 5 \\ +9 \\ \hline \end{array}$

18. $\begin{array}{r} 6 \\ +8 \\ \hline \end{array}$

19. $\begin{array}{r} 9 \\ +2 \\ \hline \end{array}$

Bonus: 10 extra points.

20. 5 + 3 = □

21. $\begin{array}{r} 2 \\ +\square \\ \hline 4 \end{array}$

22. 8 + □ = 10

23. $\begin{array}{r} 3 \\ +\square \\ \hline 6 \end{array}$

24. □ + 6 = 12

Your score ________

© School Zone Publishing Company

ADDITION FACTS

If you want to have fun with addition, you must learn your addition facts. Here they are on this page. Study them with Dee Dee, Big Chief, and Tray Fay.

1 + 0 = 1
1 + 1 = 2
1 + 2 = 3
1 + 3 = 4
1 + 4 = 5
1 + 5 = 6
1 + 6 = 7
1 + 7 = 8
1 + 8 = 9
1 + 9 = 10

2 + 0 = 2
2 + 1 = 3
2 + 2 = 4
2 + 3 = 5
2 + 4 = 6
2 + 5 = 7
2 + 6 = 8
2 + 7 = 9
2 + 8 = 10
2 + 9 = 11

3 + 0 = 3
3 + 1 = 4
3 + 2 = 5
3 + 3 = 6
3 + 4 = 7
3 + 5 = 8
3 + 6 = 9
3 + 7 = 10
3 + 8 = 11
3 + 9 = 12

4 + 0 = 4
4 + 1 = 5
4 + 2 = 6
4 + 3 = 7
4 + 4 = 8
4 + 5 = 9
4 + 6 = 10
4 + 7 = 11
4 + 8 = 12
4 + 9 = 13

5 + 0 = 5
5 + 1 = 6
5 + 2 = 7
5 + 3 = 8
5 + 4 = 9
5 + 5 = 10
5 + 6 = 11
5 + 7 = 12
5 + 8 = 13
5 + 9 = 14

6 + 0 = 6
6 + 1 = 7
6 + 2 = 8
6 + 3 = 9
6 + 4 = 10
6 + 5 = 11
6 + 6 = 12
6 + 7 = 13
6 + 8 = 14
6 + 9 = 15

7 + 0 = 7
7 + 1 = 8
7 + 2 = 9
7 + 3 = 10
7 + 4 = 11
7 + 5 = 12
7 + 6 = 13
7 + 7 = 14
7 + 8 = 15
7 + 9 = 16

8 + 0 = 8
8 + 1 = 9
8 + 2 = 10
8 + 3 = 11
8 + 4 = 12
8 + 5 = 13
8 + 6 = 14
8 + 7 = 15
8 + 8 = 16
8 + 9 = 17

9 + 0 = 9
9 + 1 = 10
9 + 2 = 11
9 + 3 = 12
9 + 4 = 13
9 + 5 = 14
9 + 6 = 15
9 + 7 = 16
9 + 8 = 17
9 + 9 = 18

Practice writing your addition facts.

© School Zone Publishing Company

BEGINNING SUBTRACTION

The answer is called the DIFFERENCE.

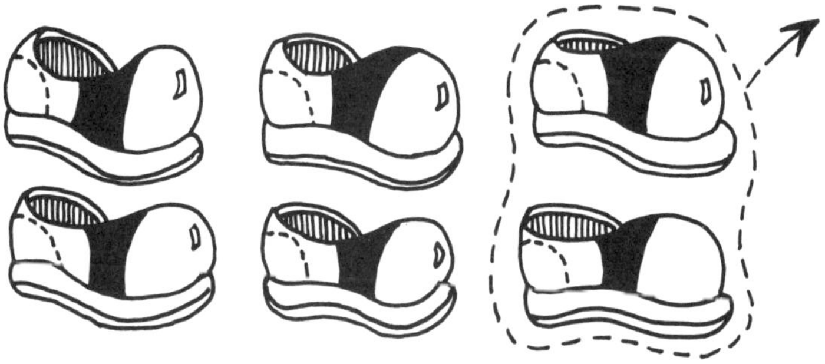

6 objects take away 2 = 4 objects left   6 — 2 = 4

4 objects take away 1 =   ___ — ___ = ___

5 objects take away 3 =   ___ — ___ = ___

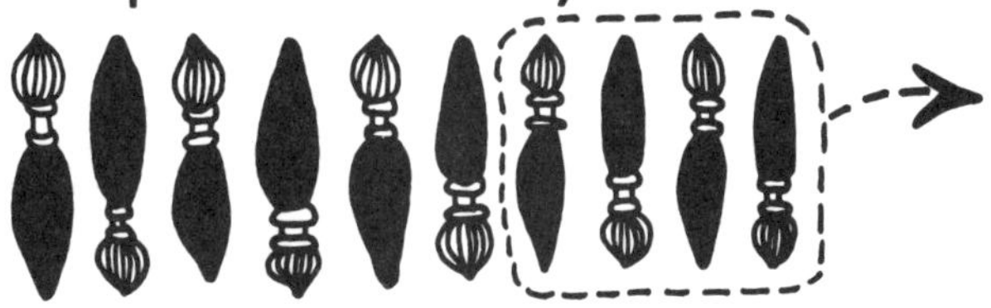

10 objects take away 4 =   ___ — ___ = ___

6 objects take away 2 =   ___ — ___ = ___

© School Zone Publishing Company

FIND THE DIFFERENCE

Horizontally

1. 7 — 4 = ______
2. 5 — 3 = ______
3. 6 — 4 = ______
4. 8 — 7 = ______
5. 10 — 3 = ______
6. 9 — 5 = ______

Vertically

7. 5 —4
8. 9 —7
9. 6 —3
10. 10 —5

Mix them

11. 3 — 2 = ______
12. 8 —4
13. 9 — 4 = ______
14. 4 —3
15. 6 — 6 = ______
16. 7 — 6 = ______
17. 5 —5
18. 4 —2
19. 10 — 5 = ______
20. 4 — 3 = ______
21. 9 — 9 = ______
22. 5 —3
23. 6 —5
24. 9 —2

Your score ______

© School Zone Publishing Company

FUN WITH SUBTRACTION

Example:

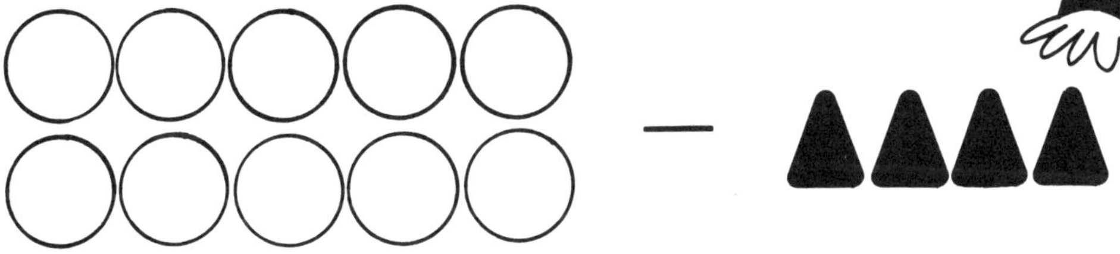

10 - 4 = 6

1. 

___ – ___ = ___

2. 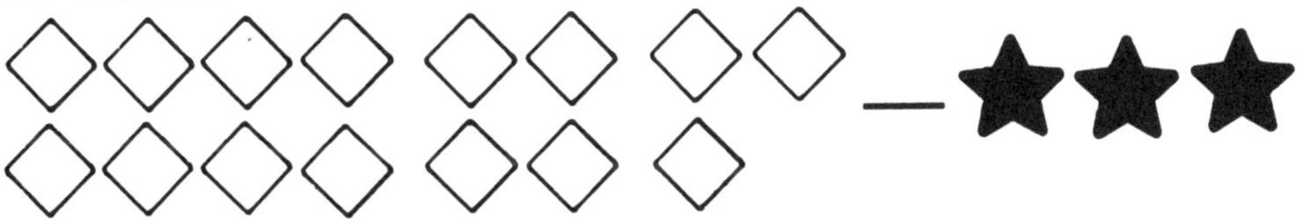

___ – ___ = ___

3. 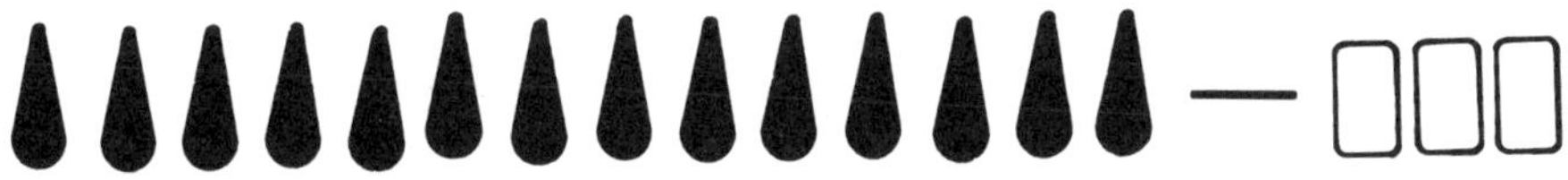

___ – ___ = ___

4. 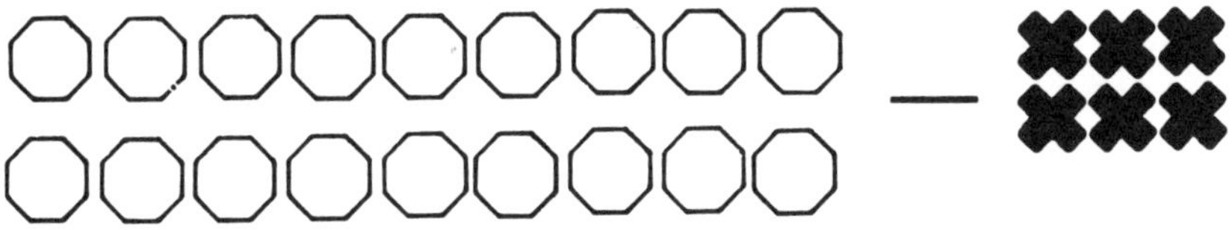

___ – ___ = ___

5. 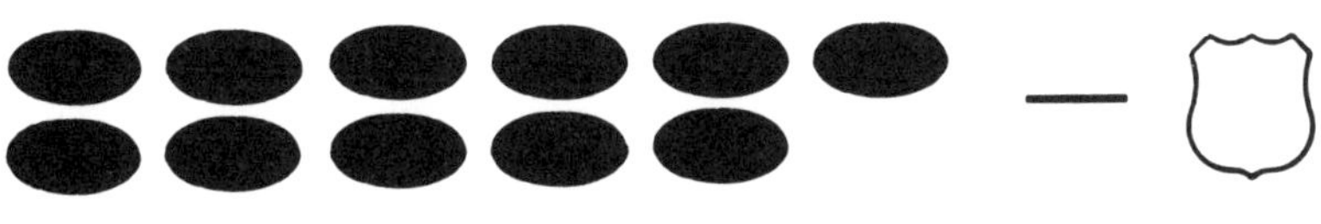

___ – ___ = ___

6. 

___ – ___ = ___

Your score ________

© School Zone Publishing Company

SUBTRACT NUMBERS UP TO TWENTY

Find the difference.

1. 9 — 5 = ______
2. 12 — 10 = ______
3. 18 — 9 = ______
4. 11 — 5 = ______
5. 15 — 9 = ______
6. 16 — 8 = ______

---

7. 15 — 7 = ______
8. 14 — 6 = ______
9. 10 — 6 = ______

10. 12
 —5

11. 13
 —3

12. 17
 —7

13. 14
 —7

14. 19
 —9

15. 11
 —1

---

16. 18
 —8

17. 15
 —5

18. 10
 —5

19. 13
 —4

Bonus: 10 extra points.

20. 9 — 5 = □

21. 11
 —6
 □

22. 10 — □ = 5

23. 18
 —□
 9

24. □ — 6 = 6

Your score ______

© School Zone Publishing Company

SUBTRACTION FACTS

Here are the subtraction facts. Study them and have fun doing subtraction. Study with Ken, Nicki, and Rogie.

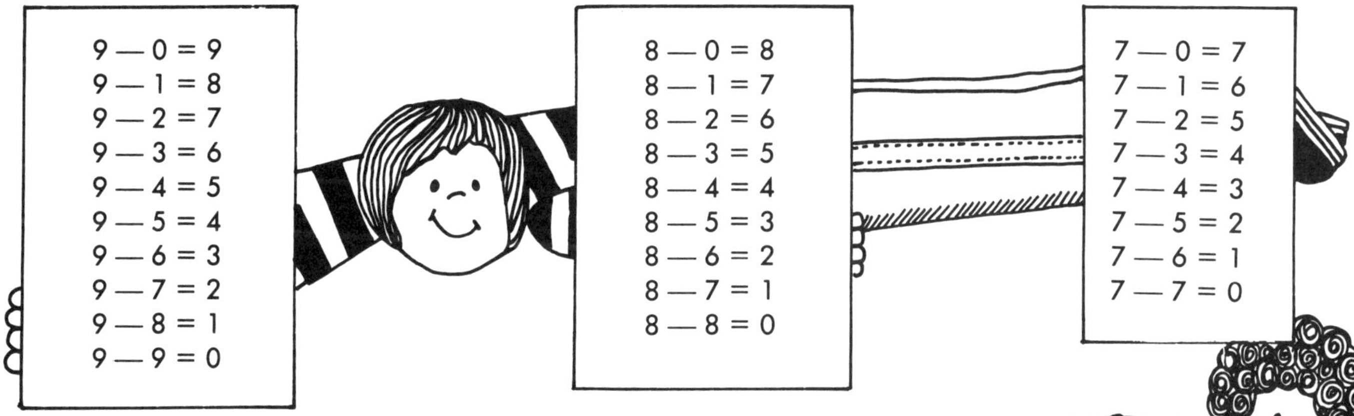

9 — 0 = 9
9 — 1 = 8
9 — 2 = 7
9 — 3 = 6
9 — 4 = 5
9 — 5 = 4
9 — 6 = 3
9 — 7 = 2
9 — 8 = 1
9 — 9 = 0

8 — 0 = 8
8 — 1 = 7
8 — 2 = 6
8 — 3 = 5
8 — 4 = 4
8 — 5 = 3
8 — 6 = 2
8 — 7 = 1
8 — 8 = 0

7 — 0 = 7
7 — 1 = 6
7 — 2 = 5
7 — 3 = 4
7 — 4 = 3
7 — 5 = 2
7 — 6 = 1
7 — 7 = 0

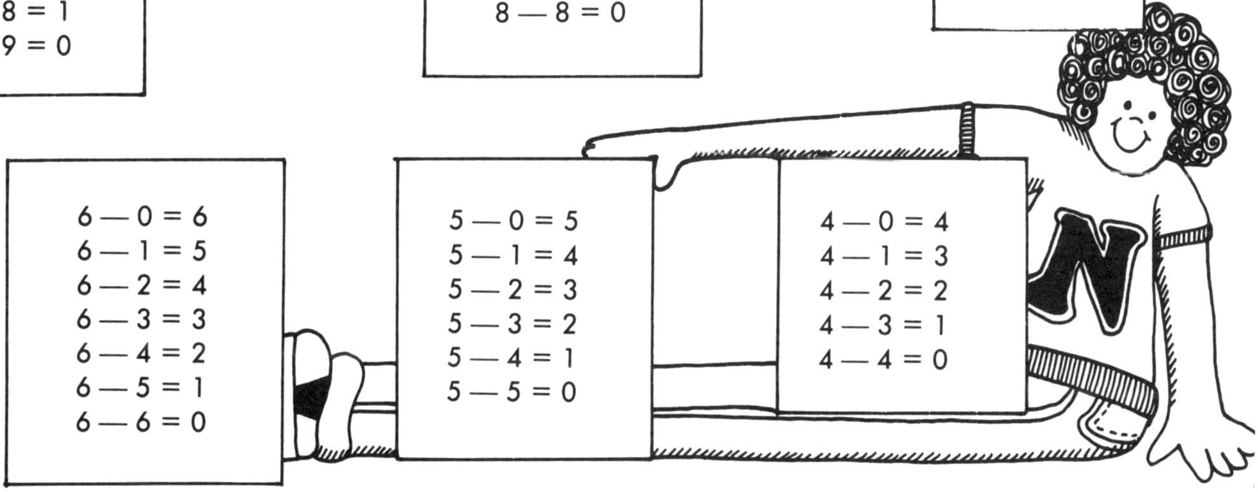

6 — 0 = 6
6 — 1 = 5
6 — 2 = 4
6 — 3 = 3
6 — 4 = 2
6 — 5 = 1
6 — 6 = 0

5 — 0 = 5
5 — 1 = 4
5 — 2 = 3
5 — 3 = 2
5 — 4 = 1
5 — 5 = 0

4 — 0 = 4
4 — 1 = 3
4 — 2 = 2
4 — 3 = 1
4 — 4 = 0

10 — 0 = 10
10 — 1 = 9
10 — 2 = 8
10 — 3 = 7
10 — 4 = 6
10 — 5 = 5
10 — 6 = 4
10 — 7 = 3
10 — 8 = 2
10 — 9 = 1
10 — 10 = 0

11 — 0 = 11
11 — 1 = 10
11 — 2 = 9
11 — 3 = 8
11 — 4 = 7
11 — 5 = 6
11 — 6 = 5
11 — 7 = 4
11 — 8 = 3
11 — 9 = 2
11 — 10 = 1
11 — 11 = 0

12 — 0 = 12
12 — 1 = 11
12 — 2 = 10
12 — 3 = 9
12 — 4 = 8
12 — 5 = 7
12 — 6 = 6
12 — 7 = 5
12 — 8 = 4
12 — 9 = 3
12 — 10 = 2
12 — 11 = 1
12 — 12 = 0

Practice writing your subtraction facts.

© School Zone Publishing Company

LET'S TRY THREE!

When adding 3 numbers, always group 2 numbers together FIRST to find the SUM.

2 ⟩ 2 + 3 = 5
3
+4 ← 5 + 4 = 9
9 ←
sum

You try it.

1.	2.	3.	4.	5.
4	9	8	5	7
1	1	5	0	4
+5	+7	+9	+8	+8

6.	7.	8.	9.	10.
8	6	5	4	8
9	3	3	6	4
+9	+2	+2	+5	+8

11.	12.	13.	14.	15.
2	9	3	9	7
7	7	2	5	3
+6	+9	+6	+1	+4

Your score ________

© School Zone Publishing Company

ADD THEM UP

When adding 2 digit numbers, always add the numbers in the ONE'S place first.

$$\begin{array}{r} 1\boxed{3} \\ +\ \boxed{5} \\ \hline \boxed{8} \end{array} \longrightarrow \begin{array}{r} \boxed{1}\boxed{3} \\ +\ \boxed{5} \\ \hline \boxed{1}\boxed{8} \end{array}$$

ones

Add the tens.

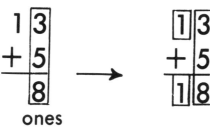

Try it. Remember to add the ones first.

1. 13 + 6	2. 10 + 5	3. 14 + 2	4. 17 + 2	5. 11 + 4
6. 16 + 3	7. 13 + 2	8. 15 + 4	9. 11 + 3	10. 13 + 5
11. 10 + 6	12. 12 + 5	13. 14 + 3	14. 11 + 8	15. 10 + 2
16. 17 + 1	17. 13 + 6	18. 15 + 3	19. 12 + 7	20. 18 + 1

Your score ________

© School Zone Publishing Company

ONES AND TENS COUNT UP

Always add the ones first. Then add the tens.

ones	tens
$\begin{array}{r} 1\boxed{2} \\ +1\boxed{3} \\ \hline \boxed{5} \end{array}$	$\begin{array}{r} \boxed{1}2 \\ +\boxed{1}3 \\ \hline \boxed{2}5 \end{array}$

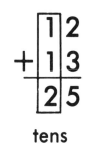

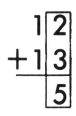

These are so easy I can do them standing on my hands!

1. $\begin{array}{r} 24 \\ +53 \\ \hline \end{array}$ 2. $\begin{array}{r} 64 \\ +25 \\ \hline \end{array}$ 3. $\begin{array}{r} 38 \\ +21 \\ \hline \end{array}$ 4. $\begin{array}{r} 66 \\ +23 \\ \hline \end{array}$ 5. $\begin{array}{r} 24 \\ +52 \\ \hline \end{array}$

6. $\begin{array}{r} 28 \\ +51 \\ \hline \end{array}$ 7. $\begin{array}{r} 43 \\ +22 \\ \hline \end{array}$ 8. $\begin{array}{r} 18 \\ +11 \\ \hline \end{array}$ 9. $\begin{array}{r} 14 \\ +10 \\ \hline \end{array}$ 10. $\begin{array}{r} 15 \\ +11 \\ \hline \end{array}$

11. $\begin{array}{r} 43 \\ +34 \\ \hline \end{array}$ 12. $\begin{array}{r} 62 \\ +34 \\ \hline \end{array}$ 13. $\begin{array}{r} 74 \\ +25 \\ \hline \end{array}$ 14. $\begin{array}{r} 84 \\ +13 \\ \hline \end{array}$ 15. $\begin{array}{r} 35 \\ +20 \\ \hline \end{array}$

16. $\begin{array}{r} 39 \\ +10 \\ \hline \end{array}$ 17. $\begin{array}{r} 26 \\ +13 \\ \hline \end{array}$ 18. $\begin{array}{r} 63 \\ +34 \\ \hline \end{array}$ 19. $\begin{array}{r} 75 \\ +24 \\ \hline \end{array}$ 20. $\begin{array}{r} 33 \\ +22 \\ \hline \end{array}$

Your score________

© School Zone Publishing Company

ADDITION RACEWAY

Play this game with a friend. Use buttons, beans, or anything as markers.

*Fill in the box in each space with the correct answer.
*Move your marker that many spaces.
*Move your marker back two spaces for every incorrect answer.
*The first one to reach FINISH wins.

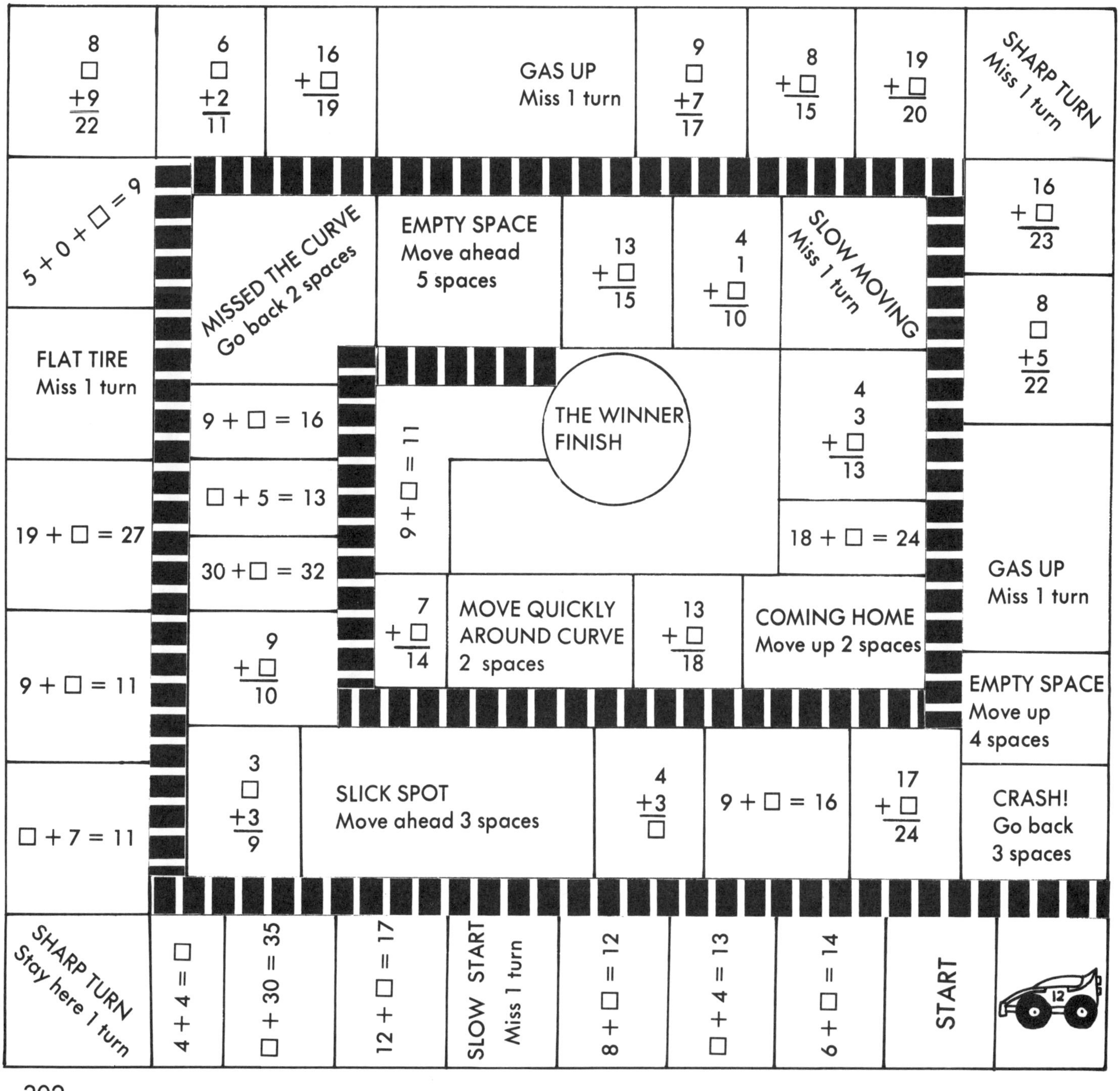

© School Zone Publishing Company

ADDITION ANIMAL

Color areas that have the same sum.
What animal did you find?

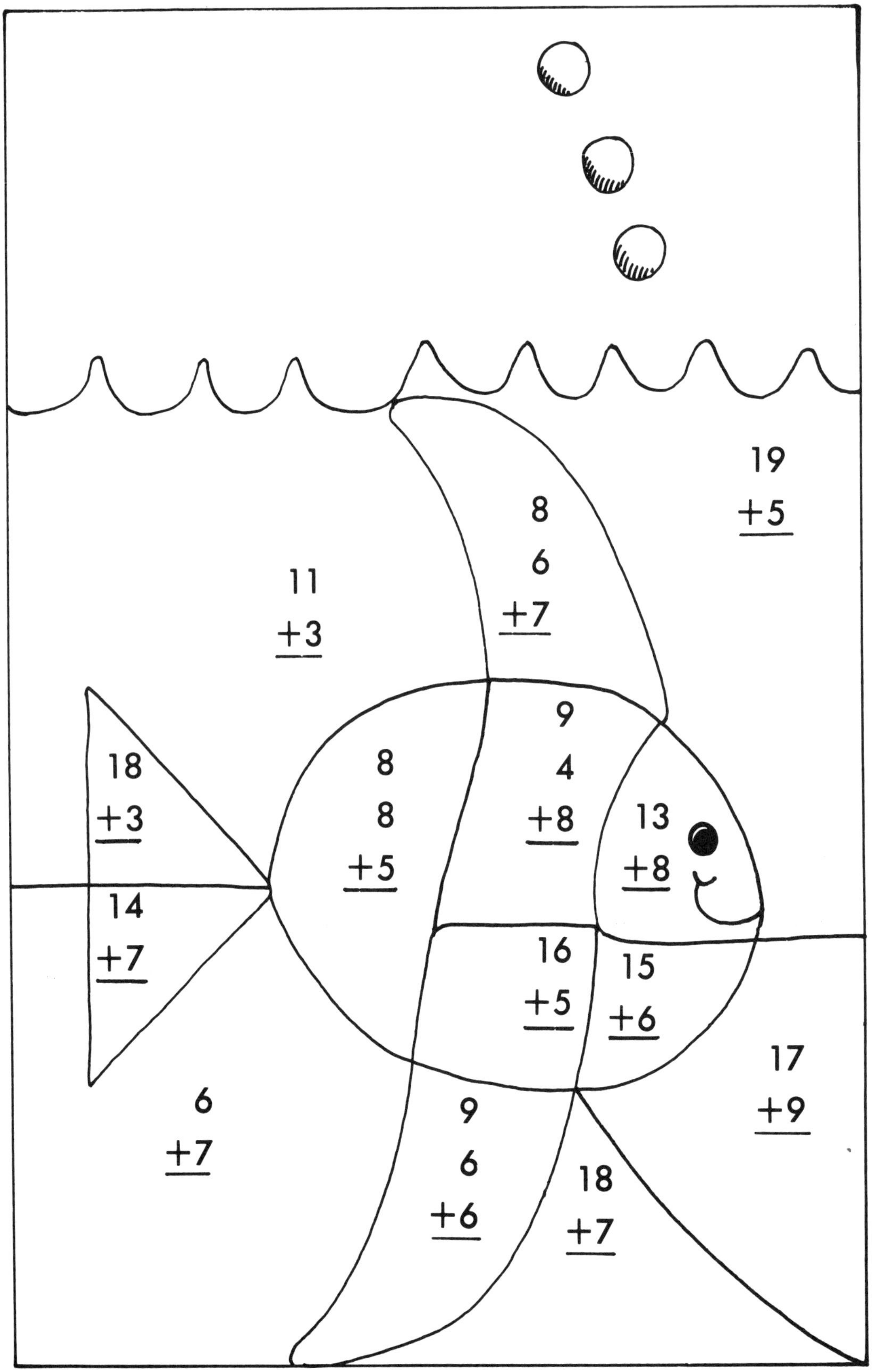

© School Zone Publishing Company

ONES AND TENS SUBTRACTION

Always subtract the ones first. Then subtract the tens.

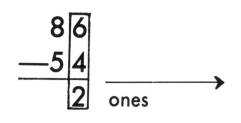

8 6		8 6	
—5 4	→	— 5 4	
2 ones		tens 3 2	→ difference = 32

Try it.

1. 39	2. 58	3. 89	4. 77	5. 65
—13	—24	—37	—43	—24
6. 24	7. 49	8. 99	9. 75	10. 93
—13	—33	—84	—53	—81
11. 44	12. 55	13. 69	14. 19	15. 25
—22	—43	—38	—13	—14
16. 32	17. 58	18. 39	19. 85	20. 77
—11	—47	—15	—74	—44

Your score __________

© School Zone Publishing Company

NINE FINE

Play this game with a friend. Use buttons, beans, or anything as markers.
*Take turns working the problems.
*Move ahead one space for each correct answer.
*Move ahead three spaces if your answer has the number 9 in it.
*If your answer is wrong, you do not move ahead.
*The first player to go around the 9 is the winner.

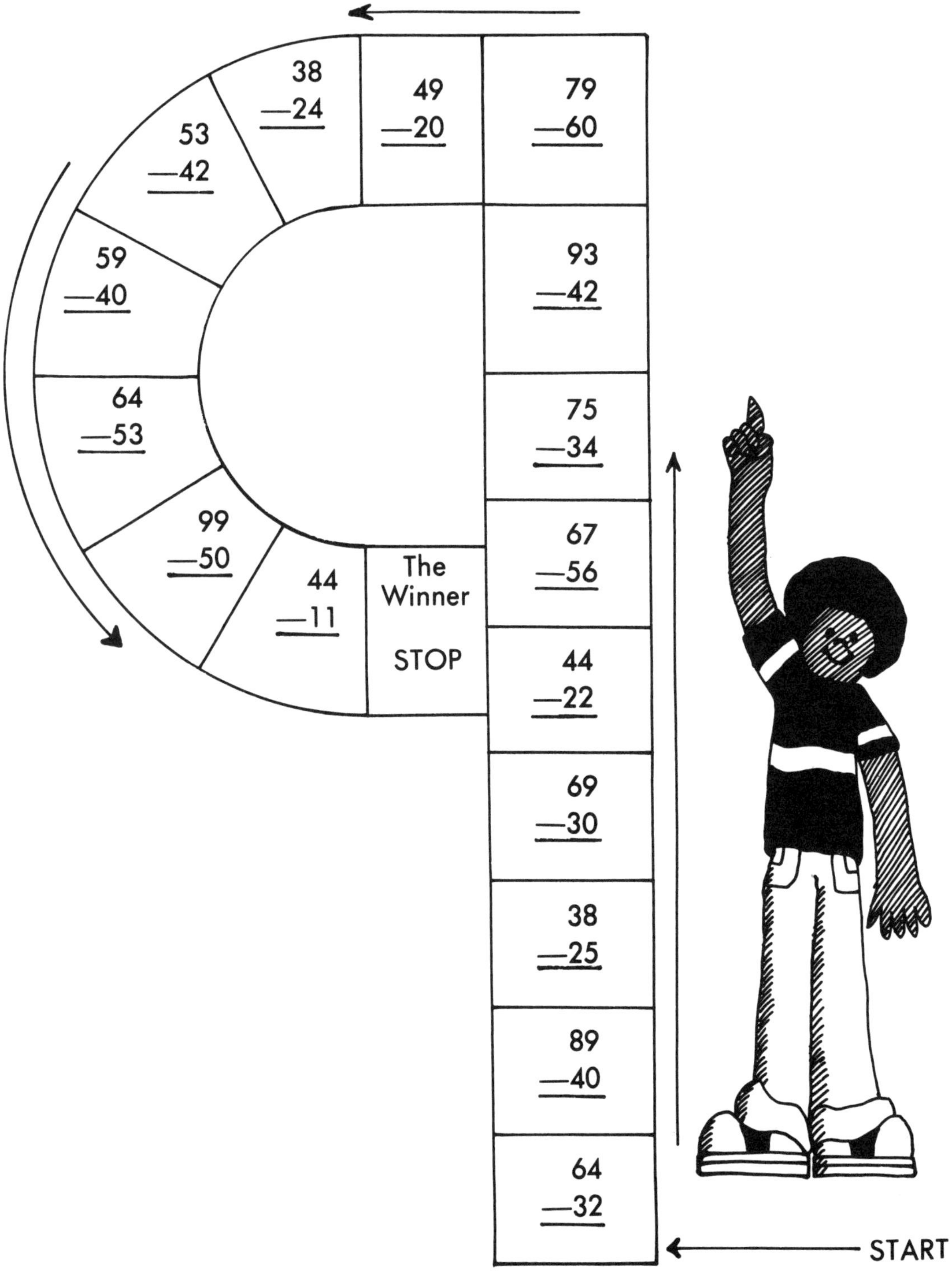

© School Zone Publishing Company

REGROUPING WITH ADDITION

Regrouping in addition means to carry.

$$\begin{array}{r} 36 \\ +26 \\ \hline 12 \end{array}$$

1 ten and 2 ones

$$\begin{array}{r} \overset{1}{3}6 \\ +26 \\ \hline 2 \end{array}$$

Give the 1 ten to the tens.

Now add the tens.

$$\begin{array}{r} \overset{1}{3}6 \\ +26 \\ \hline 62 \end{array}$$

← The answer.

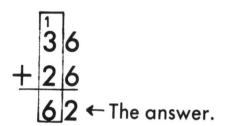

If I can do these, you can do these!

Try it.

1. 48 +24	2. 57 +34	3. 88 +13	4. 29 +66	5. 45 +28
6. 36 +36	7. 74 +16	8. 52 +18	9. 63 +29	10. 54 +46
11. 68 +33	12. 27 +54	13. 34 +66	14. 48 +25	15. 57 +15
16. 99 +22	17. 53 +37	18. 39 +56	19. 46 +79	20. 59 +33

© School Zone Publishing Company

COLUMN REGROUPING

REMEMBER: Add the ones first, then add the tens.

```
 36   Add the ones.
  5
+21
 12   1 ten + 2 ones
```

```
 1
 36   Give the 1 ten to the tens.
  5   → Add the tens.
+21
  2
```

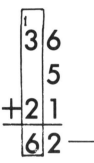

```
 1
 36
  5
+21
 62 → The answer.
```

Try it.

1. 47 + 6 + 15 =
2. 65 + 7 + 2 =
3. 53 + 19 + 4 =
4. 69 + 5 + 29 =
5. 24 + 3 + 5 =
6. 37 + 18 + 3 =
7. 74 + 8 + 17 =
8. 86 + 4 + 9 =
9. 52 + 33 + 8 =
10. 5 + 4 + 32 =
11. 83 + 29 + 7 =
12. 25 + 3 + 59 =
13. 16 + 3 + 4 =
14. 39 + 5 + 21 =
15. 43 + 2 + 4 =

© School Zone Publishing Company

PLAY WITH NUMBERS

Find the problems in the picture below. Do them. Then color the picture.

© School Zone Publishing Company

MR. ZERO

He's fun to add. Take your time and succeed with Mr. Zero.

1. $\begin{array}{r} 500 \\ +400 \\ \hline \end{array}$

2. $\begin{array}{r} 300 \\ +600 \\ \hline \end{array}$

3. $\begin{array}{r} 200 \\ +100 \\ \hline \end{array}$

4. $\begin{array}{r} 900 \\ +200 \\ \hline \end{array}$

5. $\begin{array}{r} 800 \\ +100 \\ \hline \end{array}$

6. $\begin{array}{r} 600 \\ +300 \\ \hline \end{array}$

7. $\begin{array}{r} 700 \\ +500 \\ \hline \end{array}$

8. $\begin{array}{r} 400 \\ +400 \\ \hline \end{array}$

9. $\begin{array}{r} 700 \\ +300 \\ \hline \end{array}$

10. $\begin{array}{r} 800 \\ +300 \\ \hline \end{array}$

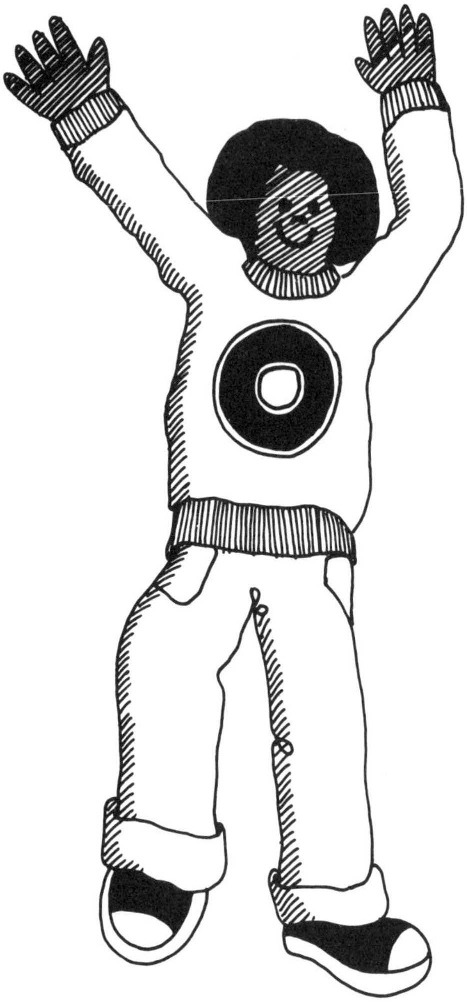

Bonus: 10 extra points.
Write your own problem with Mr. Zero.

Your score ________

© School Zone Publishing Company

1-2-3 ADD UP

Remember: Add the ones first, then add the tens. This time you must also add the hundreds.

$$\begin{array}{r} 56\boxed{2} \\ +37\boxed{6} \\ \hline 8 \end{array}$$ Add the ones.

$$\begin{array}{r} 5\boxed{6}2 \\ +3\boxed{7}6 \\ \hline 38 \end{array}$$ Add the tens. 1 hundred + 3 tens

$$\begin{array}{r} \overset{1}{5}62 \\ +376 \\ \hline 38 \end{array}$$ Give the one hundred to the hundreds.

$$\begin{array}{r} \overset{1}{\boxed{5}}62 \\ +\boxed{3}76 \\ \hline 938 \end{array}$$ Add the hundreds. ⟶ 938 is the answer.

Try it.

1.	2.	3.	4.	5.
364	257	578	799	553
+7	+115	+118	+21	+7

6.	7.	8.	9.	10.
644	524	431	897	431
+276	+118	+469	+18	+469

Your score ________

© School Zone Publishing Company

MORE!

Bonus: 10 extra points if you get the whole page correct.

1. 416 +332	2. 143 +309	3. 237 +624	4. 578 +329
5. 413 +340	6. 845 +723	7. 325 +423	8. 648 +277
9. 765 +434	10. 347 +6	11. 847 +39	12. 544 +3
13. 222 +333	14. 787 +28	15. 509 +44	16. 366 +57
17. 613 +4	18. 818 +118	19. 571 +3	20. 660 +47

Your score ________

© School Zone Publishing Company

REGROUPING WITH SUBTRACTION

Regrouping in subtraction means to borrow.

62 ← Always start with the top number. 2 take away 6.
—26 You cannot do it, because the 6 is bigger.
You must borrow from the tens.

5
~~6~~2 Borrow 1 ten from the 6 tens. That leaves 5 tens.
—26

---

5 1
~~6~~2 Put the one next to the 2. Now it is 12 ones.
—26

---

5 1
~~6~~2 Work the problem. 12 take away 6. 5 take away 2.
—26
36

Try it.

1. 68 —59	2. 45 —28	3. 94 —37	4. 43 —29	5. 42 —25
6. 65 —48	7. 82 —34	8. 32 —19	9. 54 —39	10. 76 —57
11. 81 —43	12. 54 —26	13. 92 —78	14. 41 —24	15. 37 —19

© School Zone Publishing Company

SUBTRACT WITH THREE

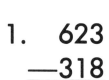

Don't forget to borrow (regroup).

```
 7 11 1
 823
−576
 247
```

This time you must borrow from the hundreds also.

1. 623 − 318	2. 952 − 636	3. 487 − 369	4. 521 − 184
5. 792 − 398	6. 345 − 169	7. 587 − 569	8. 953 − 268
9. 385 − 196	10. 672 − 564	11. 537 − 349	12. 974 − 636
13. 344 − 155	14. 673 − 484	15. 453 − 275	

Your score ________

© School Zone Publishing Company

SUBTRACT WITH MR. ZERO

```
 700 ← 0 take away 7. You cannot do it. You must borrow.
—357
```

```
 700   You cannot borrow from the tens because there is a zero.
—357   You can borrow from the hundreds.
```

```
 6 1
 X00   1 hundred from 7 hundred leaves 6 hundred.
—357   Give that hundred to the tens.
       Now you have 10 tens.
```

```
 6 9 9
 X00   But you still need to borrow for the ones.
—357   Borrow from the tens. Now you have 9 tens.
```

```
 6 9 1
 X00   Give the 1 ten to the ones. Now you have 10 ones.
—357   Let's do the problem.
 343
```

Try it.

1. 600 —357	2. 809 —426	3. 680 —475	4. 502 —296	5. 400 —119
6. 950 —748	7. 300 —145	8. 701 —550	9. 700 —555	10. 330 —142

Your score ________

© School Zone Publishing Company

500 WOW!

*2 players
*Use buttons, beans, or anything for markers.
*Take turns subtracting the problems.
*When a player gets an answer, find it in one of the boxes at the top of the page. Put a marker on the number.
*The first player to get 3 markers in a row, vertically, horizontally, or diagonally, wins the game.

245	278	67
132	234	64
323	167	141

281	56	174
184	331	312
266	237	14

1. 500 − 234
2. 500 − 359
3. 500 − 436
4. 500 − 169
5. 500 − 266
6. 500 − 333
7. 500 − 255
8. 500 − 444
9. 500 − 486
10. 500 − 433
11. 500 − 177
12. 500 − 263
13. 500 − 219
14. 500 − 326
15. 500 − 222
16. 500 − 368
17. 500 − 316
18. 500 − 188

© School Zone Publishing Company

MORE!!

Bonus: 10 extra points if you get every problem on this page correct.

1. 82 —7	2. 66 —39	3. 42 —25	4. 94 —75	5. 75 —68
6. 35 —19	7. 66 —8	8. 43 —25	9. 24 —7	10. 35 —9
11. 863 —646	12. 432 —258	13. 762 —54	14. 714 —535	15. 284 —66
16. 500 —347	17. 840 —396	18. 509 —349	19. 600 —437	20. 970 —784

Your score ____________

© School Zone Publishing Company

NUMBER BALLOONS

Tracy went to the circus. She bought a bunch of number balloons. Do the problems and find the answers on Tracy's balloons. Put the number of the problem by the balloon with the correct answer. Have fun coloring this page.

1. 68 − 59	2. 385 − 47	3. 82 − 7	4. 43 − 9	5. 300 − 145
6. 672 − 564	7. 952 − 636	8. 809 − 426	9. 45 − 28	10. 800 − 699

© School Zone Publishing Company

REVIEW

S0-EAX-197

1.  + 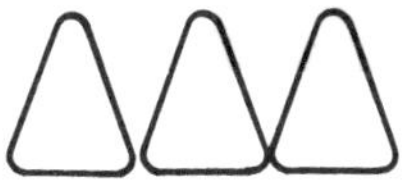 ____ + ____ = ____

2. $4 + 3 =$ ______

3. $\begin{array}{r} 6 \\ +3 \\ \hline \end{array}$

4. $7 + 7 =$ ______

5. $\begin{array}{r} 5 \\ +9 \\ \hline \end{array}$

6.  —  ____ — ____ = ____

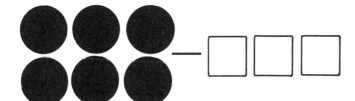

7. $7 - 4 =$ ______

8. $\begin{array}{r} 9 \\ -2 \\ \hline \end{array}$

9. $\begin{array}{r} 18 \\ -8 \\ \hline \end{array}$

10. $\begin{array}{r} 9 \\ 1 \\ +7 \\ \hline \end{array}$

11. $\begin{array}{r} 13 \\ -6 \\ \hline \end{array}$

12. $\begin{array}{r} 24 \\ +53 \\ \hline \end{array}$

13. $\begin{array}{r} 39 \\ +13 \\ \hline \end{array}$

14. $\begin{array}{r} 47 \\ 6 \\ +15 \\ \hline \end{array}$

15. $\begin{array}{r} 600 \\ +300 \\ \hline \end{array}$

16. $\begin{array}{r} 257 \\ +115 \\ \hline \end{array}$

17. $\begin{array}{r} 799 \\ +21 \\ \hline \end{array}$

18. $\begin{array}{r} 952 \\ -636 \\ \hline \end{array}$

Your score ________

© School Zone Publishing Company

Page 289
1. 3 + 4 = 7
2. 2 + 2 = 4
3. 4 + 4 = 8
4. 4 + 5 = 9

Page 290
1. 5
2. 7
3. 7
4. 6
5. 10
6. 9
7. 10
8. 5
9. 9
10. 8
11. 8
12. 6
13. 10
14. 9
15. 10
16. 10
17. 5
18. 8
19. 2
20. 3
21. 8
22. 4
23. 4
24. 6

Page 291
1. 8 + 5 = 13
2. 8 + 8 = 16
3. 6 + 6 = 12
4. 10 + 10 = 20
5. 7 + 3 = 10
6. 8 + 7 =15

Page 292
1. 12
2. 12
3. 19
4. 12
5. 14
6. 17
7. 16
8. 14
9. 18
10. 13
11. 13
12. 16
13. 11
14. 12
15. 12
16. 15
17. 14
18. 14
19. 11
20. 8
21. 2
22. 2
23. 3
24. 6

Page 294
1. 4 – 1 = 3
2. 5 – 3 = 2
3. 10 – 4 = 6
4. 6 – 2 = 4

Page 295
1. 3
2. 2
3. 2
4. 1
5. 7
6. 4
7. 1
8. 2
9. 3
10. 5
11. 1
12. 4
13. 5
14. 1
15. 0
16. 1
17. 0
18. 2
19. 5
20. 1
21. 0
22. 2
23. 1
24. 7

Page 296
1. 12 – 2 = 10
2. 15 – 3 = 12
3. 14 – 3 = 11
4. 18 – 6 = 12
5. 11 – 1 = 10
6. 16 – 6 = 10

Page 297
1. 4
2. 2
3. 9
4. 6
5. 6
6. 8
7. 8
8. 8
9. 4
10. 7
11. 10
12. 10
13. 7
14. 10
15. 10
16. 10
17. 10
18. 5
19. 9
20. 4
21. 5
22. 5
23. 9
24. 12

Page 299
1. 10
2. 17
3. 22
4. 13
5. 19
6. 26
7. 11
8. 10
9. 15
10. 20
11. 15
12. 25
13. 11
14. 15
15. 14

Page 300
1. 19
2. 15
3. 16
4. 19
5. 15
6. 19
7. 15
8. 19
9. 14
10. 18
11. 16
12. 17
13. 17
14. 19
15. 12
16. 18
17. 19
18. 18
19. 19
20. 19

Page 301
1. 77
2. 89
3. 59
4. 89
5. 76
6. 79
7. 65
8. 29
9. 24
10. 26
11. 77
12. 96
13. 99
14. 97
15. 55
16. 49
17. 39
18. 97
19. 99
20. 55

Page 304
1. 26
2. 34
3. 52
4. 34
5. 41
6. 11
7. 16
8. 15
9. 22
10. 12
11. 22
12. 12
13. 31
14. 06
15. 11
16. 21
17. 11
18. 24
19. 11
20. 33

Page 305
1. 32
2. 49
3. 13
4. 39
5. 22
6. 11
7. 41
8. 51
9. 19
10. 29
11. 14
12. 11
13. 19
14. 11
15. 49
16. 33

© School Zone Publishing Company

Page 306
1. 72
2. 91
3. 101
4. 95
5. 73
6. 72
7. 90
8. 70
9. 92
10. 100
11. 101
12. 81
13. 100
14. 73
15. 72
16. 121
17. 90
18. 95
19. 125
20. 92

Page 307
1. 68
2. 74
3. 76
4. 103
5. 32
6. 58
7. 99
8. 99
9. 93
10. 41
11. 119
12. 87
13. 23
14. 65
15. 49

Page 308
1. kite – 95
2. cloud – 104
3. swing – 113
4. tree – 40

boy on skate board – 95
ball – 109
boy with bat – 78

Page 309
1. 900
2. 900
3. 300
4. 1100
5. 900
6. 900
7. 1200
8. 800
9. 1000
10. 1100

Page 310
1. 371
2. 372
3. 696
4. 820
5. 560
6. 920
7. 642
8. 900
9. 915
10. 900

Page 311
1. 748
2. 452
3. 861
4. 907
5. 753
6. 1568
7. 748
8. 925
9. 1199
10. 353
11. 886
12. 547
13. 555
14. 815
15. 553
16. 423
17. 617
18. 936
19. 574
20. 707

Page 312
1. 9
2. 17
3. 57
4. 14
5. 17
6. 17
7. 48
8. 13
9. 15
10. 19
11. 38
12. 28
13. 14
14. 17
15. 18

Page 313
1. 305
2. 316
3. 118
4. 337
5. 394
6. 176
7. 18
8. 685
9. 189
10. 108
11. 188
12. 338
13. 189
14. 189
15. 178

Page 314
1. 243
2. 383
3. 205
4. 206
5. 281
6. 202
7. 155
8. 151
9. 145
10. 188

Page 315
1. 266
2. 141
3. 64
4. 331
5. 234
6. 167
7. 245
8. 56
9. 14
10. 67
11. 323
12. 237
13. 281
14. 174
15. 278
16. 132
17. 184
18. 312

Page 316
1. 75
2. 27
3. 17
4. 19
5. 7
6. 16
7. 58
8. 18
9. 17
10. 26
11. 217
12. 174
13. 708
14. 179
15. 218
16. 153
17. 444
18. 160
19. 163
20. 186

Page 317
1. 9
2. 338
3. 75
4. 34
5. 155
6. 108
7. 316
8. 383
9. 17
10. 101

Page 318
1. 3 + 3 = 6
2. 7
3. 9
4. 14
5. 14
6. 6 – 3 = 3
7. 3
8. 7
9. 10
10. 17
11. 7
12. 77
13. 52
14. 68
15. 900
16. 372
17. 820
18. 316

© School Zone Publishing Company